Johann Reinhold Forster, Per Löfling, Marcel Bossu

Travels Through That Part of North America Formerly Called Louisiana

Johann Reinhold Forster, Per Löfling, Marcel Bossu

Travels Through That Part of North America Formerly Called Louisiana

ISBN/EAN: 9783337185121

Printed in Europe, USA, Canada, Australia, Japan

Cover: Foto ©Andreas Hilbeck / pixelio.de

More available books at **www.hansebooks.com**

TRAVELS

THROUGH

LOUISIANA.

TRAVELS

THROUGH THAT PART OF

NORTH AMERICA,

FORMERLY CALLED

LOUISIANA.

By Mr. BOSSU, Captain in the French Marines.

Translated from the FRENCH, By JOHN REINHOLD FORSTER, F.A.S.

Illustrated with NOTES relative chiefly to NATURAL HISTORY.

TO WHICH IS ADDED BY THE TRANSLATOR
A SYSTEMATIC CATALOGUE of all the known Plants of English North-America,
OR, A
FLORA AMERICÆ SEPTENTRIONALIS.

TOGETHER WITH
An ABSTRACT of the most useful and necessary articles contained in
PETER LOEFLING's TRAVELS
THROUGH Spain and Cumana in South America.
Referred to the Pages of the original Swedish Edition.

VOL. I.

Ornari res ipsa negat, contenta doceri. *Horat.*

LONDON:
Printed for T. DAVIES in Russel-Street, Covent-Garden.
M DCC LXXI.

T O

WILLIAM CONSTABLE, Esq;

of BURTON-CONSTABLE.

S I R,

THE zeal with which you promote the great cause of learning, and especially that of Natural History, the Polite Arts and Antiquities, intitle you to the regard and homage of every one who is conversant with Arts and Sciences: but the favour you were so kind to bestow upon me, before you proceeded on the tour through the different parts of Europe, encourages me to take this early opportunity to congratulate you on your return to your philosophic retirement, and publicly to acknowledge the gratitude and attachment which will ever prompt me to think myself happy in my weak endeavours to approve my conduct and sentiments to my friends and benefactors.

May

DEDICATION.

May you always enjoy perfect health, and all the rational and moral bleſſings of this life; and, after a long ſeries of years, diſtinguiſhed by actions of benevolence, friendſhip, and virtue, exchange theſe tranſitory enjoyments for everlaſting felicity. Theſe are the ſincere and invariable wiſhes of him who ſubſcribes himſelf, with the trueſt regard,

SIR,

LONDON, Oct. 5.
1771.

Your moſt obliged

obedient humble ſervant,

JOHN REINHOLD FORSTER.

PREFACE.

THE prefent publication appears with a view to fupply the Englifh reader with a good account of a country, which now enjoys the happinefs to be under the mild influence and fway of the Britifh fceptre; and, if properly adminiftered and peopled, might in time become one of the great fupports of that power, which makes *Great Britain* refpected over all the globe. The country here defcribed is fufceptible of great improvements, capable to fupply the mother-country with immenfe ftores of raw materials for her manufactures, and to take in return the products of our induftry; a commerce which, connected with religious and civil liberty, is the only bafis on which the grandeur of this nation can be laftingly founded with any degree of probability.

The Catalogue of North American plants is a mere attempt, to make the curious more attentive to the American fpontaneous products, and which will give a higher degree of certainty of fuccefs to the plantations of fuch plants as were recommended to the public, by the ingenious and great promoter of Natural Hiftory and Plantations *John Ellis*, Efq; in a *Catalogue of fuch foreign plants as are worthy of being encouraged in our American colonies for the purpofes of medicine, agriculture, and commerce.*

The

PREFACE.

The English names affixed to the greater part of the plants, will make it more eafy to the common people to know and to ufe them, bring the fcience more down even to the loweft capacities, fix the hitherto vague and multifarious denominations of plants in various parts of America, and obviate that confufion and drynefs already too common in the ftudy of that ufeful branch of knowledge.

Loefling's defcriptions of the Spanifh and South American plants are the only things in his journal which deferve the attention of a curious reader; the letters publifhed along with them in the Swedifh, are compliments of a grateful pupil to his tutor, and queries and *dubia* relative to botany, and therefore not worth a tranflation. The Englifh public has now all the voyages and publications of the Linnæan fchool; *Hoffelquift, Ofbeck, Toreen, Kalm,* and *Loefling* make the whole of them.

The French word *outarde* fignifies commonly a *buftard*, but in North America they give that name to a kind of geefe, which I therefore beg to correct, vol. i. p. 96.; having but lately got an information about it, from a gentleman who is juft returned from North America.

The *Sardines* mentioned vol. i. p. 2. are not, as I have fufpected in the note, the *pilchards*, fo common on our weftern coafts; but a kind of herring, not yet defcribed, peculiar to the neighbourhood of *Belle-Ifle*, and the coaft of French Bretany.

TRAVELS
THROUGH
LOUISIANA.

LETTER I.

To the MARQUIS de l'ESTRADE.

The Author's Departure for America; Description of the Town of Cape François; *Cruelties of the Spaniards towards the Natives of the Isle of St. Domingo; working of the Mines; true Origin of the Mal de Naples.*

WHEN I had the honour of taking my leave of you, I was ordered to communicate to you every particular that should appear remarkable to me in this new world; you farther desired of me an account of all interesting subjects which might happen on

VOL. I. B the

the paſſage. I am glad that my ſtay at *Cape François* affords me an opportunity of fulfilling an engagement which is dear to me, becauſe its execution may prove agreeable to you.

I was at *Belle-Iſle* in 1750, *M. Le Chevalier de Groſſoles* commanded at that place; he gave me a letter from the Count *d'Argenſon*, from which I learnt, that his Majeſty had made me Lieutenant in the Marines; this Miniſter gave me orders to ſet out immediately for *Rochefort*; accordingly I went on board the firſt fiſhing ſmack deſtined to carry the Anchovies * *(Sardines)* to *Rochelle*, which are caught on the Coaſt of *Bretany*, and which are the chief ſupport of the inhabitants of *Belle-Iſle*.

In

---

* The *true Anchovies* are caught in the Mediterranean; and thoſe few that now and then appear in the ſeas near *England* or *France*, are rather rare examples; they are certainly not ſo numerous that a profitable fiſhery of them could be inſtituted. The *Sardine* of our Author, therefore, ſeems to be the *Pilchard*, a fiſh that is very copiouſly caught on the coaſts of *Cornwall* and *French Bretany*. *Linnæus* has no peculiar ſpecific name for this fiſh, though the great *Engliſh* natural hiſtorian, *Ray*, in his Syn. piſc. 104, had pointed out the characters of this ſpecies; which now is done more fully by Mr. *Pennant*, in his Britiſh Zoology, III. p. 291. F.

In November we weighed anchor before the *Palace**, (which is the name of the town on this ifland); and the very firft night of our voyage we had fuch a violent ftorm on the coaft of *Poitou*, that our little veffel being beat about and furrounded by the waves, we expected every moment to go to the bottom: The crew confifted of a pilot, and three failors from Lower *Bretany*, who are commonly called *Sea-wolves* †; and are fo well accuftomed to this element, that they brave the hardeft weather. The wind having increafed, our captain was obliged to put in at the *Ifle de Dieu*, fituated between *Poitou* and the county *d'Aunis*. We ftaid there eight days; at the expiration of which, the fea being calmed, we fet fail again, and continued our voyage to the Ifle of *Rhé*; from whence I croffed a channel of the fea about three leagues broad, that feparates the ifle from the continent, and arrived at *Rochelle*, and the day after I came to *Rochefort*. I was directed to addrefs myfelf to the intendant of the department of the marine, who is M. *le Normant de Méfi*, a man of real merit, and deferving of the place he occupies, by his talents and the goodnefs of his heart: he told me, that, as foon as I fhould have equipped myfelf for my voyage, I was to go to *Rochelle*,

---

* Le Palais. † *Loups de mer.*

and embark in the ship called the *Pontchartrain*, of 400 tuns. M *le Normant* had freighted this ship for the King's account, in order to transport four companies of the marines, whom we took in at the citadel on the isle of *Rhé:* they were destined to reinforce the garrison of *New Orleans*.

We set sail from *Rochelle* the 26th of December, and had contrary winds for above a fortnight on the coast of Spain. We were already willing to put in at *Corunna*, in order to be sheltered from the violence of the winds; when happily the wind shifted; and, towards the end of January, we were in sight of *Madeira*, an isle belonging to *Portugal* *; it is called the queen of islands, on account of its fertility and the excellence of its soil; it has near twenty leagues in circumference, produces good wines, and very fine fruits.

On the 15th of February we passed the tropic of Cancer. The next day the sailors spent in
some

---

* It is an African island in the Atlantic ocean, and situated to the north of the Canary islands; which latter were discovered in 1417, by a Norman gentleman called *Jean Bethencourt*, who bore the title of King of the Canaries, and made the conquest of them to the Spaniards, who possess them now.

LOUISIANA. 5

some ridiculous ceremonies, which they oblige those to undergo who never passed the line before: they are baptised with sea-water; but may avoid this too abundant aspersion by making a small present to the boatswain.

Two months after leaving *Rochelle* we arrived at Cape *François*, in the isle of *St. Domingo*; which is that part of *America* where the Spaniards have first built towns and forts.

The town lies at the bottom of a promontory: it is defended by a fort cut in the rock, at the entrance of the port. This fortress, which has a good store of artillery, projects into the sea; and by that means forms a cape, from whence the town takes its name. Its inhabitants are European merchants, Creoles, and negroes; the last being employed to cultivate sugar-canes, coffee, indigo, cacao, cotton, cassia, tobacco, and various other products.

The French and Spaniards have divided the island between them; the latter possess the western part of it*. *San Domingo* is the capital of the

---

* Since that time the Spaniards have given their share of this island to the French. F.

the ifland; it is the feat of a bifhop, whom the King of Spain appoints.

This ifland is celebrated by the origin of the *mal de Naples*, or venereal difeafe. Authors difagree fo much on this fubject, and have told the ftory in fo many different ways, that I think I fhall not do amifs to reprefent it in its true light.

Nicolas de Obando was governor of this ifle, towards the end of the fifteenth century, during the reign of King *Ferdinand* of *Arragon* and *Ifabella* of *Caftile*: he had ftrict orders to work at the converfion of the fubdued Indians; he diftributed them among the Spaniards, giving a hundred of them to one man, fifty to another; and calling this proceeding a *repartimiento*, (a divifion). I believe you will agree with me, Sir, that this is a very fingular method of making converts in *America*; fuch maxims are quite contrary to the true fpirit of the Chriftian religion*.

Thefe

---

* " The King Don *Ferdinand*, being informed of thefe
" diforders, had turned all his attention towards remedying
" them; and his care chiefly regarded the Indians, whom
" he wifhed to protect and convert, as it has always been the
" maxim of the Catholic kings. He gave feveral orders,
" and

These Spaniards, greedy of gold, forced the wretched Indians to work in the mines, and kept them almoſt buried in the earth for eight or nine months together. This hard labour, the ſulphureous vapours which continually roſe from the mines, and the famine to which they were reduced by the impoſſibility of cultivating their grounds, ſo corrupted the maſs of their blood, that their faces became tinged with a ſaffron colour; a kind of puſtules came out on every part of their body, and cauſed them inſupportable pains. They ſoon communicated this ſickneſs to their wives, and ſo of courſe to their enemies; and they all periſhed for want of a remedy.

The afflicted Spaniards hoped, that this kind of peſt would not follow them to *Europe*, whither they went for the change of air; but they were deceived; and, on their return, they gave the Europeans the diſtemper they got from the *Americans*.

How-

" and publiſhed laws, that they ſhould be inſtructed with
" mildneſs, diſintereſtedneſs, and by example: but as an
" arrow falls without force at the bottom of the aim, when
" it is beyond the reach of the arm that ſhot it; ſo, all the
" methods which he made uſe of to make his deſigns ſuc-
" ceed, loſt their force as they got to a greater diſtance."
Don Antonio de Solis.

However, Providence pitied thefe wretched iflanders: an Indian woman, the wife of a Spaniard, difcovered, fome time after, that a kind of wood called *guayacan,* was a fufficient cure for their diftemper*.

It is but too true, Sir, that evil produces evil. The Spaniards have facrificed millions of men in the new world; they have laid wafte countries of vaft extent, in order to ufurp the gold of the Indians.

Gold and filver give as much trouble and fatigue to thofe who work them out of the mines, as they afford contentment and eafe to their poffeffors. A Spanifh engineer told me, that twenty-nine years were fpent in fearching, in the mountains of *Potofi,* for the famous vein of *Crufero,* which is two hundred and fifty yards deep. Such is the hard and fupernatural labour which power and defire of riches exacts, and which is executed

---

* Notwithftanding what our author fays concerning the origin of this difeafe, it is well known, that the inhabitants of South and North America had the difeafe when the Europeans came to them; but they well knew how to cure it, though they carefully kept this knowledge from their European enemies; and it has but lately been difcovered, that in the fouth the *Guayacum,* and in the north the *Stillingia fylvatica,* together with other plants, are the Indian fpecifics. F.

executed by neceffity and fervitude, in order to extract gold from the bowels of the earth. The wretched workmen who are employed there, enjoy neither the air of our atmofphere, nor the light of the fun, and bury themfelves in infectious and cold abyffes; of which the exhalations are fo unwholefome, that they caufe fwoons and giddinefs to the workmen as foon as they offer to go in. They make ufe of candles to light them in thefe dark fubterraneous places: the metal is generally hard in them; they break it in pieces with hammers, load it on their fhoulders, and mount upwards on ladders made of twifted hides of oxen, with wooden fteps, contrived in fuch a manner, that whilft one goes up on one fide, another may defcend on the other: thefe ladders are divided into ten fets. A man generally carries two *arobas* of metal on his back *, wrapped up in a piece of cloth: he that goes firft has a candle faftened to his thumb; and they all hold themfelves with both hands on the ladder, in order to be able to go upwards for the fpace of 250 feet.

The general hiftory of *America* tells us, that the nations of *Florida* took the facks with filver, and threw them far from themfelves as ufelefs. The *Mexicans*, on the contrary, were fond of gold;

---

* An Aroba is 25 pounds, *poids de Marc.*

gold; though, as *Jofeph d'Acofta* fays, in his univerfal hiftory of the Indies, " it is true that " their avarice was not arrived to that pitch " where ours is ; and that, notwithftanding " their being idolaters, they never have worfhip- " ped gold and filver fo much as fome bad " Chriftians have done, who have committed " the moft atrocious crimes for the fake of that " metal."

The fame author relates the following anecdote, which perfectly characterizes man's ftupid defire after riches. " A Spanifh monk, confi- " dering the height of the famous volcano of " *Guatimala*, took it into his head, that that " which he faw inflamed muft needs be a mafs of " gold, fince it had burnt for many ages toge- " ther without being confumed. Mifled by this " falfe principle, he invented fome kettles, " chains, and other inftruments, with which " he intended to draw the liquid gold from this " kind of well : but the fire difappointed him ; " for the chain and kettle were fcarce entered " into this infernal orifice, but they immediate- " ly melted down. However," fays our author, " this man perfifted in inventing new methods " for fetching up the gold after which he thirfted " fo much ; but one day happening to come too " near the mouth of the volcano, the exhalations
" from

" from it killed him, when he expected to have
" succeeded in his whimsical design. Thus
" blind mortals hasten their death by too great a
" pursuit after the luxuries of this life."

But to return to the Indians of *Saint Domingo*. The history of that isle informs us, that a *Cacique* * called *Poncra*, being harassed by the Spaniards, resolved to flee from his village, which the enemies found abandoned, and where they took three thousand marks of gold, which had been left there. *Vasco Nunez de Balboa*, the successor of *Nicolas de Obando*, sent his people to the Cacique, with orders to assure him, that he should not fear to return, because he should be his friend; but that if he did not come back, he should go and hunt for him, and cause him to be devoured by his dogs †.

Poncra

---

* A cacique is a petty prince or king of the Indians.

† The Spaniards had brought over with them from *Europe* some mastiffs, which they had taught to hunt the Indians; as soon as they were let loose upon these wretches, they tore out their bowels, and devoured them. One of these dogs called *Barémel* was very much dreaded all over the island; and though he was guarded by a shield against the arrows of the Indians, they, it is said, at last killed him, by piercing his eyes with darts, which was a kind of triumph for them.

Antonio

Poncra was frightened by his threats, and did not venture to difobey. He brought with him three of his vaffals. *Nunez de Balboa* employed in vain all the cunning imaginable to bring him to difcover the place where they got the gold, which he had heard contained great quantities of that metal: good ufage and punifhments were equally infufficient to bring him to confefs what perhaps he did not know. As to the three thoufand *marks* of gold which had been found, *Poncra* faid, that thofe who had amaffed them died in the times of his fathers, and that he had not thought it worth while to fend people to fearch for more, having no need of it. This unhappy Cacique was given up to the fury of the dogs, that devoured him with his three companions.

Some time after, a Spaniard fell into the hands of the fubjects of the unhappy *Poncra*; they reproached him with the exceffive thirft of his countrymen after gold, and the injuftices it led them

---

Antonio de Herrera, in his firft *Decas*, relates, that this fierce creature, whofe inftinct was fingular, guarded a narrow pafs in the ifle of *St. Domingo*; and that one day an Indian woman, being defirous of paffing by him, addreffed him in thefe words: *Signor Dog, do not hurt me; I carry this letter to the Chriftians:* he adds, that *the dog immediately fmelled at her, piffed at her,* (thofe are his very words) *and fuffered her to pafs without doing her any harm.*

LOUISIANA. 13

them to commit; that this avidity alone forced them from their country, and brought them acrofs numberlefs perils to that ifland, to difturb its inhabitants, who lived peaceably before in their huts, under the protection of the *Great Spirit* *.

After this fhort harangue, they melted fome gold, and poured it into his mouth and ears, faying, *Thou dog, fince thou art fo willing to pof-fefs it, glut thyfelf*.

It muft, however, be owned, Sir, that, if the Mexican hiftory fhews us nothing but horror, that of *St. Domingo*, on the other hand, furnifhes us with inftances of generofity.

Don Pedro de Magaratit, formerly a commandant here for the King of Spain, was offered a couple of living turtle-doves, by an Indian in a great famine. The general took them, paid the Indian handfomely for them, and begged part of the garrifon to go with him to the higheft part of the town; where, being arrived, he faid to them, holding the little creatures in his hand, " Gentlemen, I am forry that people
" have

---

* Thus the Indians call the Supreme Being.

"have not brought me provisions sufficient to "treat you all ; I cannot resolve to satisfy my ap- "petite, whilst you are starving:" and as he had spoke these words, he let the birds fly away.

An infinite number of other instances may be added to this, which do no less honour to the inhabitants of this isle. There are several that deserve to be recorded in history; and among those that I have been told, I cannot help thinking the following story worth your notice. An old inhabitant of St. Domingo had acquired a considerable fortune there by his labour, industry, and trade. His conduct and manners remained unaltered by prosperity; and he only valued his riches, because they enabled him to serve others.

Whenever a ship arrived from France, he ran to the coast to see the passengers land, and generally conducted them to his home. One day he saw several young people, who expected to make their fortune as soon as they arrived; they had letters of recommendation, on which they depended so much, that they took little notice of the good planter, who accosted them; he left them, wishing them all kind of prosperity:
some

some time after he met them again looking very sad and discontented with the reception they had found. Gentlemen, says he to them, you are not recommended to me, and you did not rely on me. I am your fellow-creature, and you want assistance; come to my house, you will there find a table and a lodging at your service; and during that time perhaps something may offer, that will suit your inclinations. The young people were enraptured, and accepted his offers; they followed him to his house, where they found a table spread for twenty persons, and served by as many Negro servants. One of the new comers asked whether they were at a wedding, and was surprised to hear that this was nothing extraordinary. The master of the house kept them in his house for some time; his advices, and the pains he took about them, soon procured them very advantageous situations.

You will easily believe, Sir, that so good a master was loved and respected by all his slaves, who looked upon him as upon their father. This man was very far from being animated by the brutal avidity of some planters, that force their wretched slaves to such hard labour, that they refuse to marry, in order to avoid generating slaves to such masters, who treat them,

when

when old and infirm, worfe than their dogs and horfes*.

As to the inhabitants of the French iflands in the Weft Indies, I can affure you they are very generous towards ftrangers: a perfon may even travel in the interior parts of the country, without the leaft expence to himfelf; if his countenance be free and open, and his behaviour decent, he is fufficiently qualified for a favourable reception in every habitation.

It is with great juftice that we reckon the *Creoles* noble in France: their fentiments are fo noble and delicate in every ftation of life, that they perfectly deferve that appellation.

Man is every where the fame; he is equally fufceptible of good and evil; education corrects his vices, but does not give him virtue; the
fame

---

* I have feen a planter, whofe name was *Chaperon*, who forced one of his negroes to go into a heated oven, where the poor wretch expired; and his jaws being fhrivelled up, the barbarous *Chaperon* faid, I believe the fellow laughs, and took a poker to ftir him up. Since that time he is grown the fcare-crow of all the flaves; who, when they have done fomething amifs, are threatened by their mafters with, *I will fell thee to Chaperon.*

same Being has created the civilized man and the savage, and has endowed them with the same qualities, as you will find in the sequel of my correspondence. If I cannot amuse you with my stile, at least I shall make my narrative interesting, through the singularity of the facts I intend to relate.

I am, SIR, &c.

Cape François, the 15th of February 1751.

LETTER II.

To the same.

The Author's Departure from Cape François *for* Louiſiana. *Short Deſcription of the Harbour of the* Havannah. *Of the famous Gulph of* Mexico; *and of* New Orleans.

SIR,

E weighed anchor the 8th of March laſt; and on the 15th we were in ſight of *Cuba*, which is the moſt temperate of all the *Antilles*. The *Havannah* is the ſtore of all the riches of America, on account of its ſituation, and the extent and convenience of its harbour, which can contain upwards of a thouſand ſhips. It is the common *rendez-vous* of the Spaniſh fleets returning to Europe; and it is defended by three forts. *Cuba* is two hundred leagues long, and between twenty-five and thirty broad; ſixteen years have been ſpent in diſcoveries to aſcertain whether it was an iſle or

continent:

LOUISIANA.

continent: it lies under the tropic of Cancer, that is, in twenty-three degrees and a half north latitude. Near the middle of the ifland, to the fouthward, are a number of little ifles very clofe to each other, which are called the Garden of the Queen *.

During the equinox we fuffered a very violent ftorm between Cape *Catoche* and Cape *Antonio*; the latter, which we doubled on the twenty-third, is at the weftern point of the ifle of *Cuba*. I was very fea-fick, having never been at fea on fo long a voyage; but the defire of ferving my country in a new land, fufficiently compenfated all the hardfhips I underwent on my paffage. The winds changed, the fea became fmooth, and, a few days after, we entered into the famous gulph of *Mexico*, where we met with a prodigious quantity of floating timber, coming from *Louifiana* down the river *Miffifippi*: thefe logs of wood are feen for above two hundred leagues at fea, and ferve as guides to the entrance of the river in hazy and foggy weather; it being very difficult to get into it, on account of the rocks and fhoals in the neighbourhood of its entrance.

---

* Jardin de la Reyna.

In the firſt days of April we perceived the fort *Baliſe* at the mouth of the *Miſſiſippi*. Mr. *le Moine d'Iberville*, a Canada gentleman, diſcovered, in 1698 *, this mouth of the river, which M. *de la Salle* miſſed in 1684. Our veſſel ſtruck upon the bar; we fired a gun to call the pilot, and at the ſame time the captain diſembarked the artillery of the ſhip, and the two hundred regular troops which were on board for the ſervice of the colony of *Louiſiana*; which made the veſſel ſo much lighter, that ſhe came afloat again.

On the 4th of April, we ſet on ſhore eighteen officers at Fort *Baliſe* †, where M. *de Santilly* commanded: this officer treated us to the beſt of his power, while we ſtayed at his poſt, which is entirely ſurrounded with marſhes full of ſerpents and crocodiles.

The *Marquis de Vaudreuil*, governor of *Louiſiana*, being informed of our arrival, ſent ſeveral boats

---

* Mr. *d'Iberville*, governor of *Louiſiana*, conducted the firſt colony thither in 1699: after his death the country had no governor for a long while: the ſecond was M. *de la Motte Cadillac*; and the third, M. *de Bienville*, youngeſt brother of the firſt.

† They reckon thirty leagues from this place to *New Orleans*, on account of the bendings in the river.

boats to fetch us, and to bring us refreshments; we diftributed our foldiers on board them, and, by failing and rowing, we got to *New Orleans* on Eafter-day. The Marquis *de Vaudreuil* is to receive twenty-four companies of marines, to augment the forces in *Louifiana*; thefe troops come on board of merchant-fhips, freighted for the King's account; there are likewife fome female recruits enlifted in *France*, who come to people thefe climates. Induftrious foldiers, who chufe to marry thefe girls, get their difmiffion, and a certain number of acres of ground to cultivate: they get victuals from the King for three years together, and he makes them a prefent of half a pound of gun-powder, and two pounds of fhot every month; of a gun, a hatchet, a pickaxe, and corn to fow their fields; with a cow, a calf, cocks and hens, &c.

The Marquis *de Vaudreuil* has diftributed the twenty-four new companies in the different parts of the colony, without any regard to perfons; fo that every one may equally fhare the advantages and the difadvantages. As to the detachment near the *Illinois*, a poft five hundred leagues diftant from *New Orleans*, it has fallen to the fhare of the company to which I belong. I have the honour of being among the officers which M. *Rouillé*, the fecretary of ftate for the marine, has

has recommended to the Marquis *de Vaudreuil*; and I am made perfectly sensible of the deference shewn to such a recommendation. I can assure you, Sir, that the General's table is of great use to me, and to all those that are lately arrived, and have not had time to take any fixed lodgings. The affluence is very great; but the governor does the honours of his table in so noble and generous a manner, that he acquires the esteem and friendship of all the officers, who justly stile him the father of the colony. M. *Michel de la Rouvilliere*, who superintends the markets *, likewise contributes to render life agreeable to us, by the just prices he fixes upon the victuals of the country, and by every thing relative to his office.

We expect to set out for the *Illinois* the 20th of August next; Mr. de *Macarty*, who is to go with us, has been appointed commandant of the detachment by the court. The different nations which I shall be obliged to visit during this long voyage, will furnish me amply with materials for a description of the fine river *Mississippi*, and the people on its banks.

In the mean while, I intend to give you a description of *Louisiana* in general; but I believe I do

---

* *L'ordonnateur.*

LOUISIANA. 23

I do not need to be very prolix on this subject, as you probably know most of the plans and accounts that have been published of it. Let me only observe to you, that *New Orleans*, the streets of which run all in streight lines, is now much greater and more populous than formerly. There are inhabitants of four sorts, *viz.* Europeans, Americans, Africans or negroes, and *Mestizos* *. The latter are those born of Europeans and the natives of this country, whom we call savages. The *Creoles* are those that are born here of a French man and French woman, or of European parents.

The Creoles in general are very brave, tall, and well made; they are well disposed for cultivating the arts and sciences; but as they cannot make great progress therein for want of good masters, the rich and well-meaning fathers send their children to *France*, as to the best school in the world, for all sorts of acquirements.

As to the fair sex, whose only art is that of pleasing, they are already born with that advantage here, and have no need to acquire it in Europe.

---

* Métifs.

New Orleans and *Mobile* are the only towns where they speak the French pretty pure. The negroes are brought thither from Africa, and are employed in cultivating the grounds, which are excellently adapted to the culture of indigo, tobacco, rice, maize, or Indian corn, and sugar-canes, of which they have already made plantations that have succeeded very well. Thus the merchants, tradesmen, and strangers, who live here, enjoy as it were an enchanted abode, rendered delicious by the purity of its air, the fertility of its soil, and the beauty of its situation. *New Orleans* lies on the banks of the *Missisippi*, which is one of the greatest rivers in the world; because, for 800 leagues together, it passes through known countries. Its pure and delicious water * runs for the space of forty leagues between a number of habitations, which form an elegant sight on both its shores; where the pleasures of hunting and fishing, and all other enjoyments of life, are abundant.

The capuchins are the first monks that went over to *New Orleans* as missionaries in 1723. Their superior was the vicar of the parish; these good

---

* M. le *Normant de Méfi*, being *Intendant* of the marine at *Rochefort*, always drank this water at his table. It has the quality of contributing to the fecundity of women.

LOUISIANA. 25

good friars only employ themselves in affairs relative to their station in life.

Two years after, the Jesuits settled in *Louisiana*. These cunning politicians have found means to get the richest settlement in the whole colony, which they have obtained through their intrigues.

The Ursuline nuns were sent thither almost at the same time. The occupation of these pious girls, whose zeal is truly laudable, is the education of young ladies; they likewise receive orphans into their community, for which the King pays them fifty *écus* a-head pension. These nuns are likewise charged with the care of the military hospital.

My stay here has as yet been so short, that I have not been able to give you any account of the nations which inhabit the banks of the river; however, I will endeavour to give you an idea of the character and turn of the *Chitimachas*, who are settled on a river or branch which bears their name, to the westward of *New Orleans*: I believe the anecdote will prove interesting to you, though this nation is very near extinct.

In

In 1720, one of their nation, having hid himfelf in a lonely place on the banks of the *Miffifippi*, had murdered the *Abbé de St. Côme*, who was then the miffionary of the colony. M. *de Bienville*, who was then governor, made the whole nation anfwerable for it; and, to fpare his own people, he employed feveral nations of his allies to attack them.

Thefe Indians were worfted; the lofs of their beft warriors forced them to afk for peace: the governor having granted it them, on condition that they would bring the head of the murderer, they punctually executed that condition; and afterwards prefented the *calumet* or pipe of peace * to M. *de Bienville*.

The following is a relation of what I have heard concerning the ceremonies of this folemn embaffy.

They arrived at *New Orleans*, finging the fong of the calumet, which they difplayed to the wind,

---

* The calumet is a long pipe, with a head of red, black, or white marble, and a pipe of a reed two and a half or three feet long. The Indians fend it by deputies to thofe nations with whom they will renew or treat of peace. It is adorned with the feathers of the white eagle; it is a fymbol of peace and plenty amongft them; and one may go every where without fear, with the calumet in hand, becaufe nothing is held more facred.

wind, and in a certain cadence, to announce their embaſſy; and they were dreſſed out with their beſt ornaments, as is always uſual amongſt them on ſuch occaſions. The chief of the deputation ſaid to the governor: *How happy am I to find my-ſelf in thy preſence; thou haſt long been angry with our nation; we have been informed of what thy heart has told thee, and we have heard with great joy, that it was willing to give us fine days.* They then ſat down on the ground, leaning their faces on their hands, the ſpeaker without doubt to recover his breath, and the others to keep ſilent. During this interval every body was ordered not to talk, nor to laugh whilſt the harangue laſted, becauſe they would be affronted at it.

The ſpeaker, ſome moments after, aroſe with two others; one of them filled the pipe of the calumet with tobacco, the other brought fire; the firſt then lighted the pipe; the ſpeaker ſmoked a while, and then preſented the pipe to M. *de Bienville*, that he might do the ſame; accordingly the governor, and all the officers that compoſed his retinue, ſmoked out of this calumet, each according to his rank: as ſoon as this ceremony was over, the old orator took back the calumet, and put it in M. *de Bienville's* hands, in order to be preſerved by him. The ſpeaker

speaker remained standing, and the other ambassadors sat down near the present which they had brought, and which consisted of roe-buck and doe skins, and in some other furs, all dressed white, as a sign of peace.

The speaker or chancellor was dressed in a robe of several marten-skins sewed together; it was fastened to his right shoulder, and passed under his left arm; he wrapped himself up in this robe, and began his speech with a majestic air, addressing himself to the governor: " My
" heart laughs for joy on seeing myself before
" thee; we have all of us heard the word of
" peace which thou hast sent us: the hearts of
" our whole nation laugh for joy on that occa-
" sion; the women, forgetting that instant all
" that passed, have danced; and the children
" have leapt like young roe-bucks. Thy words
" shall never be forgotten, and our descendants
" will remember it as long as the ANCIENT
" WORD * shall last: as the war has made us poor,
" we have been obliged to make a general hunt
" or chace, in order to bring thee some furs:
" but we were afraid of going to any great di-
" stance, lest the other nations should not yet
" have heard thy word; nor are we come hither
" but trembling all the way, till we saw thy face.
                                              " How

---

* Thus they call *traditions*.

"How glad are my eyes and my heart to be-
"hold thee this day. Our prefents are fmall,
"but our hearts are great to obey thy word; at
"thy commands thou fhalt fee our legs run and
"leap like thofe of the ftags, to do as thou fhalt
"pleafe."

Here the orator paufed a little; then raifing
his voice, he gravely continued his difcourfe.

"How beautiful is the fun to-day, in com-
"parifon with what it was when thou wert an-
"gry with us! How dangerous is one villain!
"Thou knoweft that a fingle man has killed
"the *chief of the prayer* *, whofe death has caufed
"that of our beft warriors: we have only old
"men, and women with their children remain-
"ing, who all ftretch out their arms towards
"thee as to a good father. The gall that for-
"merly filled thy heart, has given way to ho-
"ney; the great fpirit is no longer irritated
"againft our nation; thou haft required the
"head of a villain from our hands, and in order
"to obtain peace we have fent it thee.

"The fun was red before, all the roads were
"full of thorns and briars; the clouds were
"black, the water troubled and ftained with
"our

---

* So they call our miffionaries.

" our blood; our women lamented without inter-
" miffion the lofs of their relations, and durft not
" venture to go and fetch wood for preparing
" our victuals; at the leaft fhriek of the birds
" of night all our warriors were on foot; they
" never flept without their arms; our huts were
" abandoned, and our fields lay fallow; we had
" all of us empty ftomachs, and our faces look-
" ed long and meagre; the game and wild-fowl
" fled far from us; the ferpents angrily hiffed
" at us; and the birds that perched near our
" habitations feemed, by their doleful notes, to
" fing us fongs of death.

" To-day the fun is bright, the fky is ferene,
" the clouds are vanifhed, the roads covered
" with flowers; our gardens and fields fhall
" henceforth be cultivated, and we will offer
" their firft-fruits to the great fpirit; the water
" is fo clear that we fee ourfelves in it; the fer-
" pents fly from us; the birds amufe us by the
" fweetnefs and harmony of their fongs; our
" wives and children dance, and forget to eat and
" to drink; the whole nation laughs for joy, to
" fee us walk on the fame road with thyfelf and
" the French; the fame fun fhall light us, we
" fhall have but one and the fame fpeech, and
" our hearts fhall make but one; we will kill
" them that fhall kill the French; our warriors
                                           " fhall

" shall hunt to make them subsist, and we will
" eat together: Will not that be good? what
" dost thou say to it, father?"

To this discourse, which was spoken with a
firm tone of voice, with grace and decency,
and even, if I may be allowed the expression,
with the most majestic deportment, M. *de Bienville* answered in a few words, in the common
language, which he spoke pretty fluently; that
he was very glad that their nation had recovered
their senses; he gave them something to eat;
and, as a mark of friendship, he put his hand
into that of the speaker, and so sent them home
satisfied.—Since that time they have always been
inviolably attached to the French, and furnish
New Orleans with game.

My third letter will prove more interesting;
however, I hope I have hitherto fulfilled my
promises; and am,

S I R, &c.

*New Orleans, the 1st
of July* 1751.

LETTER III.

To the same.

Description of the religious Customs and Ceremonies of some Nations which inhabit the Banks of the great River Missisippi. *Conspiracy of the Natches against the French.*

SIR,

I AM now arrived at the place where the great nation of the *Natches* formerly lived, of which the public news have said so much. It is asserted, that this formidable nation gave laws to others, on account of the great extent of their country. They inhabited all the space of land between the river *Menchak*, which is about fifty leagues from the sea, and the river *Hoyo*, which is near 460 leagues from the sea.

On

LOUISIANA.

On the 20th of August we set out from *New Orleans* on our voyage to the *Illinois*, in six boats, on board of which were the four companies about which I wrote to you in my preceding letter, commanded by *M. de Macarty*. We are obliged to row up against the current of the river *Missisippi*, on account of the many windings of that river, which runs between two great forests, the trees of which appear to be as ancient as the world.

The first places you come to on your voyage are two villages peopled with Germans, being the rest of a grant made, in 1720, by the King to Mr. *Law*. This colony was to consist of Germans and Provençals, to the amount of 1500 persons; the ground for it was laid out near a wild nation called the *Akanças*; it was four leagues square, and the colony was erected into a dutchy. They had already transported thither the ammunition and stores for a company of dragoons, and merchandises for the value of upwards a million of *livres*; but Mr. *Law* failed, and the India company, which was at that time established in Louisiana, took possession of all the goods.

The colonists separated, and the Germans settled ten leagues above *New Orleans:* they are very laborious, and are looked upon as the providers and victuallers of the town. The two villages are under [the direction of a Swedish captain *.

Two leagues further you find a nation called *Colla-piſſas*, who are diſtinguiſhed by their attachment to the French; they are now reduced to a very ſmall number; their true name is *Aquelon Piſſas*, that is, the nation who hear and ſee.

Next you meet with the *Oumas*, who adore the ſun. This nation, with moſt of the others in America, believes, that the Supreme Being reſides in the ſun, and that he deſires to be revered in that vivifying orb, as the author of nature: they ſay, there is nothing here that can be compared to him, and that this wonder by enlightening the earth, ſpreads joy and abundance on it Upon theſe principles they worſhip him, as the viſible image of the greatneſs and goodneſs of a deity, that condeſcends to make himſelf known among men, by diſtributing his benefactions amongſt them.

Fifteen

---

* It is Mr. *Arinſbourg*, who was at the battle of Pultava in 1709, with Charles XII. This old officer is the head of a numerous family eſtabliſhed in Louiſiana.

LOUISIANA. 35

Fifteen leagues above the *Oumas*, in going up the river, you arrive at the *Cut point*. This place is about forty leagues distant from *New Orleans*. The soil of it is very fertile, and covered with fruit-trees. There are a number of Frenchmen in this part of the country, who apply themselves to the culture of tobacco, cotton, rice, maize, and other corn; the colonists likewise trade in building-timber, which they carry down the river to *New Orleans* upon rafts.

Upon the left shore of the river, a little above the *Cut-point*, you see the village of the *Tonikas*, an Indian nation who have ever been attached to the French. Their chiefs have always exerted themselves to be our allies in war; the last of them, who was very brave, received a dangerous wound in an expedition against the *Natches*: the King, on receiving an account of this affair, honoured him with a commission, as brigadier of the armies of red men; and further presented him with a blue ribbon, from which hung a silver medal, with a representation of *Paris*: he likewise received a gold-headed cane.

After the massacre of the French by the *Natches*, whereof I intend to give you an account in its place, a part of that nation pretended to be desirous of making peace with the grand chief of the *Tonikas*: the latter communicated this to the commander-general of the French, to whom he was very much attached; the *Natches* prevented the anſwer, and aſſaſſinated the *Tonikas*, beginning with their grand chief; his enemies, who feared our advice and our forces, made haſte to ruin and deſtroy a great number of his ſubjects. We ſhall always lament, together with theſe good Indians, the loſs of a man, whoſe great qualities would do honour to a civilized nation.

After eighty leagues navigation from the capital of *Louiſiana*, we arrived at the poſt of the *Natches*, which, about twenty years ago, was very conſiderable, but is very inſignificant at preſent.

The fort is ſituated on an eminence, which commands the river *Miſſiſippi*, from which it is about the diſtance of a cannon-ſhot. The ground, which in this country is always riſing higher, would be one of the moſt fertile, if it were cultivated; tobacco, cotton, and maize ſucceed very well in it.

I have made ſome ſtay at this poſt, which is commanded by the Chevalier *d'Orgon*, a natural

ſon

LOUISIANA.

son of the Prince *de Lambesc*, of the house of Lorrain.

The *Natches* who lived here formerly were a very considerable nation. They formed several villages, that were under some peculiar chiefs; and these last again, obeyed one grand chief of the whole nation. All these princes bore the name of *Suns*; there were five hundred of them, all relations of the great Sun, their common sovereign, who carried on his breast the image of the sun, from which he pretended to trace his origin, and which was adored under the name of *Wachil*, which signifies *the great fire* or the *supreme fire*.

The manner in which the *Natches* rendered divine service to the sun, has something solemn in it. The high-priest got up before sun-rising, and marched at the head of the people with a grave pace, and the calumet of peace in hand; he smoked in honour of the sun, and blew the first mouthful of smoke towards him. On the appearance of that luminous body, all the by-standers began to howl by turns after the high-priest, and contemplated it with their arms extended to heaven. Then they threw themselves on the ground; and their women brought their children,

children, and taught them to keep in a devout attitude.

About their harvest-time, which happened in July, the *Natches* celebrated a great feast. They began with blacking their faces; and did not eat till three hours after noon, having previously purified themselves in the baths; the oldest man in the nation then offered to their deity the first fruits of their crops.

They had a temple in which they kept up an eternal fire; the priests took great care to preserve it, and for this purpose they were only allowed to make use of the wood of one kind of tree;- if unhappily the fire was extinguished, all the people were in the greatest consternation, and the neglectful priests were punished with death: but such an event happened very seldom; for the keepers of this celestial fire could easily renew it, by fetching common fire under pretext of lighting their calumets; for they were not allowed to employ the holy fire for that use.

When their sovereign died, he was accompanied in the grave by his wives, and by several of his subjects. The lesser Suns took care to follow the same custom; the law likewise condemned

demned every *Natchéz* to death, who had married a girl of the blood of the Suns, as soon as she was expired. On this occasion, I must tell you the history of an Indian, who was no ways willing to submit to this law : his name was *Etteacteal*; he contracted an alliance with the Suns; but the consequences which this honour brought along with it, had like to have proved very unfortunate to him. His wife fell sick; as soon as he saw her at the point of death, he fled, embarked on a piragua on the *Mississippi*, and came to *New Orleans*. He put himself under the protection of M. *de Bienville*, the then governor, and offered to be his huntsman. The Governor accepted his services, and interested himself for him with the *Natches*, who declared that he had nothing more to fear, because the ceremony was past, and he was accordingly no longer a lawful prize.

Etteacteal, being thus assured, ventured to return to his nation; and, without settling among them, he made several voyages thither : he happened to be there when the Sun, called the *Stung Serpent*, brother to the great Sun, died; he was a relation of the late wife of *Etteacteal*, and they resolved to make him pay his debt. M. *de Bienville* had been recalled to France, and the sovereign of the *Natches* thought

thought, that the protector's absence had annulled the reprieve granted to the protected person; and accordingly he caused him to be arrested. As soon as the poor fellow found himself in the hut of the grand chief of war, together with the other victims destined to be sacrificed to the *Stung Serpent*, he gave vent to the excess of his grief. The favourite wife of the late Sun, who was likewise to be sacrificed, and who saw the preparations for her death with firmness, and seemed impatient to rejoin her husband, hearing *Etteacteal*'s complaints and groans, said to him, Art thou no warrior? He answered, Yes, I am one. However, said she, thou cryest, life is dear to thee; and as that is the case, it is not good that thou shouldst go along with us, go with the women. *Etteacteal* replied, True, life is dear to me; it would be well if I walked yet on earth till to the death of the great Sun, and I would die with him. Go thy way, said the favourite, it is not fit thou shouldst go with us, and that thy heart should remain behind on earth; once more get away, and let me see thee no more.

Etteacteal did not stay to have this order repeated to him; he disappeared like lightning: three old women, two of which were his relations, offered to pay his debt; their age and
their

their infirmities had difgufted them of life; none of them had been able to ufe their legs for a great while. The hair of the two that were related to *Etteacteal*, were no more gray than thofe of women of fifty-five years in France. The other old woman was a hundred and twenty years old, and had very white hair, which is a very uncommon thing among the Indians: none of the three had a quite wrinkled fkin. They were difpatched in the evening, one at the door of the *Stung Serpent*, and the other two upon the place before the temple *.

The generofity of thefe women gave *Etteacteal* life again, acquired him the degree of *confidered*, and cleared his honour, which he had fullied by fearing death. He remained quiet after that time; and, taking advantage of what he had learnt during his ftay among the French, he became a juggler, and made ufe of his knowledge to impofe upon his countrymen †.

The

---

* A cord is faftened round their necks with a flip knot, and eight men of their relations ftrangle them, by drawing four one way and four the other; fo many are not neceffary, but as they acquire nobility by fuch executions, there are always more than are wanting, and the operation is performed in an inftant.

† The jugglers in this country perform the functions of priefts, phyficians, and fortune-tellers, and chiefly pretend to pafs for forcerers.

The morning after this execution, they made every thing ready for the convoy; and the hour being come, the great master of the ceremonies appeared at the door of the hut adorned suitably to his quality; the victims who were to accompany the deceased prince into the mansion of the spirits, came forth; they consisted of the favourite wife of the deceased, of his second wife, his chancellor, his physician, his hired man, that is his first servant, and of some old women.

The favourite went to the great Sun, with whom there were several Frenchmen, to take leave of him: she gave orders for the Suns of both sexes that were her children to appear, and spoke to the following effect:

"Children, this is the day on which I am to
" tear myself from you arms, and to follow
" your father's steps, who waits for me in the
" country of the spirits; if I were to yield to
" your tears, I would injure my love, and fail
" in my duty. I have done enough for you, by
" bearing you next to my heart, and by suck-
" ling you with my breasts. You that are de-
" scended of his blood, and fed by my milk,
" ought you to shed tears? Rejoice rather that
" you are *Suns* and warriors; you are bound to
" give examples of firmness and valour to the
" whole

" whole nation: go, my children, I have pro-
" vided for all your wants, by procuring you
" friends; my friends, and thofe of your father,
" are yours too; I leave you amidft them;
" they are the French, they are tender-hearted
" and generous, make yourfelves worthy of
" their efteem, by not degenerating from your
" race; always act openly with them, and never
" implore them with meannefs.

" And you Frenchmen," added fhe, turning
herfelf towards our officers, " I recommend my
" orphan-children to you; they will know no
" other fathers than you; you ought to protect
" them."

After that fhe got up; and, followed by her
troop, returned to her hufband's hut, with a
furprifing firmnefs.

A noble woman came to join herfelf to the
number of victims of her own accord, being engaged, by the friendfhip fhe bore the *Stung Serpent*, to follow him into the other world. The
Europeans called her the *haughty* lady, on account of her majeftic deportment, and her
proud air, and becaufe fhe only frequented the
company of the moft diftinguifhed Frenchmen;
they regretted her much, becaufe fhe had the
know-

knowledge of several simples, with which she had saved the lives of many of our sick. This moving sight filled our people with grief and horror. The favourite wife of the deceased rose up, and spoke to them with a smiling countenance: "I die without fear," said she, "grief does not " embitter my last hours, I recommend my " children to you; whenever you see them, " noble Frenchmen, remember that you have " loved their father, and that he was till death " a true and sincere friend of your nation, whom " he loved more than himself. The disposer of " life has been pleased to call him, and I shall " soon go and join him; I shall tell him that I " have seen your hearts moved at the sight of " his corps: do not be grieved; we shall be " longer friends in the *country of the spirits* than " here, because we do not die there again *."

These words forced tears from the eyes of all the French; they were obliged to do all they could to prevent the *great Sun* from killing himself; for he was inconsolable at the death of his brother,

---

* At the hour intended for the ceremony, they made the victims swallow little balls or pills of tobacco, in order to make them giddy, and as it were to take the sensation of pain from them; after that they were all strangled, and put upon mats, the favourite on the right, the other wife on the left, and the others according to their rank.

brother, upon whom he was used to lay the weight of government, he being great chief of war of the Natches. *i. e.* Generalissimo of their armies; that prince grew furious by the resistance he met with; he held his gun by the barrel, and the *Sun*, his presumptive heir, held it by the lock, and caused the powder to fall out of the pan; the hut was full of *Suns*, *Nobles*, and *Honourables* *, who were all trembling: but the French raised their spirits again, by hiding all the arms belonging to the sovereign, and filling the barrel of his gun with water, that it might be unfit for use for some time.

As soon as the Suns saw their sovereign's life in safety, they thanked the French, by squeezing their hands, but without speaking; a most profound silence reigned throughout, for grief and awe kept in bounds the multitude that were present.

The wife of the great Sun was seized with fear during this transaction. She was asked whether

---

* The established distinctions among these Indians were as follows: The *Suns*, relations of the great Sun, held the highest rank; next came the *Nobles*; after them the *Honourables*; and last of all, the common people, who were very much despised. As the nobility was propagated by the women, this contributed much to multiply it.

whether she was ill; and she answered aloud, "Yes I am;" and added, with a lower voice, "if the Frenchmen go out of this hut, my hus- "band dies, and all the Natches will die with "him; stay then, brave Frenchmen, because "your words are as powerful as arrows; be- "sides, who could have ventured to do what "you have done? But you are his true friends "and those of his brother." Their laws obliged the *great Sun*'s wife to follow her husband in the grave: this was doubtless the cause of her fears; and likewise the gratitude towards the French, who interested themselves in behalf of his life, prompted her to speak in the above-mentioned manner.

The *great Sun* gave his hand to the officers, and said to them: "My friends, my heart is so "overpowered with grief, that, though my "eyes were open, I have not taken notice that "you have been standing all this while, nor "have I asked you to sit down; but pardon the "excess of my affliction."

The Frenchmen told him, that he had no need of excuses; that they were going to leave him alone, but that they would cease to be his friends unless he gave orders to light the fires

again

again*, lighting his own before them, and that they should not leave him till his brother was buried.

He took all the Frenchmen by the hands; and said, " Since all the chiefs and noble officers
" will have me stay on earth, I will do it, I will
" not kill myself; let the fires be lighted again
" immediately, and I'll wait till death joins me
" to my brother; I am already old, and till I
" die I shall walk with the French; had it not
" been for them, I should have gone with my
" brother, and all the roads would have been
" covered with dead bodies."

This prince only survived the *Stung Serpent* one year, and his nephew succeeded him. The reign of that young prince proved very unfortunate to the colony. You shall see, Sir, by the sequel of this letter, that the colony owes its safety only to the mother of this sovereign; she got from him the secret of the general conspiracy against our nation, whom she loved very much.

I must do justice to the Indians; the project which they formed of destroying all the French
here,

---

* The great Sun had given orders to put out all the fires, which is only done at the death of the sovereigns.

here, was not the refult of natural inconftancy or fickle temper; it was the bad conduct of an officer, who infulted a people whom he ought to have treated gently, that roufed their anger. Free born men, living peaceably in the country where their anceftors fettled, could not bear the tyranny which the ftrangers exercifed over them, who were come to fettle amongft them. The *Sieur de Chepar*, commandant of the poft of the *Natches*, neglected to gain the efteem of the French and the Indians under his care; he abufed thofe who would not enter into his criminal conduct, and trufted the moft important pofts to ferjeants and corporals who were entirely devoted to him. You can eafily conceive, Sir, that the military difcipline was entirely fubverted by preferences of this kind, which are fo contrary to fubordination.

M. *Dumont*, the fecond officer, made *remonftrances*, which were not attended to, and to which he gave no other anfwer than by putting him in irons. As foon as he was fet at liberty, he went down to the capital to lay his complaints before M. *Perrier*, then governor of *Louifiana*. M. *de Chepar* was recalled to give account of his conduct; he was to be broken, but his intrigues and his patrons ferved him, he was acquitted and fent back to his poft.

Inftead

LOUISIANA. 49

Inſtead of being corrected by this mortification, he conducted himſelf as before, and became the object of deteſtation and abhorrence of both the French and Indians; he irritated the latter, and forced them to come to the moſt violent extremities. M. *de Chepar*, deſirous of making his fortune in a ſhort time, ſummoned the *Sun* of a village called the *Apple*, to retire with his people, and to leave him the ground which he occupied, becauſe he wanted to make himſelf a habitation on it, which ſhould turn out to good account. The *Cacique* repreſented to him, that the bones of his anceſtors were repoſed there: his remonſtrances proved uſeleſs; the French commandant ordered the *Great Sun* to cauſe the village to be evacuated, and even threatened to ſend him loaded with irons to *New Orleans* in caſe of non-compliance. Perhaps this officer thought, he could treat the chief as a ſlave; he did not reflect, that he ſpoke to a man accuſtomed to command, and whoſe authority was deſpotic over his ſubjects.

The Great Sun heard him, and retired without ſhewing any paſſion; he aſſembled his council, where it was reſolved, that M. *de Chepar* ſhould be told, that before they could evacuate the *Apple* village, they muſt make the plan of another, and that this required two *moons* time.

This refolution was notified to the governor, who fent back the meffengers, and threatened them with the fevereft punifhments, if the village of the Apple was not put in his hands within a very fhort term. This anfwer was brought to the council, where the old men were of opinion that they ought to gain time, during which they fhould confult upon the means of getting rid of thefe troublefome ftrangers, who were going to become tyrants. As they knew M. *de Chepar* to be very felfifh, they agreed to propofe it to him, to grant them a delay of feveral months, during which each hut was to give him a tribute in Indian corn or maize, in game, and in furs. The avarice of the governor made him fall into the fnare; he accepted the propofition, but pretended however that he only did it in order to oblige the nation, whom he loved on account of their conftant friendfhip with the French. The *Great Sun* was not impofed upon by this artful difintereftednefs; he ordered his council to meet again, and informed them, that the term they had defired had been granted, and that it was neceffary they fhould make good ufe of it, confider of the means of getting rid of a heavy tribute, and above all of the tyrannical domination of the French. He obferved, that fuch an enterprize required an inviolable fecret, folid meafures, and, above all, a great deal of cunning;

cunning; he recommended it to them, that they should in the mean while increase the proofs of confidence and friendship to the French; reflect upon what was to be done, and return to the council as soon as they had hit upon some project which might be attended with certain success.

During five or six days the nobles and old men consulted with each other, and met again unanimously resolved to destroy all the French. The oldest man in the council, having saluted his chief, spoke to the following effect:

" We have long experienced, that the neigh-
" bourhood of the French does us more harm
" than good; we old men perceive it, but our
" youths do not see it; the European goods
" please the young people, but of what service
" are they? They seduce our wives, corrupt
" the manners of the nation, debauch our girls,
" and make them proud and idle. The young
" men are in the same case; the husbands must
" over-work themselves, merely to satisfy the
" luxury of their wives. Before the French
" came into these countries, we were men; we
" were contented with what we had; we walk-
" ed boldly on all the roads, because we were
" our own masters; but now we only go by
" groping,

"groping, for fear of finding thorns in our
"way; we go like flaves, and fuch we fhall
"foon be, fince they ufe us as fuch already.
"As foon as they fhall have power enough,
"they will no longer keep in bounds, they will
"load us with irons; has not their chief threat-
"ened to offer that indignity to ours; and is
"not death preferable to flavery *?"

Here the orator paufed; and, after taking
breath, continued as follows:

"What fhall we wait for? Shall we fuffer
"the French to multiply till we can no longer
"refift them? What will the other nations fay
"of us? We pafs for the moft fenfible among
"the *red* men †, and they will have reafon to
"fay that we have lefs fenfe than other people.
"Why fhall we wait longer? Let us fet our-
"felves at liberty, and let us fhew that we are
"true men. We muft begin this day to pre-
"pare for it; we muft order our wives to get
"victuals in readinefs, without telling them the
"reafon.

---

* Nature alone has taught thefe favages to refpect their fovereign, and to cherifh liberty.

† Thus the Indians call themfelves, to diftinguifh themfelves from the Europeans who are white, and from the Africans who are black.

LOUISIANA. 53

" reafon. Let us bring the *calumet* of peace to
" all the nations of this country, and tell them
" that the French ftrive to fubdue this whole
" continent; and that, as they are ftronger in
" our neighbourhood than any where elfe, we
" fhall be the firft whom they will load with
" their yoke. As foon as they fhall have fuffi-
" cient forces, they will load all the other na-
" tions with it ; let us convince them how much
" it is their intereft to prevent this misfortune,
" which cannot be avoided but by exterminating
" them ; let all the nations join us in this un-
" dertaking ; let us deftroy the French every
" where on the fame day, and at the fame hour;
" let the time of the maffacre be that of the ex-
" piration of the term their chief has granted
" us : thus we can free ourfelves from the tri-
" bute which we have laid on ourfelves ; and
" thus the victuals which we brought them, will
" come into our poffeffion again : On that great
" day of liberty our warriors fhall have their
" fire-arms with them ; the *Natches* fhall fpread
" among the French, there fhall be three or
" four of us in each houfe to one Frenchman ;
" they fhall borrow fire-arms and ammunition
" of them, under pretence of a general chace
" on account of fome great feaft, and they fhall
" promife to bring back fome game. Some
" guns fired near the houfe of the governor of
" the

" the fort, ſhall be the ſignal for them to fall
" upon the French. In order to make all the
" advantage we can of this blow, the other na-
" tions muſt ſecond us; they muſt make the
" ſame maſſacre of the Frenchmen at their ſe-
" veral ſtations; to be ſure of that, we muſt
" make ſome bundles of rods, containing an
" equal number, give each of them a bundle,
" and keep one; let them take notice of the
" number of days they are to wait; every morn-
" ing one rod muſt be cut in pieces and thrown
" into the fire, and when there will be but one
" left, the time of the ſlaughter is come; it
" muſt begin at the firſt quarter of the day (*i. e.*
" at nine o'clock in the morning); we ſhall fall
" upon our tyrants all at once; they ſhall be
" overwhelmed on all ſides; and when they are
" once deſtroyed, it will be an eaſy matter to
" prevent thoſe from ſettling among us that
" come from the old continent, acroſs the great
" lake. It muſt be recommended before all
" things, to be exact in drawing a rod from the
" bundle every day; the leaſt miſtake can have
" dangerous conſequences; we ſhall charge
" ſome wiſe man with it, and we muſt beg our
" neighbours to imitate us."

Here the orator gave over, and the old men
approved of his propoſal; the *Sun* of the *Apple
village*

village applauded above all; he was the moſt hurt by the injuſtice of M. *de Chepar*; his private revenge would accordingly be the moſt ſatisfied, he feared to ſee it fail, and therefore repreſented to the council the conſequences of indiſcretion, and even engaged them to keep the ſecret of this conſpiracy from the *female Suns* *. It now remained to make the grand chief of the *Natches* enter into their ſcheme; notwithſtanding the great deſire he had to be rid of the French, the project ſeemed too violent to him; the Sun of the Apple took upon himſelf to determine him to it; he was reckoned a man of ſenſe and penetration, and on that account was in great repute with the nation: he ſucceeded; he remarked to the great Sun the neceſſity of this meaſure, by telling him what he had to fear for himſelf; the French governor of the fort had threatened him, that he would ſoon drive him from his village; the great Sun was young, and conſequently a weak man, he that ſpoke to him was a cunning one, the deſign was approved of: the next morning, when the Suns came to ſalute their ſovereign, they received orders to go

* The Indians have two words to denote male and female Suns, (after the manner of the Engliſh words *prince*, *princeſs*) which the French author has happily expreſſed by *Soleil* and *Soleille*.

to the village of the Apple, under some pretence or other, without raising any suspicion that they went thither in pursuance of some order; this was executed as required. The seducing genius of the Sun of the Apple attracted them all, and they all promised to enter into the conspiracy. A council of Suns and old men was immediately formed; the project was proposed there again, and carried unanimously; the old men were appointed ambassadors to the other nations; they had warriors to accompany them, and it was forbidden under pain of death to speak of this to any person. They set out immediately all at once, and unknown to the French.

Notwithstanding the profound secret that was kept among the Natches, the common people was uneasy at the councils of Suns and noble old men that had been held; it is not uncommon in every country in the world, to see subjects endeavour to penetrate the secrets of the court. However, the curiosity of the people could not be satisfied; none but the female Suns (or princesses) had a right in this nation to enquire why they kept their proceedings secret from them. The young wife of the great Sun was but eighteen years old, and cared very little about it; only the female Sun called the *Stung Arm*, mother of the sovereign, and a woman of good sense (which she was not ignorant of) could take it ill, that they kept the secret from her. She shewed her discontentment to her son, who answered, that the embassies were sent out for the sake of renewing alliances with other nations, with whom they had long been at peace, and who might think themselves despised if they were longer neglected. This dissimulated answer seemed to appease the Sun *Stung Arm*, but it did not take off her uneasiness; on the contrary it redoubled, when she saw, upon the return of the ambassadors, that the Suns assembled in secret with those deputies, to hear how they had been received, whereas such councils were generally held in public.

The princess was vexed at this: What, said she to herself, they hide from me what the whole nation ought to know: if her prudence had not checked her anger, she would have given vent to it then. It was happy for the French that she thought herself thus despised; she justly feared to augment the impossibility of coming at the secret, if she laid open her displeasure. Her genius suggested her the means of satisfying her curiosity; she prevailed upon the great Sun, her son, to go with her to see a relation who lived in the village of the Apple, and who she had

heard

heard was very ill. Under pretence of leading him the fineſt road, ſhe took him on the longeſt, which was indeed the leaſt frequented. She had a good deal of penetration; ſhe imagined, that the motive of this ſecret aroſe from their carrying on ſomething to the diſadvantage of the French; what confirmed her conjectures, were the preparations which the Sun of the Apple was making. Finding herſelf in a ſolitary place with her ſon, ſhe ſpoke to him in the following words:

"Let us ſit down here, for I am tired, and
"I have likewiſe ſomething to ſay to thee;" as
ſoon as they were ſeated, ſhe added, " Open
" thy ears to hear me; I never taught thee to
" lie, and I always told thee, that a liar did not
" deſerve to be ranked among men, and that a
" lying *Sun* deſerved to meet with the greateſt
" contempt, and even from women; therefore
" I believe thou wilt tell me truth. Tell me
" then, are not all the Suns brothers? How-
" ever, they all keep off from me, as if my lips
" were cut off, and I could not retain my words;
" or doſt thou think that I ever ſpoke in my
" ſleep. I am in deſpair to ſee myſelf ſlighted
" by my brothers, but above all by thee.
" What, art thou not my own offspring? Haſt
" thou not ſuckled at my breaſt? And have I
" not

" not fed thee with my pureſt blood? Does not
" the ſame blood run in our veins? Couldſt
" thou be a Sun if thou wert not my ſon? Haſt
" thou forgotten, that, without my care, thou
" wouldſt have been dead long ago? Every
" body, and I myſelf have told thee, that thou
" art the ſon of a Frenchman *; but my own
" blood is dearer to me than that of ſtrangers.
" I now walk by thy ſide like a bitch, without
" being looked upon; I wonder that thou doſt
" not kick me away with thy foot: I am not ſur-
" priſed that the others hide themſelves from
" me; but thou, who art my ſon, canſt thou
" do it? Haſt thou ever ſeen a ſon miſtruſt his
" mother in our nation? Thou art the only
" one of that temper. There is ſuch an uproar
" in the nation, and I am ignorant of the cauſe
" of it, I who am the old Sun; art thou
" afraid that I ſhould rebuke thee, or make thee
" the ſlave of the French, againſt whom you
" act? O! I am tired of this contempt, and
" of walking with ſuch ungrateful people."

The

---

* This princeſs had, for a long time, loved an officer of our nation; there was no doubt of his being the father of the great Sun, and that took off nothing of the reſpect that his ſubjects owed him; the women gave nobility among them, and they were contented if they were ſure of a man's mother, they cared very little to know who was his father.

The fon of this Sun was quite ftruck with her difcourfe; he was moved by it to tears, and heard thefe remonftrances with the ufual tranquility of an American, and with the refpect due to a princefs; he afterwards anfwered her to the following purport. " Thy reproaches are " arrows which pierce my breaft, and I do not " think I ever fcorned or defpifed thee; but haft " thou ever heard it faid, that the refolves of " the council of the old men may be revealed? " Is it not the duty of all men to keep fecrets, " and I who am a fovereign ought not I to fet " an example? The great Sun my wife has " not been informed of the fecret any more than " thyfelf. Though it is known that I am a " Frenchman's fon, I have not been miftrufted; " they have well imagined, that thy great ge-
" nius would find out the fecret of the council; " but when it was kept from the great Sun my " wife, was it fit that thou fhouldft be informed " of it? But fince thou haft gueffed it all, " what can I tell thee further? Thou knoweft " as much of it as myfelf, fo fhut thy mouth."

" I was dubious," faid fhe, " about whom " you were taking fo many precautions; but " fince it is againft the French, I fear you have " not taken your meafures well to furprife " them: for I know they have a great deal of
" fenfe,

" sense, though the governor of this station has lost his; they are brave; they have goods in sufficient quantity to make all the other nations act against us. If you had a mind to attack only the red men, I should sleep with more security; I am no more young*; an old woman's life is a trifle, but thine is dear to me. If your old men have thought it as easy a matter to surprise the French as the red men, they are grossly mistaken; the French have resources which we have not, thou knowest they have the *speaking substance* (i. e. paper)."

Her son told her, that she had nothing to fear with regard to the measures which had been taken. After telling her all that I have just now informed you of, he told her that the bundle of rods was in the temple, upon the flat piece of wood (or the table).

When the princess was sufficiently informed of every particular, she pretended to approve of the proceedings; and, leaving her son entirely easy, she only meditated on the means of rendering this barbarous design abortive; she had but little time left, for the day fixed for the massacre was near at hand.

This

---

* Her lover was already dead some time.

This woman could not confent to fee all the French deftroyed in one day by the confpiracy of the *Natches*; fhe therefore undertook to bid them keep upon their guard; for that purpofe fhe made ufe of fome Indian girls who had French lovers, but fhe commanded them exprefsly not to fay that they acted by her orders.

The *Sieur de Macé*, enfign of the garrifon of the fort at the Natches, received advice by a young Indian girl who loved him; fhe told him crying, that her nation was to maffacre all the French. M. *de Macé*, amazed at this difcourfe, queftioned his miftrefs: her fimple anfwers and her tender fears left him no room to doubt of the plot: he went immediately to give M. *de Chepar* intelligence of it, who put him under arreft for giving a falfe alarm; feven of the inhabitants of the fort, inftructed by the fame means, coming to afk his leave to take up arms, in order to prevent a furprife, were put in irons; the governor treated them as cowards, and was vexed that they endeavoured to infpire him with any miftruft againft a nation that fhewed fo much friendfhip: the regularity of their payments kept up his fecurity: he did not fufpect the politics of the Indians; he blindly defpifed them, nor did he think men of their kind capable of fo much cunning.

The

The Sun *Stung Arm* faw with grief, that her cares for the confervation of the French were ufelefs; fhe was determined to ferve them in fpite of themfelves; fhe could not preferve them all, and therefore fhe endeavoured to leffen the number of victims as much as poffible; fhe fecretly went to the temple*, fhe drew a couple of rods out of the bundle unnoticed by the priefts; her intention was to forward the day fixed for the execution of the confpiracy; fhe forefaw that the maffacre which would happen at the *Natches* would foon be fpread far about, that the French who were fettled among the other nations would be informed of it, and be upon their guard. That was the only thing that remained for her to do, and fhe fucceeded in it; the Natches found they were come to their laft rod, without perceiving the impofture; they boldly began the intended flaughter, in the perfuafion that their allies would act at the fame time.

The 28th of December 1729, at eight in the morning, the Indians fpread among the French; fome difcharges of guns, that were to ferve as a fignal, were fired near the door of M. *de Chepar's* houfe;

---

* Only the Suns among the women could go into the temple.

houfe; and immediately they fell upon the French every where at the fame time.

Meff. *de Rolly*, chief factors of the Weft India company, were killed firft. M. *de la Loire des Urfins* houfe made fome refiftance; his fervants killed eight *Natches* before they were overpowered. M. *des Urfins* himfelf, who juft was taking a ride, but returned at the firft firing of the guns, was ftopped by a troop of Indians: he defended himfelf very bravely, killed four of them, and died pierced with wounds. This is all that the entreprife coft the Indians: they murdered near two thoufand perfons; only twenty-five or twenty-fix negroes efcaped, and moft of them were wounded. One hundred and fifty children, ninety women, and as many negroes, were taken prifoners, in hopes of felling them to the Englifh in *Carolina*.

During this carnage the great Sun was quietly fitting under one of the India company's ware-houfes; they brought him firft of all the head of the governor, then thofe of the chief Frenchmen, which he ordered to be ranged round the firft. All the others were put in heaps; the corpfes were not buried, and became the prey of vultures; they cut open the bodies of women big with child, and murdered

almoft

almost all those that had children at the breast, because their cries and tears importuned them; they made all the rest slaves, and treated them with the greatest indignity.

Some people pretend, that M. *de Chepar* had the misfortune to perish last of all, and to be the spectator of this horrible slaughter: he then found, but too late, how wise the advices were that had been given him. The Indians told him, that a *dog* as he was did not deserve to die by the hands of warriors: he was given up to the *stinking fellows* *, who killed him with arrows, and afterwards cut off his head.

Such was the death of a man who only followed his own head, his cruelty, his avarice, and his ambition. As no Frenchman escaped from his massacre, it cannot be exactly ascertained what kind of death they made the Governor undergo; it is enough to know, that his enemies were a barbarous people, whom he had irritated. A good administration would have attached them to the French, who drew great advantages from them: thus the fault of one man can draw after it the ruin of a whole colony; one cannot be suf-

---

* The common people among the Natches are called *Mi-hé-Michéquipi*, which signifies *stinking fellow*.

sufficiently cautious in the choice of those who are to be sent as governors into those parts. The Indians, notwithstanding the ideas we have of them, are not always easily managed; politics and wisdom must necessarily be employed, in order to obtain their friendship; they will not be offended with impunity, this history is a proof of it; nothing could be better conducted than the plot of the *Natches*; and how unhappy had it been, without the interposition of Providence! The Sun *Stung Arm* was worthy of the greatest acknowledgements, but it is not well known how they have been made to her.

The nations who entered into the plot with the *Natches*, not knowing the stratagem by which the stroke had been advanced, believed they were betrayed: The *Chactaw* nation imagined, that the *Natches* were unwilling to give them their share of the plunder of the French; and, to convince the latter that they had no part in the conjuration, they joined them in order to chastise the *Natches*. These returned the French women and the negroes whom they had taken; some time after they were attacked in their intrenchments, but escaped by the help of a thunder-storm, and quitted the country. About a thousand of them were taken and brought to *New Orleans*, and afterwards sold to the isle of

St. Domingo. Among thefe prifoners was the *Great Sun*, his wife, and his mother, who related to the French the above detail of the plot. The *Great Sun* difowned the maffacre; he faid that his nation had abufed his youth, in order to ftrike this blow; that he had always loved the French; that it was their own chief who had compelled the *Natches* to this defperate action, by his extortions upon a free nation. The French were contented with his difavowal; they treated him and his mother and wife with gentlenefs; but as they did not return to their nation, they foon died with grief. Since that time this country is not inhabited: the *Natches*, being purfued by the French, and being too weak to refift them, took refuge among the *Chicachas**, where they found an afylum.

We ftill have a fort here, but the colony is far from being brilliant; the means of eftablifhing it would be to attract other Indians to it. This is all, Sir, which I can relate to you concerning this part of the country. I fhall now foon leave it, and continue my voyage; and I conclude my letter, by renewing to you the proteftations of thofe fentiments which you know me capable of. And am, S I R, &c.

At the Natches, Sept.
10. 1751.

† Chickafaws.

68   TRAVELS THROUGH

LETTER IV.

To the same.

The Author arrives at the Akanzas. *Unhappy Death of the People of* Ferdinando Soto. *Reflections on the Folly of Men who seek for a Mountain of Gold. Origin of the famous* Dorado. *Short Account of the tragic Death of M.* de la Salle.

SIR,

FTER failing about a hundred and twenty leagues to the north of the Natches, up the *Miſſiſippi*, without meeting with any habitation on the road, we arrived among a nation famous for their friendship for the French, and known formerly from the expedition of *Ferdinando Soto*. I spoke to an old Indian chief of this country, who told me, he saw M. *de la Salle* here in 1682, when he discovered the great river *St. Louis*, known

under

under the name of *Miſſiſippi*, or, as the Indians pronounce it, *Meſhaſſepi*, which ſignifies *all the rivers*, or the *great river*.

M. *de la Salle* paſſed by this nation in coming down the river: he made acquaintance with them, and took poſſeſſion of their country in the name of *Louis le Grand*, of glorious memory *; after fixing the croſs and the arms of France there, he followed the courſe of the *Miſſiſippi*, which enters into the famous gulph of *Mexico*. He took the latitude at its mouth, which he found to be twenty-nine degrees north; he ſailed up again afterwards to the river of *Illinois*, from whence he went to *Canada*, and from thence he returned into *France*.

---

* If tyranny, oppreſſion, and unbridled ambition are ſufficient to immortalize a prince, it is certain *Lewis* XIV. has a juſt claim to be called *great*. It was his happineſs to have great miniſters in the firſt part of his life, in a time when the greater part of Europe had very few manufactures; but he was weak enough to give ear to the advices ſuggeſted to him by the Jeſuits, and a ſuperannuated and bigotted miſtreſs: this overturned the ſyſtem of grandeur for which the miniſters had laid a good foundation, and Lewis had the misfortune to ſee all the rival nations around him grow powerful and rich, by the emigration of his oppreſſed Proteſtant ſubjects, and thus he outlived his own greatneſs: his death was the moſt fortunate event for France in her weak and exhauſted ſtate. F.

On his arrival at court, he imparted his discovery to Meff. *Colbert* and *de Seignelai*, who obtained for him a commiffion from the King, importing, that all the countries which he fhould difcover from *New Bifcay* to the *Illinois*, and the people, both French and Indians, that fhould be in thofe countries, fhould be under his orders.

It was at the fame nation, called *Akanzas*, that Mr. *Joutel* arrived, who fet out after the death of M. *de la Salle*, with guides to find out the *Miffifippi*. This is the only officer who has left us an account which may be credited. I think I ought to give you an abftract of it; you will find the hiftory of M. *de la Salle* in it, and of the end of his unlucky expedition.

In regard to *Ferdinand Soto*'s voyage, I fhall but juft mention, that the general hiftory of the Weft Indies informs us, that this great officer, proud and enriched by the conqueft of *Peru*, after imbruing his facrilegious hands in the blood of the unfortunate family of the *Incas*, intended to penetrate into this country with the braveft of his foldiers, to fubdue the nations that inhabit the neighbourhood of this river, of which I am going to give you a defcription; but he did not know the interior parts of this vaft continent; perhaps he expected to find effeminate

nations

nations in it, as in South America; he was mistaken in his hopes, part of his people were killed with clubs by the Indians, who flayed the principal officers of his army, and afterwards exposed their skins on the door of their temple, which so frightened the Spaniards that they re-imbarked immediately for Europe.

The historian says, that *Ferdinand Soto* died of the shame which the bad success of this enterprize had brought on him, in 1543; and, since that time till 1682, this fine country has been inhabited by no Europeans.

The fate of M. *de la Salle* has been no happier than that of *Ferdinand Soto*.

There is no virtue in man which is not blended with some faults; this is generally the fault of human nature; and what increases our humiliation, the greatest virtues are often accompanied by the greatest vices. You will easily perceive this, Sir, by the short extract from M. *Joutel's* Journal.

M. *Robert Cavelier de la Salle* set sail from *Rochelle* the 24th of July 1684, with a squadron of four ships, commanded by M. *de Beaujeu*, a captain of a ship. Two hundred and eighty-five

five persons, together with thirty volunteers *
and some gentlemen, and a number of workmen
and girls embarked with him. M. *de la Salle*
was on board M. *de Beaujeu*'s ship, in whom he
reposed no manner of confidence. Whatever
that officer proposed to him, he always answered
with an air of haughtiness, *This is not the King's
intention*; he certainly did not take the proper
steps to interest a man in his undertaking, whose
assistance he wanted to make it succeed. Every
one accordingly began to judge disadvantage-
ously of an expedition, the chiefs of which seemed to act by very different principles; and time
has unhappily confirmed it.

The 28th of December 1684, the squadron
discovered the continent of *Florida*; and M. *de
la Salle* having heard much about the current
that set in to the eastward in the Mexican gulph,
he made no doubt but that the mouth of the
Missisippi was far to the west; an error that was
the cause of all his misfortunes. Accordingly
he bore away westward; but he advanced very
little, because he went near the shore from time
to

---

* Among these were three priests of *St. Sulpitius*, one of
them M. *de la Salle*'s brother, *Chedeville* his relation, and
Majulte, besides four recollects, who were to establish the
missions among the Indians. There were likewise two of
his nephews, *Moranget* and *Cavelier* fourteen years of age.

to time, and failed along the coaft, to try whether he could not difcover what he fought for.

The 2d of January 1685, the fquadron was, according to conjecture, pretty near the mouth of the *Miſſiſippi*; and on the 10th they paffed by it, without perceiving it. M. *de la Salle*, being perfuaded that the fquadron was but juft oppofite the *Appalachian* mountains, continued his voyage without fending his long-boat on fhore.

It is faid, that people fhewed him the mouth of the river, and that he would not fo much as take the trouble of getting a certainty, becaufe he had taken it into his head, that it could not be the place which was pointed out to him. His obftinacy could not be conquered nor juftified.

He certainly did not know, or did not think of it, that the greateft men in the world have often been, in part, indebted for their greateft fuccefs to people of inferior merit; and that thofe are the wifeft, who profit by the advice and underftanding even of thofe that are lefs endowed than they themfelves.

Some time after, upon fome hints which the Indians on the coaft gave him, he wanted to return;

turn; but M. *de Beaujeu* refused to do him that favour. They pursued the same course; and the squadron, in a few days, came to *St. Bernard*'s bay, without knowing it. This bay is one hundred leagues to the westward of the mouth of the *Missisippi*; they cast anchor there, and sent the boats upon discovery, in order to try to get knowledge of the place they were in. They found a very fine river, with a bar at the mouth of it, where there is not above ten or twelve feet water. This discovery was made after many times sailing backwards and forwards, and after several meetings of the council, in which nothing was concluded, because whenever one proposed any thing, the other was sure to oppose it.

M. *de la Salle*, who believed he was near the *Missisippi*, and whom M. *de Beaujeu*'s presence constrained more than it did him any service, resolved to land all his people in that place. Having taken this resolution, on the 20th of February he sent orders to the commander of the ship *La Flute* to land the heaviest goods, and to go up into the river. He intended to be present at the execution of his orders; but the Marquis *de la Sablonniere*, and five or six Frenchmen, having been taken by the Indians as they walked in the woods, he hastened to free them.

He

LOUISIANA. 75

He was not yet far from the fhore, when, cafting his eye towards the bay, he faw the *Flute* manœuvring in fuch a manner as to beat againft the rocks; his bad luck, fays *Joutel* in his relation, prevented his returning to avoid that misfortune. He continued his journey towards the Indian village, where his people had been carried to; and when he came there, he heard a cannon fired. He took this as a fignal to give him notice, that the *Flute* was loft; and his conjecture proved true.

Thofe who were witneffes to this accident plainly took it to be the effect of a premeditated defign of M. *de St. Aigron*, who commanded that veffel. This lofs had many difagreeable confequences, as it contained the ammunition utenfils, tools, and in general all that is neceffary to a new fettlement. M. *de la Salle* haftened to the place where the fhip was loft, and found every body in a total inaction. He begged M. *de Beaujeu* to lend him his boat and canoe, which he obtained very eafily.

He began with faving the crew; next he got the powder and flower, afterwards the wine and brandy; he brought on fhore about thirty barrels: had the boat of the *Flute* been able to

affift

aſſiſt that of the ſhip *Le Joli*, almoſt every thing would have been ſaved; but that was ſunk on purpoſe, and the night being come, they were obliged to defer the unlading till the next morning. Some hours being paſt, the wind, which came from the ſea, grew more violent, and the waves increaſed; the *Flute* beating againſt the rocks burſt, and a quantity of goods fell out through the opening, and were carried away by the ſea. This was only perceived at break of day; thirty more barrels of wine and brandy were ſaved, together with ſome barrels full of flower, meat, and peaſe: all the reſt was loſt.

To increaſe the misfortune, they were ſurrounded on all ſides by Indians; who, notwithſtanding the care that was taken to prevent their profiting any thing by the general confuſion, took away ſeveral things which had been preſerved from the wreck. The theft was not perceived till they were retired with the booty. They had left ſeveral of their canoes on the ſhore, which were ſeized upon: very weak repriſals indeed, which coſt much more than they were worth. The Indians came at night to take their canoes; they ſurpriſed thoſe who were left to take care of them, and, finding them aſleep, they killed two volunteers, whom M. *de la Salle*

regretted

regretted very much, and wounded his nephew and another person.

So many misfortunes, one after another, disgusted several persons who were upon the expedition; and, among others, Meff. *Doinmaville* and *Mignet*, two engineers, who were willing to return to France, to which the discourses of M. *de la Salle*'s enemies contributed greatly; for they never ceased to cry down his conduct, and tax his project as a silly and rash undertaking. He, on the contrary, never shewed more resolution and firmness; he constructed a warehouse surrounded with good intrenchments; and taking it into his head, that the river, in which he was, might possibly be one of the branches of the *Miſſiſippi*, he prepared to go up in it.

They immediately began erecting a fort; as soon as the work was somewhat advanced, M. *de la Salle* gave *Joutel* orders to finish it, left him the command of it, and about one hundred men: he took the rest of his people, about sixty in all, with himself, and embarked on the river, with the resolution of going up as high as he could. *Joutel* stayed but a short time after him in the fort which had been begun; every night the savages were roving in the neighbourhood; the French defended themselves against them,

them, but with losses that weakened them. On the 14th of July, *Joutel* received an order from M. *de la Salle* to join him with all his people.

Many good stout men had been killed or taken by the Indians; others were dead with fatigue, and the number of sick increased every day; in a word, nothing could be more unhappy than M. *de la Salle*'s situation. He was devoured with grief; but he dissimulated it pretty well, by which means his dissimulation degenerated into a morose obstinacy. As soon as he saw all his people together, he began in good earnest to think of making a settlement, and fortifying it. He was the engineer of his own fort, and being always the first to put his hand to work, every body worked as well as he could to follow his example.

Nothing was wanting but to encourage this good-will of the people, but M. *de la Salle* had not sufficient command of his temper. At the very time when his people spent their forces with working, and had but just as much as was absolutely necessary to live upon, he could not prevail on himself to relax his severity a little, or alter his inflexible temper, which is never seasonable, and less so in a new settlement. It

is

is not sufficient to have courage, health, and watchfulness, to make any undertaking succeed; many other talents are requisite. Moderation, patience, and disinterestedness, are equally necessary. It is useful to dissimulate now and then, to prevent making evil worse. Gentleness is the best method which every commander can follow.

M. *de la Salle* punished the least faults with an unheard-of cruelty; and seldom any word of comfort came from his mouth to those who suffered with the greatest constancy. He had of course the misfortune to see all his people fall into a state of languor and despondency, which was more the effect of despair, than of excess of labour or scantiness of good nourishment.

Having given his last orders at his fort, he resolved to advance into the country, and began to march on the 12th of January 1687, with M. *de Cavelier* his brother, *Moranget* and the young *Cavelier* his nephews, Father *Anastatius* a Franciscan friar, *Joutel, Duhaut, L'Archeveque de Marne*, a German whose name was *Hiens*, a surgeon named *Liétot*, the pilot *Teffier, Saget*, and an Indian who was a good huntsman. I mention them all, because they shall be spoke of in the sequel.

As they advanced further into the country, they found it inhabited; and when they were but forty leagues from the nation of the *Cenis*, they heard that there was a Frenchman among thofe Indians. It was a failor from Lower *Bretany*, who had loft himfelf when M. *de la Salle* firft came down the *Miſſiſippi*: this poor'wretch lived among the *Cenis* fince 1682, having been adopted by them. He did not hope to fee Europe again, nothing but chance could procure him the means of returning thither: *Joutel* went to fetch him from amongft thofe Indians. He only quitted them to be witnefs of a crime.

The 17th of May, *Moranget* being on a hunting party, and having, as it is faid, abufed with words *Duhaut*, *Hiens*, and the furgeon *Liétot*, thofe three men refolved to get rid of him as foon as poffible, and to begin with the fervant of M. *de la Salle*, and his Indian huntfman who was called *Nika*, who both accompanied *Moranget*, and could have defended him. They communicated their defign to *L'Archeveque* and the pilot *Teſſier*, who approved of it, and defired to take part in the execution. They did not fpeak of it to the Sieur *de Marne*, who was with them, and whom they wifhed to have been able to get away. The next night, whilft the three unhappy victims whom they would facrifice to their

revenge

revenge slept very quietly, *Liétot* gave each of them several blows with the hatchet on the head. The Indian and the servant died immediately. *Moranget* raised himself so as to sit upright, without speaking a word; and the murderers obliged the Sieur *de Marne* to dispatch him, threatening to kill him too if he refused; thus, by making him an accomplice of their crime, they wanted to secure themselves against his accusing them.

The first crime is always followed by uneasiness; the greatest villains find it difficult to conquer it: the murderers conceived, that it would not be easy to escape the just vengeance of M. *de la Salle*, unless by preventing him; and this they resolved upon, after deliberating on the means of effecting it. They thought the safest way was to meet him, and surprise all that accompanied him; and so open themselves a way for the murder which they intended to perpetrate.

So strange a resolution could only be inspired by that blind despair, which hurries villains into the abyss which they dig for themselves: an unexpected incident became favourable to them, and delivered into their hands the prey which they fought for. A river that separated them from the camp, and which was considerably increased since they passed it, kept them two days: this retardment, which at first seemed an obstacle to their project, facilitated the execution of it. M. *de la Salle*, wondering that his nephew did not return, nor either of the two men that were with him, determined to go and seek them himself. It was remarked, that he was uneasy when he was going to set out, and inquired with a kind of uncommon concern whether *Moranget* had quarrelled with any one.

He then called *Joutel*, and intrusted him with the command of his camp, ordering him to go his rounds in it from time to time, and to light fires, that the smoke might bring him on his road again, in case he should lose his way; he likewise bid him give no body leave to absent himself. He set out on the 20th, attended by Father *Anastasius* and an Indian. As he approached to the place where the assassins had stopt, he saw some eagles soaring pretty near the place, and concluded that there was some carrion: he fired his gun; and the conspirators, who had not yet seen him, guessing that it was he who was coming, got their arms in readiness. The river was between them and him: *Duhaut*

and

and *L'Archeveque* croſſed it; and ſeeing M. *de la Salle* advancing ſlowly, they ſtopped. *Duhaut* hid himſelf in the long graſs, with his gun cocked, *L'Archeveque* advanced a little more: and a moment after, M. *de la Salle* knowing him, aſked him where his nephew was? He anſwered, that he was lower down. At the ſame inſtant *Duhaut* fired; M. *de la Salle* received the ſhot in his head, and fell down dead.

It was the 20th of May 1687 that this murder was committed near the *Cenis*. Father *Anaſtaſius*, ſeeing M. *de la Salle* drop down at his feet, expected that the murderers would not ſpare him, though they ſhould have no other view in it than to get rid of a witneſs of their crime. *Duhaut* came near him to quiet him, and told him, that what they had done was an act of deſpair, and that they had long thought of revenging themſelves on *Moranget*, who had endeavoured to ruin them. Father *Anaſtaſius* informed M. *Cavelier* of his brother's death; that gentlemen told them, that if it was their intention to kill him likewiſe, he would forgive them his death before hand, and he only demanded, as a favour, a quarter of an hour to prepare himſelf for death. They replied, that he had nothing to fear, and that nobody complained of him.

Joutel was not then in the camp; *L'Archeveque*, who was his friend, ran to inform him, that his death was certain if he shewed any resentment of what had happened, or if he pretended to take advantage of the authority with which M. de la Salle had invested him. *Joutel*, who was of a very gentle temper, anfwered, that they should be content with his conduct, and that he believed that they ought to be pleased with the manner in which he had hitherto behaved; and then he returned to the camp.

As foon as *Duhaut* faw *Joutel*, he called out to him, that every one should command by turns. He had already taken all the authority into his hands; and the first use he made of it, was to make himself master of the magazine. He divided it afterwards with *L'Archeveque*, saying, that every thing belonged to him. There were about thirty thousand livres worth of goods, and near twenty-five thousand livres both in coin and in plate.

The affaffins had force and boldness on their side; they had shewn themselves capable of the greatest crimes, accordingly they met with no refiftance at first. They soon divided, and quarrelled among themselves; they found difficul-

ties

ies in dividing the treasure; they came to blows, and *Hiens* fired his pistol at *Duhaut*'s head, who reeled, and fell four yards from the place where he stood. At the same time *Rutel* the sailor, whom *Joutel* fetched from the *Cenis*, fired a gun at *Liétot*. That wretch lived yet several hours, though he had three balls in his body; so the two assassins, one of M. *de la Salle*, and the other of his nephew *Moranget*, were themselves the victims of that spirit of fury, which they had inspired to this unhappy colony.

The Indians knew not what to think of these murderers; they were quite scandalized by them. They were in the right, and could with more reason treat those Frenchmen as barbarians, than we had to consider them as such. Be that as it will, such was the tragic death of *Robert Cavelier, Sieur de la Salle*, a man of abilities, of a great extent of genius, and of a courage and firmness of mind which might have carried him to something very great, if, with these good qualities, he had known how to get the better of his sullen, morose mind, to soften his severity, or rather the roughness of his temper, and check the haughtiness with which he treated not only those who depended entirely upon himself, but even his associates. The most unhappy thing for the memory of this famous man is, that he has not been pitied by any body, and that the bad success that has attended his undertaking has given him the appearance of an adventurer among those who only judge from appearances. Unhappily they are commonly the greatest number, and their voice is, in a manner, the voice of the people. He has further been reproached with never taking advice from any body, and with having ruined his private affairs by his obstinacy *.

Thus ended this unlucky undertaking; many things conspired to make it abortive: it would at least have had part of the wished-for success if a settlement on the mouth of the Missisipp had been the only thing in view, as many people thought it was. It is certain, that when M. *d* *Beaujeu* abandoned M. *de la Salle* in St. *Bernard'* *Bay*, the latter soon found out, that he was to th

---

* In order to diminish the villainy of the deed of *Duhaut* it has been spread, that M. *de la Salle* had killed your *Duhaut* with his own hands, and that he had treated several others in the same manner; that it was despair and revenge that animated the conspirators, who feared to perish them selves by his injustice and severity. One ought to be much the more upon one's guard against such calumniating discourses, as it is but too common to increase the faults the unhappy, and to attribute to them even those which th really have not.

the westward of the river he sought for; if it had been his intention to find it, he might on his first journey to the *Cenis* have obtained guides from those Indians, because they granted some in the sequel to *Joutel* *; but he wished to come near the Spaniards, in order to take cognizance of the mines of *St. Barbara*, and to seek likewise a *Dorado*. By endeavouring to do too much, he not only did nothing at all, but made all his people perish, and perished himself, and was pitied by nobody.

Before I conclude this letter, let me add some reflections on the folly of men.

The avidity of the Spanish captains must have been very great, as it engaged them to seek for an imaginary *Dorado* or mountain of gold, whilst the whole country they were in abounded in all parts

---

* The Sieur *Joutel* found the *Missisippi* by means of the Indians, who brought him to the *Akanzas*, and from thence into *Canada*, ; where he arrived, accompanied by one priest, a Recollet friar, a soldier, a sailor, a colonist, and an Indian, who composed a strange sort of caravan. They were all that returned from this expedition. The remains of this unhappy colony perished either through the Indians or through the Spaniards, who took them prisoners, and set them at work in their mines.

parts with that metal. This is a proof, that all the treasures in the world are incapable of satisfying man, as soon as avidity has once gained the empire in his heart.

The Spaniards were not contented with the riches of *Peru*; they must still go to discover a *Dorado*, that is, a country where the rocks and stones are all of gold. The Indians, in order to flatter the avidity of their enemies, and at the same time to get them out of their country, never ceased amusing them with accounts of the gold, silver, diamonds, and pearls with which that country abounded. Their desire of getting rid of their unwelcome guests, induced them to spare nothing towards persuading them of the existence of this pretended country. The Spaniards believed these accounts, in which they were interested; and this is said to be the origin of the famous *Dorado*, which has made so much noise in the world.

The report was current, that, after passing a long chain of mountains covered with snow, one entered upon a vast plain exceedingly well peopled, in which was the *Dorado* that every one wished to discover.

Quesada,

Quesada, with two hundred and fifty brave soldiers, set out immediately in search of it. On *St. James*'s day they perceived, from the top of a mountain, some vast plains which resembled a sea; and when they were descended to the foot of the mountain, they built there a town, and called it *San-Yago*, in remembrance of the day on which they discovered the plain; they likewise surnamed it *Las Atalayas* *, in order to point out the design of their journey, which was to discover the *Dorado*. This town exists still in the place, which is marked in the maps as a monument which seems to engage posterity to go out upon the discovery of this unknown treasure. *Quesada* passed through the woods of *Ayrico* with excessive trouble, and arrived at *Timana* in 1543, having lost almost all his people.

Orellana undertook the same voyage in that year; he set out from *Peru*, descended the river *Maragnon* or of the Amazons, came to the coast, and neglected nothing towards arriving at the mountain of gold; but all his pains were useless, and he gained no more honour by the under-

---

* *Atalayar* signifies to discover, or to spy, in Spanish: *Atalaya*, a tower or fort from whence one discovers: *Las Atalayas* is the plural.

undertaking than that of having completed one of the moſt horrible voyages that ever were heard of. About the ſame time *Philip de Ure*, fearing that *Queſada* would profit alone by this diſcovery, ſet out from *Coro* in the province of *Venezuela*, together with *Aquito*, the Lieutenant *Velalcazar*, and one hundred and twenty men; but a *Cacique* having told him, that moſt of the people of *Queſada* had periſhed in the undertaking, he went to the ſouthward along the river *Guabari*, and ſtopped, as Father *Simon* and Father *Piedrahata* aſſure us, at the firſt ſettlement of *Omaguas*, in a very bad plight. But what will not men undertake for the ſake of gold! *Auri ſacra fames, quid non mortalia pectora cogis* * ?

But to what purpoſe is all this philoſophy.— The ſtay which I intend to make here, will enable me to ſend you a new letter on the ſubject of the moſt intereſting particulars of the politics and form of government of the nations who inhabit this country. I am,

SIR, &c.

At the Akanzas,
Oct. 29. 1751.

---

* Here follows a dull quotation from a Spaniſh author upon this ſubject, which we thought proper to omit. F.

LOUISIANA. 91

LETTER V.

To the same.

Description of the Manners of the Nation of Akanzas, their Religion and Manner of carrying on War; the Goodness and Fertility of their Country.

SIR,

I Hope the description I shall give of this Indian nation, by drawing your attention upon their particular character, will convey a general idea of all the nations of North America. There is indeed very little difference among them, in regard to their customs and their way of thinking, and especially in regard to a Supreme Being, which in their language they call *Coyocopchill*, which signifies *the great Spirit*, or the *Master of life*.

The

The *Akanzas* live on the banks of a river that bears their name; it arifes in *New Mexico*, and falls into the *Miffifippi*. Thefe Indians are tall, well made, brave, good fwimmers, very expert in hunting and fifhing, and entirely devoted to the French, of which they have given marks on feveral occafions.

I fpoke, in my preceding letter, of an old man of this nation, who faid he had feen M. *de la Salle*. This good Indian added, that from that time he conceived a very great efteem for the French; that they were the firft nation of white men he had feen, and fince that time he had always recommended it to his nation, whofe chief he was, never to receive any other European allies than the French, who were immediately received at his requeft: in reality thefe people never would have any thing to do with the conjuration of the general maffacre of the French colony at the *Natches*. I muft do thefe good Indians that juftice; they are always at war with the *Tchicachas* (Chickfaws) who gave the *Natches* a retreat.

The country of the *Akanzas* is one of the fineft in the world; the foil of it is fo fertile, that it produces, without any culture, European

wheat,

LOUISIANA.

wheat, all kinds of food, and good fruit, unknown in *France*; game of all kinds is plentiful there; wild oxen *, stags, roebucks, bears, tygers,

---

* The here enumerated animals, we intend to make better known, by adding the names in Dr. Linnæus Syft. Nat. and Mr. Pennant's Syn. of Quadr. or his British Zoology.

1. WILD OXEN. Bos Bifon, *Linn.* American ox, *Penn. Syn. Quad.* 8.

2. STAGS. Cervus Elaphus, *Linn.* Stag deer, *Penn. Syn. Quad.* 49.

3. ROEBUCKS. As it is dubious whether this species is in *North America*, this is probably the Dama Virginiana, Ray. *Syn. Quad.* 86,; or Virginian deer, *Penn. Syn. Quadrup.* 51.

4. BEARS. Urfus Arctos, *Linn.* Black bear, *Penn. Syn. Quad.* 190.

5. TYGERS. There are no true tygers in all the new continent, and what is called thus muft be the Cugacurana of *Marcgrave*, and *Ray. Syn. Quad.* 169. or Brown cat, *Penn. Syn. Quad.* 179.

6. LEOPARDS. Felis Pardus, *Linn.* Panther, *Penn. Syn. Quad,* p. 171. note. Mr. Pennant has proved, from very good authorities, that this species is found in America, contrary to what M. *de Buffon* says; who, though a very great naturalift, by far fuperior to many who make free

with

tygers, leopards, foxes, wild cats, rabbets, turkies, grous, pheafants, partridges, quails; turtles, wood-pigeons, fwans, geefe, buftards, ducks

---

with him, is however a man who never departs from an opinion which he once has embraced, and which he will carry by his eloquence in fpite of the moft creditable authorities to the contrary.

7. FOXES. Canis Vulpes, *Linn.* Fox, *Penn. Syn. Quad.* 152. with all its varieties, the crofs fox, the black fox, and the brand fox.

8. WILD CATS. Felis filveftris tigrina, *Briffon. Quad.* 193. Cayenne Cat, *Penn. Syn. Quad.* 182.

9. RABBETS. There were originally no rabbets in America, but they were imported by the Spaniards, and are now greatly increafed; whether thefe, here called rabbets, on the river *Miffifippi*, are the true rabbets, or whether they are that kind of hare which is peculiar to North America, cannot be decided. The North American hare feems to be the Alpine hare, *Penn. Syn. Quad.* 249; it is lefs in fize than the European common hare, and a medium between hare and rabbet, according to Kalm's *North Amer.* I. p. 105.

10. TURKIES. Meleagris Gallopavo, *Linn.* Le dindon, *Planches enluminées*, 97.

11. GROUS. There are about feven different kinds of grous in *North America*.

(a) Tetrao

LOUISIANA.

ducks of all kinds, teals, divers, snipes, water-hens, golden plovers, stares, thrushes, and other birds which are not known in Europe.

On

(a) Tetrao Phasianellus, *Linn.* The long-tailed grous, *Edward*, 117.
(b) —— Canadensis, *Linn.* The spotted grous, *Edw.* 71.
(c) —— Lagopus, *Linn.* The white grous, *Edw.* 72. *Pl. enl.* 129.
(d) —— Cupido, *Linn.* The pinnated grous, *Cat.* III. 1.
(e) —— Umbellus, *Linn.* The ruffed grous, *Edw.* 248.
(f) —— Canace, *Linn.* The striated grous, *Pl. enl.* 131. & 132, *Briss.* I. 203. t. 20. f. 1. 2.
(g) —— Togatus, *Linn.* The shoulder-knot grous, *Pl. enl.* 104. *Briss.* I. 207. t. 22. f. 1.

Which of these are found so far south as *Louisiana* cannot be determined.

12. PHEASANTS. This is so vague a denomination, that it is next to impossible to find out which kind of pheasant the author means; for there is but one pheasant in *America*, in *Cayenne*, and *Guiana*, and therefore it is dubious whether this bird is found so far north as *Louisiana*: I am therefore inclined to believe, the author meant the *long-tailed grous*, which bears a great similarity to a pheasant, and is found as far as *Virginia*, which is not above three or four degrees more north than the *Akanzas*.

13. PARTRIDGES. This seems to be the American partridge, *Cat.* III. 12. Tetrao Virginianus, *Linn.*

14. QUAILS.

On my arrival at the *Akanzas*, the young warriors received me with the dance of the calumet. It is necessary that I should inform you, that

---

14. QUAILS. Tetrao Mexicanus, *Linn.* Lousiana quail, *Pl. enl.* 149.

15. TURTLES. Columba Canadensis, *Linn.* Canada turtle, *Pl. enl.* 176.

16. WOOD-PIGEONS. Columba migratoria, *Linn.* Migratory pigeon. *Kalm*, II. p. 82. t. 2. Columba Carolinensis, *Linn.* Caroline pigeon, *Cat.* I. 24.

17. SWANS. Anas Cygnus, *Linn. Br. Zool.* p. 440. *Edward* 150.

18. GEESE. Anas Anser, *Linn.* Wild goose, *Br. Zool.* 447. Anas crythropus, *Linn.* White fronted goose, *Br. Zool.* 450. *Edw.* 153. Anas Canadensis, *Linn.* Canada goose, *Edw.* 151. *Pl. enl.* 346.

19. BUSTARDS, Otis Tarda, *Linn.* This is the first time that I find a bustard mentioned among the American birds. As they are not uncommon in France, I am inclined to think the author's account to be true; and as he has already mentioned the turkies before, it is not likely that he should confound the bustard and turkey.

20. DUCKS of all kinds. There are at least twenty kinds of ducks known to be in America. Vid. *Forster's Catalogue of North American animals*, p. 16. 17.

21. TEALS.

LOUISIANA. 97

that dancing enters into all sorts of tranfactions with thefe nations; they have religious, phyfical, merry, ceremonious, warlike, pacific, nuptial, funeral, playful, hunting, and lewd dances: the laft is abolifhed fince our arrival in America.

The dance of impudicity was performed privately and in night-time, by the light of a great fire. All that entered into the lafcivious affembly,

---

21. TEALS. I fuppofe the author means by teals the leffer kinds of ducks, as the harlequin, pied, brown, white-faced, blue-wing, &c. and common teal.

22. DIVERS are of four kinds in North America. Vid. *Forfter's Cat. N. Amer.* 16.

23. SNIPES. There are likewife feveral birds of this kind in *North America*; fo that without a more detailed denomination, it is impoffible to determine the fpecies.

24. WATER-HENS. Of this kind is the Rallus Carolinenfis, *Linn.* the Carolina rail, and the common water-hen, or Fulica chloropus, *Linn.* in N. Amer.

25. GOLDEN PLOVERS. Charadrius apricarius, *Linn.* *Edw.* 140.

26. STARES. Sturnus Ludovicianus, *Linn.* *Pl. enl.* 256. *Briff.* II. 449. t. 42. f. 1. *Cat.* I. 13. This bird has miftakenly appeared in the books of the modern ornithologifts under

bly were obliged to *strike against the post* *, that is, to swear that they never would reveal what they had seen or done in this dissolute ball: the dancers of both sexes appeared quite naked there, in attitudes and gestures of prostitution, accompanied with songs of the same kind, which you must excuse my transcribing, though, in the language of the Indians, they are purely pieces of genteel wit.

The *Akanzas* have expert fellows among them, who would perhaps amaze our jugglers. I saw

---

under two names: *Brisson* calls it, in II. 242. an American ouzel; and II. 449. he represents it as a Louisiana stare. *Linnæus* makes likewise two birds of it; he calls it a lark, p. 289. Alauda magna, and p. 290. a stare, Sturnus Ludovicianus; but, upon comparison, it may be easily determined, that both are but a stare, and that it ought to be erased from among the *Larks* and *Ouzels*.

27. THRUSHES. There are at least seven *North American* thrushes, which of them are upon the river *Mississippi* cannot be determined for want of information, F.

* Whenever the Indians swear or take oaths, they take a club with which they strike against a post, calling to mind their fine actions in war, and promising to keep their word religiously: an oath of this nature is irrevocable among them: every Cacique swears to lead his nation well, and strikes the post; without taking that oath, he cannot be installed in the dignity.

saw one of them, who, in my prefence, performed a trick which will appear incredible to you; after fome wry mouths, he fwallowed a rib of a ftag feventeen inches long, held it with his fingers, and drew it out of his ftomach again. He went to *New Orleans* to fhew his agility to the governor and the officers of the garrifon; this the Indians call acting the phyfician.

The *Akanzas* declare war with the following ceremonies. They make a feaft in the hut of the chief, where dog's flefh is ferved up, which is the principal food of warriors; becaufe they fay, that a creature which is fo brave as to be killed in the defence of his mafter, muft give them valour. He that kills one of the enemy's dogs is likewife received as a warrior; but he muft bring the fcalp of the dog, that is, the fkin from the head, as if it were the fcalp of a man, without which the others would not believe him. The Indians have dogs in great numbers, both for hunting, and to fecure them from being furprifed by the enemies.

After the feaft of which I have fpoken, the great chief calls together an affembly of warriors.

The assembly is held in the middle of the village, in a great hut made on purpose, which they call the hut of the council. The chief and most considerable men place themselves, according to their respective ranks, on mats or on tyger-skins. When they are all seated, the chief or orator puts himself into the midst of the assembly, and holds his speech with a loud voice: he represents to his nation, that it would be a shame for them not to revenge the affront they received from such or such a nation; that if they did take them to account for it, they would for the future be looked upon as women *. At that instant all the assembly applauds, by saying, *Heu! heu!* The chief then takes a bundle of rods, and presents it to the assembly; all that are desirous of going to war take one of the rods, and by this means they are enlisted.

The next morning the women run through the village, crying, " Young men and warriors " who received the rods, set out, go to war, re " venge the deaths of our relations, allies, an " friends

---

* When an Indian is called a *woman* or an *old woman*, is an affront, which signifies a man without courage, coward.

friends; and do not return till you are stained with the blood of our enemies, and bring with you their scalps *."

Then a young Indian takes the trouble to [p]aint red a club, which they call a *head-breaker*; [th]is club is brought upon the limits of the ene[m]ies country; there they cut a piece out of a [tr]ee, and with vermilion they draw on it two ar[ro]ws acrofs each other, which is their symbol of [w]ar: the red colour signifies, that the nation [de]sires revenge, and will not be satisfied till it [ha]s shed the blood of their enemies.

Before they set out, the chief of the nation [ca]lls another assembly, which is generally fol[lo]wed by a feast, to which he invites his allies. [T]he chief presents the confederates with rods, [to] engage them to march with them as auxiliary [tro]ops. At the end of the repast they sing and

H 3   dance

---

* The Indians are used to pluck the skins from their ene[mi]es heads whom they kill in battle; they count the num[ber] of the slain by these scalps, which they bring home like [tro]phies on poles. We generally give them, in goods, for [the] King's account, the value of ten crowns (écus) for each [sca]lp of our enemies.

dance the dance of war*. All the young men are painted red; it is really curious to see them dance. He that expresses by dance the discovery or the surprise, watches his enemy, keeping in a stooping posture; all at once he falls upon him, his club in hand, making horrible cries, as is done in a real action. His comrade drops as if he were thunderstruck, stiffening all his muscles as an epileptic; after which the other represents, dancing, the method of scalping the dead enemy; this is done with a knife which he has in his hand, he makes an incision on the forehead, and round the neck of his enemy; he places his long nails therein, he puts both his knees against the shoulders of the captive, and with a sudden push with his knees and pull with his hands, he takes up the skin with the hair on it, from the head. All this is represented in singing and dancing to the tune of a drum and a *chi-*

---

* The song of war is conceived in the following terms " I go to war to avenge the death of my brothers; I sha " kill, I shall exterminate, I shall plunder, I shall burn m " enemies: I shall bring away slaves, I shall devour the " heart, dry their flesh, drink their blood; I shall brin " their scalps, and make cups of their sculls;" and mo such expressions, which are full of cruelty, and shew a thir after revenge and slaughter.

a *chichikois* *, which marks the time and the cadence.

" The Indians never go to war without consulting their *Manitou* †, to whom they attribute all their good or bad luck. If the *Manitou* has not been favourable to them, they quit him without any ceremony, and take another. The chief, before he goes to war, undergoes a very rigid fasting, and paints his body black during that time. After the fast, he washes himself, and paints his body and his face red. He harangues his warriors before the false deity, after which every one prepares his baggage. Sometimes they go to war four or five hundred leagues from their own country.

Their baggage, in time of war, consists of a bear's skin, which serves as a bed; a wild ox's skin, with which they cover themselves; a tyger-cat's skin, which serves as a sack to put the calumet or tobacco-pipe in; a *head-breaker* or club;

---

* This is a gourd in which they put a kind of little beads; they likewise fasten such beads to their feet.

† False Indian deity; sometimes a dried raven or a snake; they likewise employ for that purpose amphibious creatures and quadrupeds.

club; and a little hatchet, which they make use of in order to make huts in the woods.

Their arms confist of a gun or musket, the horn of an ox to put the gun-powder in, which they hang round the body with a string, together with a little bag in which they put their balls, the flint, and a screw; besides this, a bow and a quiver full of arrows; the latter are very useful for hunting. They never employ their fire-arms at any animals, when they are upon any expedition against their enemies, left the noise might serve to discover them. They agree amongst themselves upon the method of surprising their enemies; for the Indians place all their glory in the knowledge of this kind of war, which is generally fatal to those who are the object of it.

They take very little care with regard to victuals; every one has a little bag of flour of Indian corn or maize, roasted as we do coffee, and when he is hungry he takes a spoonful of water in which some of this flour or meal is diluted, which he keeps till they are very near the enemy.

Though the Indians are sometimes three or four days without eating, they are not ill at all from it, but continue their road as before: they contract their girdle round their belly, in proportion as it grows more empty, and diminishes in size; in a word, they are indefatigable.

When the Indians have made a stroke at the enemy, as they term it, some young warriors immediately set out, to bring the news of the victory to the village. They make their arrival known, by some cries, which mark the number of prisoners, that of the dead, and that of the scalps which they bring with them. The women prepare to receive the prisoners, and to give them a hearty drubbing with sticks. They have likewise a right to decide who of the captives shall die, for they are brought before them with their hands tied, and painted black *. Those women who have lost their husbands, or sons, are at liberty to take captives to replace them. They can adopt them as husbands or as sons, and they are then immediately set free.

Those who are not adopted must be burnt at a slow fire: to that purpose their head is scalped,

---

* Those who are thus painted are to be burnt in the midst of the village, unless the women adopt them.

ed, and they are faftened to two pofts which are driven into the ground, with a piece of wood lying acrofs them *; then all the young people exercife their fury upon them, and they endure the greateft torments without complaining; on the contrary, they fing till they expire, faying that they are true men, and that they fear neither fire nor death; they laugh at their tormentors, and tell them that they do not make them fuffer enough; that if they were in their hands they would plague them much worfe; that the fire muft be applied to fuch and fuch parts, and that they are there the moft fenfible to pain. It is to be remarked, that when they difpofe themfelves to march againft their enemies, they take care to paint their bodies red; fo that, when they attack the enemy, with fuch howls as if they were bewitched, they really look like a troop of devils let loofe from hell †. They are good towards their friends, but very cruel towards their enemies.

As

---

* The captives are obliged to fing and dance round thefe pofts.

† The Indians in general, both men and women, have no hair on their bodies, befides thofe on the head; they fay, that in this particular we refemble the beafts, and they fay the fame when they fee us eat herbs and fallad.

As to religion, they believe the exiftence of a great Spirit, whom they adore under the form of a ferpent or a crocodile; they give him a kind of divine fervice. They fear the devil, whom they call a bad fpirit. They likewife adore the fun and moon. When it thunders, they imagine that the *Lord of life* fpeaks to them in an angry tone.

I muft not clofe my letter without informing you of a fingular event, which, though of very little importance, may however be very ufeful to me, during my ftay in *America*. The *Akanzas* have adopted me; they have acknowledged me as a warrior and a chief, and have given me the mark of it, which is the figure of a roe-buck imprinted on my thigh. I have willingly undergone this painful operation, which was performed in the following manner: I was feated on a tyger's fkin; an Indian burnt fome ftraw, the afhes of which he diluted with water: he made ufe of this fimple mixture to draw the roe-buck; he then followed the drawing with great needles, pricking them deep into the flefh, till the blood comes out; this blood mixing with the afhes of the ftraw, forms a figure which can never be effaced. I fmoked the calumet after that; they fpread white fkins under my feet;

on

on which I walked; they danced before me crying out for joy; they told me afterwards, that I could go to all the people who were their allies, present the calumet, and shew my mark, and I would be well received; that I was their brother, and that if any one killed me, they would kill him; now I am a noble *Akanza*. These people think they have done me all the honour due to a defender of their country, by thus adopting me: and I regard this honour almost like that which the *Marſhal de Richelieu* received, when his name was inscribed in the golden book at *Genoa* among the noble Genoese. It is true, there is some difference between an inscription and the operation I have undergone; I cannot express it to you how much I have suffered by it; I did all I could to prevent shewing how much I was affected; on the contrary, I joked with the Indian women that were present; and all the spectators, amazed at my insensibility, cried out for joy, and danced round about me, saying, I was a true man. The pain has been very violent, and I have had the fever from it for a week together. You cannot believe how fond the *Akanzas* are of me since that time. This is all I had to say upon this subject: some time this month we intend to continue our journey to the *Illinois*. As the season is much advanced,

vanced, and we have yet three hundred leagues to go, we run the rifk of being ftopped by the ice, and of wintering on the road. We have been obliged to ftop here for preparing the bifcuit neceffary for fo long a voyage; for in this feafon we muft combat both the current and the north wind. According to all appearances, I fhall not be able to write before next year. This letter fets out by a boat, which will arrive in time before the departure of a man of war for *France*, where I hope my letter will find you in good health. I beg you would let me hear from you; for I affure you, you can do me no greater pleafure.

I am, &c.

At the Akanzas, the 6th of November 1751.

P. S. I found a Meftizo Indian among the *Akanzas*; and, upon queftioning him concerning his origin, I heard that he was the fon of *Rutel*, that failor from *Bretany* who loft himfelf, when M. *de la Salle* came down the *Miffifippi* in 1682, and of whom I have had the honour of fpeaking before.

This

This demi-Indian added, that *Rutel* his father was found by the *Cenis*, an Indian nation, who adopted him; he received one of their girls as his wife, in the quality of a warrior; becaufe, having made ufe of his mufket in a battle againft fome enemies of the *Cenis*, the explofion of that weapon, which was as yet unknown to them, frightened them, and put them to flight.

This *Rutel* having afterwards taught the Indians the method of going with oars and fails in their canoes and piraguas, he enabled them to defeat a little fleet of their enemies; this manner of navigating being till then unknown to the nation, and drew their gratitude and veneration upon him; they revered him as the greateft man in the world; and the famous *Ruiter*, who, from a common failor, became Lieutenant and Admiral of the United Provinces, was perhaps lefs revered than *Rutel* was among the *Cenis*.

LOUISIANA. 111

LETTER VI.

To the same.

An Account of the Author's Navigation from the A-kanzas to the Illinois. *The King's Boat St. Louis, on which the Author was, is overset; he falls into the* Missisippi, *and an* Akanza *saves his life.*

SIR,

 AM now, thank God, arrived at Fort *Chartres*, after running many risks on this long and troublesome voyage. We set out from the *Akanzas* the 7th of November, on our voyage hither. We have gone three hundred leagues without meeting with any village or habitation. As this extent of country is absolutely uninhabited, there are happily great flocks of wild oxen, stags, and roe-bucks, to be met with, especially in this season when the wa-
ters

ters are low. Thefe animals are obliged to come in flocks to the river to drink, we often killed them as they croffed it, and likewife fome bears were thus got. The *Akanza* Indians generally come to hire themfelves to the French, in order to make them fubfift by hunting upon the road. Thefe hunters fet out in the morning in piraguas; they kill the oxen which they meet on the banks of the river, and the boats that follow after them take on board the meat, which lies ready for them on the fhore.

The Indians take care to keep the tongue, and the flefh from the back of the animals which they have killed, and to prefent thefe bits to the commander and officers of the convoy; after which a ferjeant or a corporal diftributes the flefh to the foldiers in each boat: the pleafure of hunting amply repays for the fatigues of the voyage. The game is fo common in the neighbourhood of the river *St. François* *, that, when we went on fhore in thofe parts, it was impoffible to fleep, on account of the multitudes of fwans, cranes, geefe, buftards, and ducks, that were continually going up and down in thefe watery places. On approaching the country of the *Illinois*,

---

* This river comes from the country of the *Hautaux*.

Illinois, you see, in the day-time, whole clouds of turtle-doves or wood-pigeons. A circumstance that will perhaps be incredible, is, that they often eclipse the sun; these birds, living merely upon acorns and the seeds of beech-trees, in the woods, are excellent in autumn; sometimes eighty of them are killed at one shot. What a pity that so fine a country is not inhabited, or is only inhabited by brutes!

M. *de Macarty*, an Irishman, and commander of the convoy, having had some fits of the gout, and fearing to be obliged to winter on the road, resolved to go before the rest, when we were at the juncture of the *Ohio* with the *Mississippi*, thirty leagues from the *Illinois*. He took the best rowers out of all the boats, and put them on board his boat, and, without troubling himself about the others, he left them behind, contrary to M. *de Vaudreuil*'s injunctions; however, the law of nature dictates to every body the order of assisting others mutually, in case of an attack from an enemy, or some other accident, such as happened to the boat *St. Louis*, on board of which I was. It got upon a sand-bank, and they were obliged to unload it almost entirely before they could set it a-float again, which made

VOL. I.   I   me

me lofe two days, and prevented my joining the convoy again.

To increafe my misfortunes, when I was but fourteen leagues from the *Illinois*, my boat, three days after it was ftranded, ran againft a tree, of which the *Miffifippi* is full, and efpecially in time of low water; the fhock burft the boat, and fuch a quantity of water got in, that it funk in lefs than an hour's time. By this accident I loft all I had : I ran the rifk of perifhing too ; for I had thrown myfelf into a piragua, but it was fo full of goods faved from the wreck, that it overfet; feveral foldiers were drowned, and I fhould have fhared the fame fate, had it not been for a generous *Akanza*, who, not fearing the feverity of the feafon, leapt into the water, and feized me by my riding-coat.

After thefe adventures I am at laft arrived at Fort *Chartres* : I had not been long here when I was witnefs to an event which might have had very unhappy confequences. The *Pehen guichias* and the *Ouyatanons* had agreed upon the total ruin of five French villages among the *Illinois*. M. *de Macarty* had fent me before-hand to prepare quarters for fome troops that came in

a con-a convoy. The Indians had meditated their enterprife, and intended to come before the convoy. I was then at the *Kafkakias*, where M. de *Montcharvaux* commanded, who could not juftly know the whole extent of the plot of thofe barbarians. Thefe were fpread in the houfes of the inhabitants; by their careffes, their affectation, and calling to mind the maffacre of the Natches, we fufpected their defign.

On fuch occafions as thefe, an officer feels all the weight of the command. M. de *Montcharvaux* was not difcouraged; he was feconded by M. *de Gruife*, an intelligent, brave officer. He held a council with the oldeft and moft confiderable people of the place; and did me the honour to confult me in this circumftance : it was more through his goodnefs than through neceffity, becaufe I was newly arrived, and confequently little acquainted with the fituation of affairs in that neighbourhood. I will however venture to fay, that he was pleafed with the advice I gave, though it was a very fimple one. My opinion was, that, in order to penetrate the defign of thefe Indians, we fhould keep on the defenfive, without fhewing the leaft fufpicion : that we fhould fend out fome armed inhabitants on horfeback, as if they went a-hunting; recom-

I 2 mending

mending it to them, that, after they had gone the rounds, they should return into the village full gallop, as if something had happened to them: this was to give a false alarm. There remained nothing further to be done in that case, but to examine the countenances of the Indians, who would certainly betray themselves. This advice was followed; the Indians believed the French had discovered their plot; they intended to execute it on Christmas-day, when the people came from the great mass; they had exactly inquired after that day, asking, in their way, when that day came on which the Son of the great Spirit came into the world.

As soon as they believed they were discovered, they thought only of making their escape; we fired upon them, and killed twenty-two on the spot. A serjeant, called *La Jeuneſſe*, a Creole, and a good hunter, killed four in my presence. M. *de Gruiſe*, on his side, attacked those who were in the Jesuits house, he wounded several of them, and took five alive, among whom there was one *Illinois*; they were put in irons.

M. *de Macarty* hastened to dispatch messengers to *New Orleans* to the Marquis *de Vaudreuil*, to give him an account of this expedition; the governor

LOUISIANA.

ernor sent back orders to deliver the prisoners to their countrymen, who came crying, the calumet in hand, and disavowed the plot, saying their people had lost their senses, and that the English had taken their senses from them. They received peace very thankfully, and all is quiet at present; however, for precaution's sake, the inhabitants have received orders to carry their muskets when they go to mass; and the officer of the guard to place two sentinels at the church-door during divine service.

I must not forget to mention to you, Sir, that all this passed without our having a single man killed or wounded. The Indians threw away their cloaths and their clubs to run the better; the vigilance of M. *de Montcharvaux* the commandant, and of M. *de Gruise* the major, has prevented the conspiracy, at the moment when the plot was to be executed. I am now returned to Fort *Chartres*, where we lead a pretty peaceable life; I cannot send any great news, but I will communicate some little anecdotes which may amuse you, and will at least give you an idea of our Indians.

I had hired an Indian for my hunter during winter; he belonged to the village of the *Mit-chigamias*;

chigamias; one day having got a very great quan
tity of game, inftead of bringing it to me, h
went to treat * with fome Frenchmen, wh(
gave him brandy in exchange, of which h
drank fo much as to lofe the ufe of hi
reafon. As he entered my lodgings in thi
condition, I received him very ill; I too
away the mufket which I had given him, an
turned him off by pufhing him out of doors
he came, however, into my kitchen againft m
will, lay down in it, and would not go out c
it. As foon as he was in his fenfes again, h
well conceived what a great fault he had con
mitted; and, being willing to atone for it, h
took a gun, powder, and fhot, and went ou
The next day he returns, and comes in, ver
haughtily, loaded with game: he had round h
naked body a girdle, between which all the heac
of the wild fowls were put; he loofened it, an
threw them into the middle of my room; h
then fat down near my fire, without fpeaking
he lighted his calumet, and giving it me 1
fmoke out of it, he faid, " I own I had loft ir
" fenfes yefterday, but I have found them agaii
" I a

---

* They call *treating*, the exchange or barter of Europe
merchandize againft the furs which the Indians take in hur
ing.

"I acknowledge my fault; and I beg thee to "excuse it. I agree that I had deserved the "treatment I received, being turned out of thy "hut; thou haft done well to let me come in "again, because, if the other Indians had heard "of it, they would at the leaft difpute reproach "me with having been turned out of the hut of "the chief *Great Nofe* *."

Many Europeans make no difference between the Indians and brutes, imagining that they have neither reafon nor common fenfe. However, the circumftance which I have now related, and a great many more, fufficiently fhew, that thefe people are fufceptible of fentiments of honour; they know how to do themfelves juftice when they are wronged, and know very well when they do ill. There are nations among the Europeans, of whom one may remark as ridiculous and barbarous cuftoms as among the American Indians.

To return to my hunter: you know very well, that drunkennefs debafes men to the rank

---

* An epithet the Indians gave me to diftinguifh me from the other officers, to each of whom they gave fuch denominations, relative to the good or bad qualities they obferved in them.

of brutes, and that this vice is corrected with difficulty even amongſt the French. The Indians imitate them eaſily in it, and ſay the white people have taught them to drink the *fiery water* *.

One day my Indian found the door of the King's magazine open; he ſneaked in like a ſerpent, got to a barrel of brandy, and ſhed half of it, by endeavouring to fill a bottle with it. This accident obliged me to diſmiſs him; however, as he was a good hunter, and had only one fault, his wife begged me to give him phyſic, to prevent his drinking: I willingly undertook the cure, with the aſſiſtance of his wife and relations. Once this hunter was drunk, but deſired ſtill more brandy; I got the people to tell him I had ſome, but that I was very tenacious of it. He came immediately, and aſked me for ſome: I ſaid, I had brandy, but I would not give it for nothing. He ſaid he was poor; however, if I would take his wife, he would hire her to me for a month. I anſwered, that the chiefs of the white warriors did not come to the red men to enjoy their wives; that if he would ſell me his ſon, I would willingly take him as a ſlave, and

---

* Thus they call *brandy*.

and give him in return a barrel of brandy; we made the bargain in prefence of feveral witneffes, and he delivered his fon to me.

I was ready to laugh at this farce, from the very beginning of it. I made him drink upon the bargain fome brandy, into which I had put long pepper. When he had drunk it, he was bound, and brought to fleep. When he was recovered of his drunkennefs, the Cacique of the village and his relations, who were in the fecret, came to him into his hut, where he lay upon a mat; they difplayed to him all the horror of the unnatural action he had committed by felling his own offspring. The poor Indian came crying to me, and faid, *Indagé wai panis*, *i. e.* I am unworthy of living; I do no longer deferve to bear the tender name of father. He was very angry at the brandy I had given him to drink, and which had fired all his ftomach; he called it *urine of the chief of hell*, that is, of the evil fpirit that caufed it.

His wife, who is naturally humorous, and who was diverting herfelf at his expence, afked him very coolly where his fon was? He ftill excufed himfelf, faying, that, knowing me to be very kind, he expected I would return him his

fon;

son; that he knew the grand chief of the French *, and the father of the red men, had no slaves in his empire. I told him he was in the right, but that I had adopted his son, and would take him in that quality with me to France, in order to make him a Christian, and that all the furs of his nation would not be sufficient to redeem him.

As the relations seemed to be grieved, they advised the drunkard Indian to go to the *chief of the prayer*, or the man that speaks with the great Spirit; for thus they call the priests: I told him, that if the chief of the prayer † required it, I should not be contrary to him; I would return him his son, on condition that he should be baptised, and that I should be his godfather; that as to himself, I required from him an abjuration of drunkenness, which had proved so fatal to him. He said my words were strong, and he should remember them while he lived; he begged I would adopt him as a brother, and said he was going to strike at the post ‡.

Since

---

* The French King.

† The Abbé *Gagnon*, of the order of St. Sulpitius, and chaplain of Fort *Chartres*.

‡ The Indian method of taking an oath. See Letter V.

Since that time he has never drank wine, or any fpirituous liquors; I have fent people to offer them to him, but he always refufed them, faying, that he had ftruck at the poft, and that the Lord of life would be angry with him; that I had told him that this Spirit could not be deceived: he rocollected that once I had named the number of glaffes of brandy which he had drunk, without my having feen him; to which he had anfwered, that it was very true, and that he believed that the great Spirit that fees every thing muft have told me of it. I took the following method when I wanted to know how many drams my Indian had taken. I left a clean glafs near a barrel of brandy; the Indian, being alone, was tempted to drink a glafs; after which I ordered the glafs to be wafhed in hot water, and put in its place again; and every time he drank, my people always did the fame thing. Accordingly it was very eafy for me to tell him, thou haft taken fo many drams; he was always amazed at it, and thought I was a forcerer.

I have often remarked, that the Indians are highly pleafed when the French carefs their little children; likewife, in order to make myfelf beloved and feared by them at the fame time,

when-

whenever I had reason to be displeased with their behaviour, I made use of this method: the more I seemed vexed and angry at the fathers, the more I affected friendship for their children; I caressed them, and gave them European toys. The Indians readily guessed, that as I had no reason to complain of their wives and children, I did not love them less than before, and was only vexed at those who had offended me, without extending my anger upon their families. This moved their heart, and consequently they went out, killed some wild fowls, brought them to me, and, throwing them on the floor, said, " This is to appease thee, be no longer angry " with us." I immediately answered, I willingly forget the past, when I see you come back with your wits, meaning when you do not come empty handed. A father's heart is the same all over the world; every father is pleased with the friendship which is shewn to his children, who make returns by their caresses.

You can well conceive, that a mere trifle can gain me the friendship of these people; and that it depends only upon the method of acting with them, to attach them to one's self at all events. But let this suffice for this time; I think I must recall to your mind the plan I purposed fed to follow; I only examine the fituation of the places where I ftop, and, during my ftay, I fhall apply particularly to know the genius of the people with whom I am to live for a time; and I think this ftudy not beneath a traveller. You are a foldier and a philofopher; I am perfuaded, that what I fhall give you an account of will pleafe you; for I flatter myfelf, that you depend upon the fidelity of your hiftorian : indeed, I mean to affert nothing but what I am an eye-witnefs of; for I can neither invent nor exaggerate. I am, SIR, &c.

At Fort Chartres, among the Illinois,
  the 28th of March 1752.

LETTER VII.

To the same.

Description of the War of the Nations of Foxes against the Illinois, of which the Author has been an Eye-witness. Account how the French settled among these People.

SIR,

 HAVE enquired after the manner in which the French settlement has been made here. The country of the *Illinois* was discovered by our Canadian hunters; they found its climate very good, being in forty degrees north latitude, settled on it, and made an alliance with the natives. Many people among them married Indian girls, of which the greatest part became Christians: and after the discovery of *Louisiana*, the India Company sent many families

lies

lies over hither, who lived and multiplied here. There are now five great villages of French inhabitants in thefe parts *. The moft confiderable place is called *Kafkakias*, a name of the tribe of an *Illinois* fettlement, which is about half a league from it. The Sieur *Sauffier*, an engineer, has made a plan for conftructing a new fort here, according to the intention of the court. It fhall bear the fame name with the old one, which is called Fort *de Chartres*.

The *Illinois* country is one of the fineft in the world; it fupplies all the lower parts of *Louifiana* with flower. Its commerce confifts in furs, lead and falt. There are many falt fprings †, that attract the wild oxen, and the roe-bucks, which like the paftures around them very much. Their flefh and tongues are falted, and furnifh another branch of commerce to *New Orleans*; and they cure hams, which equal thofe of *Bayonne*. The fruits are as fine as in *France*.

---

* The India Company were poffeffed of Louifiana; but they gave it back to the King in 1731. The five villages of the French are that of the *Kafkakias*, the Fort *Chartres*, St. *Philip*, the *Kaokias*, and the *Prairie du Rocher* (meadow on the rock); there is now a fixth, called St. *Genevieve*.

† Called *Salt-licks*, by the Englifh Planters. F.

The

The *Illinois* have very near the same manners and customs as the Nations I have already spoken of; they only differ in their language. They marry, and often, when they return from hunting, leave each other again, each party going a different way.

The marriage of the Indians is quite in the state of nature, and has no other form than the mutual consent of the parties. As they are not tied by any civil contract, whenever they are dissatisfied with each other, they separate, without ceremony, saying that marriage is a tie of the heart, and that they only marry in order to love each other, and help each other mutually in their wants. I have seen very happy marriages among these people; divorces and polygamy are uncommon amongst them, though the latter is allowed by the laws. An Indian may have two wives if he hunts well; sometimes one Indian marries two sisters, giving it as a reason that they will agree better among themselves, than two that are strangers to each other. The Indian women in general are very laborious; they are commonly told, when they are young, that if they be idle or heavy, they will get a wretched husband. Here avarice, ambition, and many other passions, so common among the

Europeans,

LOUISIANA.

Europeans, never ſtifle the feelings of nature, in a father's breaſt, or incline him to force his children, and much leſs to controul them in their inclinations. By an admirable ſympathy, deſerving of admiration, thoſe only are married, who love each other.

The *Illinois* Indians were formerly the moſt formidable in *Louſiana*, but the continual wars, which they have been engaged in, againſt the northren nations, have reduced them to a very ſmall number. The hatred of the *Canada Indians* againſt them, ariſes from the incurſions which the *Illinois* were uſed to make into their country, and becauſe they took and killed in theſe inroads, both the male and female beavers, which among theſe nations is reckoned a crime and cowardice, becauſe they make a great commerce with the ſkins of theſe *amphibia* *, which they exchange for European goods.

In 1752, the Indians of the tribe of *Koakias* met ſix Indians of the nation of *Foxes*, hunting †; they

---

* Beavers are quadrupeds and probably called, by our author, *amphibia* for no other reaſon, but becauſe they may be eaten as fiſh on the *jours maigres* F.

† Their true name is *Outagamis*; they inhabit the country to the weſt of the Lake *Michigan*.

they took them prisoners, though they were not at war, and resolved to burn them, that they might not give any account of them. One of the *Foxes*, or *Outagamis* was happy enough to escape from the stake he was fastened to, and being pursued by his tormentors, he leaped into a lake, and eluded their researches, by swimming under water. He remained hidden in the rushes, only putting out his head from time to time to take breath. He had the firmness to remain in that posture while his comrades were broiling. In the night time he escaped the watchfulness of the *Illinois*, who thought he was either drowned or eaten by the *armed fish* *. As he was naked and without arms, he was obliged, in order to subsist upon the road, to eat grass like a beast. Being returned to his nation, he told them what had happened to him with the *Illinois*, and the unhappy fate which they had made his fellow-travellers undergo. Their relations immediately began to grieve for them after their manner. The chief of the nation called an assembly together, for they undertake nothing without a council; the result

---

* The armed fish in *Louisiana* is exceedingly voracious. His teeth cut the iron of the fish hooks in pieces.

result was to send bundles of rods * to the chiefs of the tribes, who were their allies, among whom were the *Sioux*, the *Sakis* and the *Kikapous* who marched as auxiliary troops under the standard of the *Foxes*. The army consisted of a thousand warriors; every thing being in readiness, the general of the *Foxes* marched towards the *Illinois*, and chiefly towards the *Mitchigamias* who had given shelter to the *Koakias*.

The warriors being come together to the number of one thousand, they embarked in one hundred and eighty canoes made of birch tree bark, on the river *Ouisconsing* which falls into the *Mississippi*. By the current of the river, and the help of their oars, they were soon brought to their enemies, the *Illinois*.

They passed in good order by the fort of *Koakias* where the Chevalier *de Volsei*, an officer of my detachment, commanded. The van of this fleet of the *Foxes*, consisted of the best runners, who were to go on shore to reconnoitre. They landed

---

* As the Indians have not got the art of writing, the rods mark the number of warriors, and the day of assembling for the departure of the army.

landed about a quarter of a league from the *Mitchigamias* village, which was furrounded within a mufket fhot by a wood; their enemies being far from expecting fuch a vifit.

The *Foxes* had fixed upon *Corpus Chrifti* day for fighting the *Illinois*. They knew that the latter would come to Fort *Chartres* to fee the ceremony which is performed by the French on that folemn day; the fort was only a league from the Indian village.

Every thing being in readinefs for the attack, the general of the *Foxes* ordered ten or twelve of the beft runnners to throw away their bodies †. Thefe young men immediately fell upon the enemy's village and killed all they met as they came in, crying the cry of death, and having difcharged their arms, they fled with as much quicknefs as they came.

The *Illinois* took up their arms and purfued them; but the army of the *Foxes*, lying on the ground,

---

* This is a great holiday with the French.

† To *throw away* their bodies, is among the Indians to *expofe* their bodies *to danger*, as thofe do that are obliged to mount firft of all the breach to ftorm a place.

LOUISIANA. 133

ground, in the high grafs, difcharged all their arms and killed twenty-eight *Illinois*: at the fame time they fell upon the village, and killed men, women and children; fet fire to the village, and bound and led away the reft as captives.

The *Foxes* loft but four men in this glorious expedition, one of them being a chief with a medal *, of the nation of *Sioux*, who went with them as an ally.

I was a fpectator of this flaughter, which happened on the fixth of June 1752. I was at that time on a hill which overlooks the plain and the village of the *Mitchigamias*. I had the opportunity of faving the life of a girl of fifteen years of age, who came to bring me fome ftraw-berberries. At the time of the attack, fhe ran away, and as the enemies purfued her, fhe ran into my arms, where the barbarians did not venture to fhoot at her, for fear of hitting me.

---

* This diftinction, of which I have already fpoken, is granted by order of the King, through his general, to the moft valiant Indians, and who are moft attached to the French nation.

This account will inform you, that nothing can be more dangerous, than being taken unawares by these nations. None but those, who were gone out of curiosity to see the procession at the French fort of *Chartres*, escaped the revenge of the *Foxes*, who contented with their victory, re-embarked in their boats, and put the prisoners well bound in the van; and passing by the French fort of *Koakias*, they gave a general salute with their guns.

The chief, or admiral of the *Foxes*, had hoisted the French colours on his canoe, and was as proud of his victory, as if he had subdued a great empire.

M. *de Macarty*, our governor, has written to those in the posts of Canada, to treat with the *Foxes* concerning the ransom of the *Illinois*, whom they have taken prisoners.

These cunning Indians had conducted their undertaking so well, that we knew nothing of it till it was executed; they hid the knowledge of it from us, justly fearing that we should interpose our mediation between them and the *Illinois*, as being the friends and allies of both; but the offended nation was defirous of vengeance only.

The village of the *Mitchigamias* has loft about eighty perfons, both killed and prifoners, in this fatal affair.

On the fixteenth of *June*, I was ordered by the commandant of Fort *Chartres*, to affemble the remains of the conquered tribes of *Koakias* and *Mitchigamias*, and I held this fhort fpeech to them, by means of the King's interpreter.

I fpeak to you, my children *, on the part of your father, M. *de Macarty*, who takes a great fhare in your misfortune, at the fame time he exhorts you to take care in fowing your maize, that you may efcape the want in which you are at prefent. Here is fome maize, which he gives you, becaufe his heart fuffers to fee you weakened by hunger. He has likewife told me to give this little quantity of powder, fhot and flints; we cannot do better at prefent, becaufe we have our enemies as well as you, and we do not know when the boats will come from the great village (i. e. *New Orleans*) Your father recom-

---

* The Indians are ufed to call every officer, *my father*.

recommends it to you to go a hunting, and to take your families with you, that they may have somewhat to live upon, leaving only a certain number of men, to take care of the fields, and to prevent the wild beasts from ruining them; you must likewise take care to send one of your people from time to time, to inquire how matters stand here.

The Answer of the Chiefs of the Tribes.

" It is very well, my Father, that the great chief *
" pities us. It was a very brave action to be sur-
" prized in the manner we have been; thou hast been
" an eye-witness of it, for thou hast saved the life
" of one of our girls; our tribe have been killed
" by the *Foxes*, who have burnt our huts with our
" victuals, and taken our booty, during our re-
" treat at the *Kaskakias*. Thou must think, that
" we cannot leave any here, or they must starve,
" and would ever lament the death of our rela-
" tions, who perished in this sad action. But to
" convince our father of our fidelity, tell him,
" by means of the speaking substance (paper),
" that from time to time we shall send some one
" of

---

* Thus these nations call the superior officers of a province or district.

LOUISIANA.

" of our people to him with game to know what
" happens here.

" We hope the grand chief of the French
" will protect and help us to shelter ourselves a-
" gainst the enemy. We beg thee likewise to make
" interest with him that he may be so good as to
" send word to several families of our people,
" who stayed among the *Kaskakias*, to join us,
" in order to assist us in the common defence of
" the intended fort, of which we have drawn
" the plan on the shore of the *Missisippi*."

Speech of Chikagou, a Chief with a Medal.

" I beg, my father, that thou wouldst get our
" arms mended, and we shall decamp after that
" immediately: and that thou wilt tell the grand
" chief not to hear the bad words, which our
" enemies will not fail to throw out against our
" nation, let him remember the promise I made
" him, it shall be a true one; and I preserve his
" words in my heart."

Answer.

If what thou sayest be true, thy father will
receive thee well, and all the other chiefs will

endeavour

endeavour to pleafe thee, if thy heart agree with thy tongue. It is neceffary thou fhouldft fet out foon: confider the damage which the dogs of thy village have done among the cattle belonging to the French inhabitants *, and with what tranquility they fuffer it; that they have hitherto faid nothing about it, is in confideration of your misfortunes, which grieve them, and they cannot fee you reduced to this fad condition without being moved at it: but they begin to be tired, therefore you muft remedy it. Your father will be fatisfied when he knows that you are gone to the hunting country, becaufe his heart is afflicted to fee you fuffer hunger, and he pities his children.

As to myfelf, I heartily wifh you good fuccefs in hunting, and a plentiful crop at your return. I hope the *Great Spirit* will have pity upon you; do not flight him: recommend it to your young people not to play the fool, that is, not to deftroy the female beavers in the lakes

and

---

* The Indians have many dogs for hunting; and they themfelves having loft their provifions, their dogs were hungry, and devoured the cattle of the French. The Indian dogs are of a breed which partakes of the wolf and the dog.

and hunting places of your enemies, who will not fail to be revenged for it, as you have unhappily experienced.

Your father has written to Mr. *Adamville*, who commands at the *Peorias*, to make your peace with the *Foxes*, and to treat with them about the ranfom of your wives and children, whom they have taken prifoners; the merchandizes fhall be furnifhed for that purpofe for the account of the king, your father, grand chief of the white men and of the red men.

Among the Indians, thofe who run away or defert in an action, where their honour, and the defence of their country is at ftake, are not punifhed; but they are confidered as the difgrace of human nature. The others are continually reproaching them, that they are not men, but old women; they are defpifed by the very women, and the uglieft girls will not accept of them for hufbands, and if ever it happened that a girl fhould be willing to marry a coward, her relations would not allow of it, for fear of having men without courage, and ufelefs to their country in their family. Thefe men are obliged to let their hair grow, and to wear an *alkonan*,

like

like the women *. I faw one of them, who being afhamed of his figure, went by himfelf to fight the *Tchikachas*, who are our enemies and theirs. He came near them, creeping like a fnake, and hiding himfelf in the great grafs during three or four days, without eating or drinking. As the Englifh bring goods to the *Tchikachas* (Chickfaws) in caravans, our *Illinois* killed one of them who had ftrayed from the caravan, cut off his head, mounted his horfe, and got off. He was out three months upon this fine expedition. On his return the nation received him with due honour, and gave him a wife, that he might beget warriors. Before his departure he eat of dog's flefh, conformably to the opinion current among his people, and of which I have already had the honour of fpeaking to you.

The grand chief of the *Illinois* is defcended from the family of the *Tamaroas*, who were formerly fovereigns of this country. This Cacique or Indian king, is the fon of him that went to France with his attendants in 1720. He was prefented to the King, who gave him a medal with his portrait, which the fon now wears on his

---

* A fhort petticoat, which the Indian women make ufe of, to cover their nakednefs.

his breaſt. There was likewiſe a woman of the nation of the *Miſſouris*, who was called the princeſs of the *Miſſouris* *. The Sieur *Dubois*, a ſerjeant, and interpreter of thoſe American ambaſſadors, having been created an officer by the King, married this *Miſſourian* lady at his return. She became a widow; and afterwards married the Sieur *Marin*, a captain of the militia, by whom ſhe had a daughter, who is ſtill alive.

The Indian princeſs deſcribed to her countrymen the magnificence ſhe had ſeen at the court of France, where ſhe had been well received, and loaded with preſents; ſhe had, amongſt other things, got a fine repeating watch ſet with diamonds, which the ſavages called a ſpirit, on account of its motion, which ſeemed ſupernatural to them.

I have here ſpoken with an old Indian, who was in the retinue of the Prince *Tamaroas*; I aſked him ſeveral queſtions concerning France, and

---

* She was the daughter of the grand chief of this nation. It is ſaid ſhe was M. *de Bourinont*'s miſtreſs, who, during his command among the *Miſſouris*, never ceaſed to praiſe and extol the wonders of France, and by that means engaged ſeveral to follow him: this girl went over to the Chriſtian religion, and was baptiſed at the church of *Notre Dame*.

and especially what fine sights he had seen at *Pa-ris:* he answered, that it was the *Rue de Boucheries,* (the shambles) because there was a great abundance of flesh; and after that the *Rue St. Honoré.* When he told his countrymen that he had seen the opera, and that all the people there are jugglers or sorcerers; and that he likewise saw, upon the *Pont-Neuf,* some little men who danced and sung *, they would not believe him. When he said, that, in the great village of the French *(Paris),* he had seen as many people as there are leaves on the trees in their forests, (an hyperbole which the Indians make use of to express a great number, having no words to express a number above a hundred), they answered, that the Europeans probably had fascinated his eyes, that it was impossible, and that they had always offered the same objects to his eyes. He said that he had seen the huts of the grand chief of the French, *i. e. Versailles* and *Louvre,* and that they contained more people than there are in their country: he likewise added, that he had seen the hut of the old warriors, (the royal hospital of invalids). As this old Indian began already to doat, he agreed with the other Indians, that the French had bewitched him. Another
Illinois,

---

* A puppet-show.

Illinois, who had made the same voyage, told his countrymen, that, in the *Thuilleries*, and other public walks, he had seen men who were half women, having their hair dressed like women, wearing the same ear-rings, and great nose-gays on their breast; that he suspected they put *rouge* on their faces, and that he found they smelled like crocodiles *.

This Indian spoke with the greatest contempt of that race of mortals, whom we know under the name of *petits-maitres*, or beaus, who are born with the weakness and the delicacy peculiar to women; nature seeming to have begun making them such, and afterwards to make a mistake in the formation of their sex.

The Indian had likewise remarked the enormous height of the head-dresses of our women in that time †, and of the heels of their shoes. But what would he have said, if he had seen the extravagant width of their hoops, and their fine shape

---

* The crocodile in the *Mississippi* has follicles with musk, which smells stronger than the East Indian musk; its effluvia are so strong, that you can often smell the animal before you see it.

† During the regency.

shape forced, from their infancy, into that elegant cuirass called stays. These coquets are not less ridiculous by their artifices, than their silly adorers. You have made the observation, as I have done, in the course of your travels through Europe, that the foreigners and country gentlemen, who come to *Paris* to copy our beaus and our belles, have rendered themselves insupportable to their countrymen by this unnatural method of acting: indeed, said our American, such effeminate manners dishonour a respectable nation.

I have received a letter from the Marquis *de Vaudreuil*, in which he expresses great concern for the unhappy accident which has befallen me, by the wreck of my boat. This governor, from a pure effect of his generosity, which is natural to him, has been willing to alleviate, as much as is in his power, the fate of an unhappy officer, who lost all he had in the King's service.

He has given me leave to come to *New Orleans*, and offered me his purse and his table; I am afraid he will be gone for France by the time I arrive at *New Orleans*. It may be said with truth, that he has deserved the esteem and friendship of every body. The Indians incessantly com-

LOUISIANA. 145

compare him now to M. *de Bienville*, his predeceffor. When thefe people do not fpeak in praife of a governor, but, on the contrary, agree with all the inhabitants in detefting him, it is the ftrongeft accufation againſt him.

Before I conclude, I fhall add a word about the *Miſſouris*. Baron *Porneuf*, who has been governor of Fort *Orleans* eftabliſhed in that nation, and who knows their genius perfectly well, has informed me, that they were formerly very warlike and good, but that the French hunters had corrupted them, by their bad conduct, and by fome difunions among them; they had made themfelves contemptible by frauds in trade; they feduced and carried off the Indian women, which, among thefe people, is a very great crime; for they never pardon fuch forts of robberies. All the irregularities of thefe bad Frenchmen irritated the *Miſſouris* againſt them; and therefore, during M. *de Bienville*'s government, they maffacred the Sieur *Dubois*, and the little garrifon under his command; and as no foldier efcaped, we have never been able to know who was right and who was wrong.

The ftory I fhall tell you will convince you, that thefe people are only nominally favages, and that the French, who endeavoured to impofe upon them, have deceived themfelves. About forty years ago, when thefe Americans did not yet know the Europeans, a traveller or hunter penetrated into their country, made them acquainted with fire-arms, and fold them mufkets and gunpowder: they went out a-hunting, and got great plenty of game, and of courfe many furs. Another traveller went thither fome time after, with ammunitions; but the Indians being ftill provided, they did not care to barter with the Frenchman, who invented a very odd trick, in order to fell his powder, without much troubling his head with the confequences that might refult from his impofture to his countrymen. He thought he had done a great action in deceiving thefe poor people.

As the Indians are naturally curious, they were defirous of knowing how powder, which they called *grain*, was made in France. The traveller made them believe, that it was fown in *favannahs*, and that they had crops of it as of indigo or millet in *America*.

The *Miffouris* were pleafed with this difcovery, and fowed all the gun-powder they had left, which obliged them to buy that of the Frenchman,

man, who got a confiderable quantity of beaver-fkins, otter-fkins, &c. for it, and afterwards went down the river to the *Illinois*, where M. *de Tonti* commanded.

The *Miſſouris* went from time to time to the *favannah*, to fee if the powder was growing: they had placed a guard there, to hinder the wild beafts from fpoiling the field; but they foon found out the Frenchman's trick: It muft be obferved, that the Indians can be deceived but once, and that they always remember it; accordingly thefe were refolved to be revenged upon the firft Frenchman that fhould come to them. Soon after, the hopes of profit excited the traveller to fend his partner to the *Miſſouris*, with goods proper for their commerce; they foon found out, that this Frenchman was aſſociated with the man who had impofed upon them; however, they diffembled the trick which his predeceffor had played. They gave him the public hut, which was in the middle of the village, to depofit his bales in; and when they were all laid out to view, the *Miſſouris* came in confufedly, and all thofe who had been foolifh enough to fow gun-powder, took away fome goods; fo the poor Frenchman was rid of all his bales at once, but without any equivalent from the Indians. He complained much of thefe proceedings, and laid his grievances before the great chief, who anfwered him very gravely: That he fhould have juftice done him, but that for that purpofe he muft wait for the gun-powder harveft, his fubjects having fown that commodity by the advice of his countryman; that he might believe upon the word of a fovereign, that, after that harveft was over, he would order a general hunt, and that all the fkins of the wild beafts which fhould be taken, fhould be given in return for the important fecret, which the other Frenchman had taught them.

Our traveller alledged, that the ground of the *Miffouris* was not fit for producing gun-powder, and that his fubjects had not taken notice, that France was the only country where it fucceeded in. All his reafoning was ufelefs; he returned much lighter than he came, and afhamed of having been corrected by favage men.

This leffon did not prevent others from going to the *Miffouris*; one of them intended to play a good trick there; he got ready a piragua, which he loaded with trifles; and, being informed of the preceding adventure, he filled a little cafk

with

with aſhes and pounded charcoal, at the top of which he put ſome gun-powder. When he arrived, he put all his goods in the great hut, in order to tempt the *Miſſouris* to rob him; it happened as he expected. The Frenchman made a great noiſe, gave the Indians abuſive language, and, running to the caſk of gunpowder, he opened it, took a burning match, and cried out, I have loſt my wits, I will blow up the hut, and you ſhall come with me to the country of the ſpirits. The Indians were frightened, and knew not what to do; the other Frenchmen who came with him were out of doors, and cried out, our brother has loſt his ſenſes, and he *will* not recover them again, till he gets his goods back, or till he gets paid for for them. The chiefs went through the village, to exhort the people to pay; thoſe who had any relations in the hut joined them; the people were moved, and every one brought all the furs he had into the hut; the Frenchman then ſaid he had found his ſenſes again. The chief preſented him with the calumet, he ſmoked, and poured water upon the gun-powder to make it uſeleſs, or rather to hide his fraud from the Indians. He brought home fine furs to the value of a thouſand crowns. The Indians have ever ſince

since held him in great esteem, giving him the name of a *true man*, or *man of courage*.

I shall finish my letter with the description of a very odd and extraordinary ceremony, performed by the *Missouris*, who came hither as ambassadors, at the time when the Chevalier *de Boisbriant* commanded here. This tragic story will at the same time serve to teach officers, who, through a noble ambition, aspire to military commands, that both the theoretical and the practical part of geography ought absolutely to be understood by them; and that it is necessary they should carefully study the interior situation of a country where they are at war, in order to avoid all surprises of the enemy, and to preserve the lives of the men who are under their care. What I shall now tell, will sufficiently convince them of this necessity.

Spain saw, with great displeasure, during the regency, our settlements on the *Missisippi*: The English too, on their side, spared no intrigues to ruin this growing colony, as they do still in regard to those upon the banks of the river *Ohio*, which they say belongs to them; and they have likewise laid claim to the *Missisippi*.

In

LOUISIANA. 151

In 1720, the Spaniards formed the defign of settling at the *Miffouris*, who are near the *Illinois*, in order to confine us more to the weftward; the *Miffouris* are far diftant from *New Mexico*, which is the moft northerly province the Spaniards have.

They believed, that in order to put their colony in fafety, it was neceffary they fhould entirely deftroy the *Miffouris*; but concluding that it would be impoffible to fubdue them with their own forces alone, they refolved to make an alliance with the *Ofages*, a people who were the neighbours of the *Miffouris*, and at the fame time their mortal enemies, hoping, with their affiftance, to furprife and deftroy their enemies. With that view they formed a caravan at *Santa-Fé*, confifting of men, women, and foldiers, having a *Jacobine* prieft for their chaplain, and an engineer-captain for their chief and conductor, with the horfes and cattle neceffary for a permanent fettlement.

The caravan being fet out, miftook its road, and arrived at the *Miffouris*, taking them to be the *Ofages*. Immediately the conductor of the caravan orders his interpreter to fpeak to the chief of the *Miffouris*, as if he had been that of the *Oſages*, and tell him that they were come to make an alliance with him, in order to deſtroy together the *Miſſouris* their enemies.

The great chief of the *Miſſouris* concealed his thoughts upon this expedition, ſhewed the Spaniards ſigns of great joy, and promiſed to execute a deſign with them which gave him much pleaſure. To that purpoſe he invited them to reſt for a few days after their tireſome journey, till he had aſſembled his warriors, and held council with the old men: but the reſult of this council of war was, that they ſhould entertain their gueſts very well, and affect the ſincereſt friendſhip for them.

They agreed together to ſet out in three days. The Spaniſh captain immediately diſtributed fifteen hundred muſkets amongſt them, with an equal number of piſtols, ſabres, and hatchets; but the very morning after this agreement, the *Miſſouris* came, by break of day, into the Spaniſh camp, and killed them all except the *Jacobine* prieſt, whoſe ſingular dreſs did not ſeem to belong to a warrior: they called him a *mag-pie*, and diverted themſelves with making him ride on one of the Spaniſh horſes, on their days of aſſembly.

The

The prieſt, though he was careſſed and well fed, was not without uneaſineſs, fearing that theſe jokes would end in ſacrificing him to the *Manitou*, or deity of the Indians; therefore, one day, taking advantage of their confidence in him, he took his meaſures to get away before their faces. All thoſe tranſactions the *Miſſouris* themſelves have related, when they brought the ornaments of the chapel hither. They were dreſſed out in theſe ornaments: the chief had on the naked ſkin the chaſuble, with the paten ſuſpended from his neck, having driven a nail through it, and making uſe of it as a breaſt-plate; he marched gravely at the head of all the others, being crowned with feathers and a pair of horns. Thoſe that followed him had more chaſubles on; after them came thoſe who carried the ſtole, followed by thoſe who had the ſcarfs about their necks; after them came three or four young Indians, ſome with albs, and others with ſurplices on. The Acolothiſts, contrary to order, were at the end of this proceſſion, not being adorned enough, and held in their hands a croſs or chandelier, whilſt they danced in cadence. Theſe people, not knowing the reſpect due to the ſacred utenſils, hung the chalice to a horſe's neck, as if it had been a bell.

Repreſent

Represent to yourself the ridiculous fight which the singular order of this procession must offer to the eye, as they arrived before the house of M. *de Boisbriant* the King's lieutenant, marching in cadence, and with the great calumet of peace displayed according to custom.

The first Frenchman who saw this masquerade arrive, ran laughing to give M. *de Boisbriant* intelligence of it; this officer, who is as pious as he is brave, was overcome with grief at the fight of the Indians, and knew not what to think of the event; he feared they had destroyed some French settlement; but when he saw them near by, his sadness vanished, and he had much to do to keep himself from laughing with the rest.

The *Missouris* told him, that the Spaniards intended to have destroyed them; that they brought him all these things, as being of no use to them, and that, if he would, he might give them such goods in return as were more to their liking. Accordingly he gave them some goods, and sent the ornaments to M. *de Bienville*, who was then governor-general of the province of *Louisiana*.

LOUISIANA. 155.

As the Indians had got a great number of Spanish horses from this caravan, the chief of the *Missouris* gave the finest to M. *de Boisbriant*.

They had likewise brought with them the map which had conducted the Spaniards so ill, who came to surrender themselves, by confessing their intention to their enemies.

I shall profit of the permission which I have obtained to go down to *New Orleans*. If I find our general, and a letter from you there, it will be a double pleasure to me.

I am, SIR, &c.

At the Illinois, the 15*th
of May* 1753.

LET-

LETTER VIII.

To the same.

The Author leaves the Country of the Illinois, and goes to New Orleans. Arrival of Monsieur de Kerlerec. Departure of the Marquis de Vaudreuil. The Author's second Voyage to the Illinois. Heroic Action of a Father, who sacrificed himself for his Son.

SIR,

IN June I arrived at the Capital of *Louisiana,* where I found a letter from you, which gave me real pleasure, by informing me that you continue to enjoy your health, and it made up for the loss I had of our dear governor's presence; when I came hither I heard he was already gone to France; and to compleat my misfortunes, Mr. *Michel de la Ruevilliero* was dead of an apoplexy; he had wrote

wrote to me that he had with forrow heard of the lofs of my boat, and that notwithftanding it was not the king's cuftom to re-imburfe fuch expences, yet he would repair this lofs with pleafure for my relief: that I fhould make an exact account of all I had loft, and join to it a certificate from M. *de Macarty*, the commander of the convoy: this was, he faid, an indifpenfable neceffity, that this article may at leaft have fome appearance, and thus be entered in the accounts; he promifed that as foon as he fhould have this paper, he would fettle what I was to receive. The Marquis de *Vaudreuil* had recommended me at his departure to his fucceffor M. *de Kerlerec*, who has not paid any attention to his recommendation; his qualities are quite the reverfe of thofe of his predeceffor; but this new governor alledges, that he is not come fo far, merely for the fake of changing the air. He kept me at *New Orleans*, and only allowed me to rejoin my garrifon in 1754, with the convoy which M. de *Faverot* commanded. I could not find any room to embark my provifions for the voyage, on account of the number of goods every one was allowed to take as a venture, and which filled the king's boats: I made my juft reprefentations on this fubject to M. *de Kerlerec*, who made me fuffer all kinds of difagreeable circumftances stances on this occasion. After which, having asked me what venture I took with me, I answered, that I understood nothing of commerce; that being a soldier, his majesty had sent me to *Louisiana* to serve him, and that I placed all my glory in that service, at last M. *de Kerlerec* gave me leave to join my garrison.

I left *New Orleans* the seventeenth of August, but the boats, as I have already said, were so much laden with ventures, that being overtaken by the frost, we could not get to the *Illinois*, but were obliged to winter on the road; and the convoy only arrived in January, 1755, which occasioned extortions and immense costs for the king's account. The fatigue of so long a voyage ruined my health so much, that I was reduced to the utmost extremity. I was conducted on foot by Indians, and when I was tired, they carried me in a dressed ox hide, made in the form of a hamock, hung upon a great pole, as a litter. They changed succeffively, and in this manner I came once more to the old fort *Chartres*, where I lay in a hut, till I could get a lodging in the new fort, which is almost finished. It is built of free stone, flanked with four bastions, and capable of containing a garrison of three hundred men. I

asked

LOUISIANA. 159

aſked M. *de Macarty*'s leave to go to change the air at the *Kaokias*, who are a day's journey from Fort *Chartres*, and the road to it is either by water or by land. In this poſt there is a little fort on the left ſide of the *Miſſiſippi*, it is the great road of the *Illinois* to *Canada*, and the center of commerce of *New France*, or *Louiſiana*, which is conſiderable in furs.

The prieſts of the order of St. *Sulpicius*, to whom the iſle and town of *Montreal* belong, have eſtabliſhed a miſſion here under the name of the *Holy Family of Jeſus*. There are but three prieſts. I have been particularly acquainted with the Abbé *Mercier*, a Canadian by birth, and vicar of the whole country of *Illinois*. He was a man of probity, whoſe friendſhip could not fail of being of uſe to me, by the knowledge he had acquired of the manners of the Indians, who were edified by his virtue and diſintereſtedneſs. He ſpoke the language of the country, and on account of the fluency with which he expreſſed himſelf in it, he was highly eſteemed among the Indians, who conſult him in all matters. He has ſpent forty five years in cultivating the Lord's vineyard in theſe diſtant countries, and the Indian nations of theſe parts

have

have always refpected him. A man of his character could never have lived long enough for the happinefs of thefe people. This worthy apoftle of *Louifiana*, fell into a confumption in Lent, and he died of it one Friday at half an hour after eleven at night, expiring as a Chriftian hero. He had an admirable prefence of mind, and I have regretted him very much. The French and the Indians were inconfolable; the latter fent their deputies according to their cuftom to lament him on his tomb. They came in fwarms, and as foon as they arrived near the houfe of the late Abbé, they cried out aloud and made doleful lamentations. Thefe poor people were in a great confternation, and grief was painted on their faces. Thefe people, whom we call favages, know the true virtue in man; this man had worked almoft during his whole life for their welfare; they called him their father and the chief of the prayer.

What a difference is there between this miffionary and another anterior to him, who falfely attributed to himfelf the difcovery of *Louifiana*; I mean the father *Hennepin*, a Recollet friar, of whom I fhall fpeak to you. In 1683, he publifhed a relation, the title of which is not right: for

for the country which the Recollet, and the Sieur *Decan* difcovered in going up the *Miffifippi* from the river of *Illinois* to the fall St. *Anthony*, does not belong to *Louifiana*, but to *Canada*. The relation of a fecond voyage of father *Hennepin*, in the *Recueil des Voyages du Nord*, bears a title which is equally falfe : voyage to a country greater than Europe, between the frozen ocean, and new *Mexico* ; for though they have gone very far up the *Miffifippi*, they have ftill been at a great diftance from the frozen ocean. When the author publifhed this fecond relation he had quarrelled with M. *de la Salle* ; it feems that he was actually forbid returning to *America*, and that the difpleafure this reftriction gave him, prompted him to retire to Holland, where he publifhed a third work, intitled a new defcription of a very great country, fituated in *America* between new *Mexico* and the frozen ocean, with reflections on M. *de la Salle*'s undertakings and other things concerning the defcription and hiftory of *North America*.

The author there not only vents all his ill-nature on M. *de la Salle*, but likewife throws it upon *France*, pretending to have been ill-treated by the nation. He means to fave his honour by declaring that he was born a fubject of the Catholic

tholic king *; but he ought to reflect that it
was at the expence of France that he travelled
in *America*, and that it was in the name of his
moſt Chriſtian majeſty, that he and the Sieur
Decan took poſſeſſion of the countries which
they had diſcovered. He did not fear
to advance, that it was with the conſent of
his Catholic majeſty, his firſt ſovereign, that
he dedicated his relation, to William the
Third, king of Great Britain, in which he
ſolicits that monarch to conquer theſe vaſt regi-
ons, and to ſend Miſſionaries thither, to teach
the Indians the Chriſtian religion; a proceeding
which excited the ridicule of the Catholics, and
ſcandalized the Proteſtants, who were ſurprized
to ſee a prieſt who called himſelf a miſſionary,
exhort a Proteſtant ſovereign to found a Roman
church in *America*. All his works are beſides
written in a pompous ſtile, which ſhocks the
reader, and offends him by the liberties which
the author takes, and by his indecent invectives.
Father *Hennepin* thought he might make uſe of
the privilege of a traveller; but he has likewiſe
been much cried down by his fellow-travellers,
who have often declared, that he was very un-
faithful

---

* Father Henneppin was a native of *Douay*.

faithful in all his accounts. It appears that there was more vanity in his undertaking, than true zeal in making profelytes in A-merica.

Whilft I was at the *Koakias*, fome Indians of the nation of *Ofages* arrived there; their *Manitou*, or falfe deity, was a dried ferpent, of a monftrous fize. Thefe people faid that this prodigious animal had committed great devaftations in their country; that it fwallowed a tyger-cat all at once; that confequently they had declared war againft it, and were gone to attack it. They followed it by the track, but neither balls nor arrows could penetrate its body, which was covered with very hard fcales, like thofe of a crocodile. They fucceeded at laft in putting it to death by fhooting balls and arrows at it, which blinded it. He that had killed it carried the mark or impreffion of it on his body, in the fame manner as the *Akanzas* imprinted the roe-buck on my thigh. They make this lafting mark in the following manner. They firft draw with black, or with gun-powder the figure of the animal or object they mean to reprefent, on the flefh; after which they fting the fkin in the out-line, with one or more needles till the blood; the figure is then flightly wafhed

M 2 over

over with a fine fpunge dipt in a folution of rock falt, which mixes the blood with the black, contracting the fkin which has been ftung, and renders the figure indelible. This is not done without fome pain ; but as it is a kind of knighthood to which they are only intitled by great actions, they fuffer with pleafure, in order to pafs for men of courage. Thefe marks of diftinction multiply in proportion to the fine actions they do in war.

If one of them fhould get himfelf marked, without having previoufly diftinguifhed himfelf in battle, he would be degraded, and looked upon as a coward, unworthy of an honour which only belongs to thofe who generoufly expofe their lives in defence of their country. The Indians only value the fons of Caciques, in as much as they are brave and virtuous after the example of their fathers and anceftors.

I faw an Indian, who, though he had never fignalized himfelf in defence of the nation however chofe to get a mark on his body, in order to deceive thofe who only judged from appearances. He would pafs for a man of courage with a view to obtain one of the prettieft girls of the nation in marriage, who, favage as fhe was

was however not without ambition. As he was on the point of concluding the match with her relations, the warriors, full of indignation on seeing a coward boast with a mark due only to military merit, held an assembly of chiefs of war, in order to punish such audaciousness. The council agreed, that, to obviate such an abuse, which would confound brave men with cowards, he who had wrongfully adorned himself with the figure of a club on his skin, without ever having struck a blow at war, should have the mark torn off, that is, the place should be flayed, and that the same should be done to all who would offend in the same case.

As there was no pardon to hope for, his condemnation being pronounced by an act of this Indian senate, who is jealous of maintaining the honour of the nation, I offered, in commiseration of the poor wretch, to cure him in the French manner; I said I would take off the skin and the mark without hurting him, and that my remedy would change the blood into water. The Indians, ignorant of my secret, believed I jested with them: therefore, counterfeiting their jugglers, I gave the pretended bravo a calabash full of syrup of the maple-tree, into which I had put a dose of opium; and, whilst he was asleep,

I applied Spanish flies to the figure of the club which he bore on his breaft, and over them fome plantain leaves, which caufed tumours; the fkin and the mark went off, and a watery matter came out. This method of proceeding furprifed the Indian jugglers, who were ignorant of the Spanifh flies, or Cantharides, which are very common in *North America*. They give a light in night-time; and even the fmalleft types can be read, by holding the infect near to the letters, and following the lines.

There is often a fimilarity in the manners of the Indians and of the Europeans, though they may appear ever fo different amongft themfelves. The following example is a proof of it. An officer belonging to the regiment of the *Ifle de France*, having fallen in love with a young lady at *Paris* in 1749, the mother of the lady told him, that fhe would willingly give him her daughter, provided he was adorned with the crofs of *St. Louis*. In order to accelerate his marriage, love infpired him with the thought of taking that diftinction from himfelf, which the King alone can give away. The lady already looked upon him as her fon-in-law; but a few days after, the falfe chevalier is met by an officer of his regiment, who, being before him in the fervice, is

furprifed

surprised to see him obtain the cross before himself. The new chevalier told him, that, with protections, one could get at every thing. The officer, who knew nothing of the other's views, goes immediately to M. *d'Argenson*, and represents to him the injustice done to him, by giving the order of St. Louis to his junior officer. The minister denies it, and sends for the list of promotions, in which the officer is not comprised: accordingly he is taken up, and brought before the tribunal of the Marshals of France. A court was held at the hospital of invalids, wherein Marshal *Belle-isle* presided. The false chevalier was sentenced to have the cross taken from him, to be degraded, and to be confined in a fortress during twenty years.

The Indian women are allowed to make marks all over their body, without any bad consequences; I have seen some of them who had marks even on their breasts, though that part be extremely delicate; but they endure it firmly, like the men, in order to please them, and to appear handsomer to them.

To return to the *Manitou* of the *Osages*, I wished to have this pretended relic in my possession, in order to adorn your collection of natural

tural curiosities with it; I was willing to treat about it with the Indian priest who served it, offering him European goods in return, and representing to him that the adoration of this animal was an abuse; that he ought, as we do, to worship the *Great Spirit*, or *Author of Nature*; but this cunning priest of the devil, in owning that his superstitious countrymen adored every thing uncommon, told me, that he expected to make a great profit of his *Manitou*; that, being a physician, and a juggler besides, he could easily make them believe that his deity eat with the evil spirit at night, and that they must bring him victuals into his hut, and fine furs to dress him out.

Thus this impostor, by his artful discourses, gives weight to the errors and prejudices of these ignorant people. These fellows make them believe, that they converse with the devil at night, whom the Indians are much afraid of, because he can only do harm; whereas they say the *Great Spirit*, being good, can do them no hurt.

I shall finish my letter by an account of the tragic death of an Indian of the nation of *Gollapissas*, who sacrificed himself for his son; I have
admired

admired this heroic deed, which raises human generosity to the highest pitch.

A *Chactaw*, speaking very ill of the French, said, that the *Collapissas* were their *dogs*, i. e. their slaves; one of these, vexed at such abusive language, killed the *Chactaw* with his gun. The nation of *Chactaws*, which is the greatest and most numerous on this continent, armed immediately, and sent deputies to *New Orleans* to ask from the governor the head of the murderer, who had put himself under the protection of the French. They offered presents to make up the quarrel, but the cruel nation of *Chactaws* would not accept any; they even threatened to destroy the village of *Collapissas*. To prevent the effusion of blood, the poor unhappy Indian was delivered up to them. The Sieur *Ferrand*, commander of the German settlement on the right shore of the *Mississippi*, was charged with this commission. The rendez-vous for this purpose was given between the village *Collapissa* and the settlement of the Germans; and the sacrifice was performed there as follows:

The Indian was called *Tichou Mingo*, i. e. Cacique's servant. He stood upright, and held a speech, according to the custom of the people, saying,

saying, " I am a true man, that is, I do not
" fear death; but I pity the fate of a wife and
" four children, whom I leave behind me very
" young, and of my father and mother, who
" are old, and for whom I got subsistence by
" hunting *. I recommend them to the French,
" because I die for having taken their part."

He had hardly spoken the last word of this
short and pathetic speech, when his good and
tender father, penetrated with his son's filial
love, got up, and spoke to the following effect:
" It is through courage † that my son dies; but
" being young, and full of vigour, he is more
" fit than myself to provide for his mother, wife,
" and four little children; it is therefore necef-
" fary he should stay on earth to take care of
" them. As to myself, I am near the end of my
" career, I have lived long enough, and I wish my
" son may come to the same age, in order to
" educate my little children. I am no longer fit
" for any thing, some years of life more or
" less are indifferent to me. I have lived as a
" man,

---

* He was the best hunter in the nation.

† Courage is a word which, in their language, signifies
something great or extraordinary.

" man, and will die as such; therefore I go to
" take his place *."

At these words, which expressed paternal affection in a very strong and moving manner, his wife, his son, his daughter-in-law, and their little children, shed tears round the brave old man; he embraced them for the last time, and exhorted them to be faithful to the French, and to die rather than to betray them by any meanness unworthy of his blood: at last he told them, that his death was a necessary sacrifice to the nation, which he was contented and proud to make. With these words he presented his head to the relations of the dead *Chactaw*, and they accepted it: after that he laid himself on the trunk of a tree, and they cut off his head immediately with one stroke of a hatchet.

Every thing was made up by this death; but the young man was obliged to give them his father's head †; in taking it up, he said to it,

" Pardon

---

* These nations follow the *lex talionis*, death is avenged by death; and it is sufficient to substitute any one of the nation, if even he were not a relation of the criminal; slaves only are excepted.

† They put it on a pole, and carried it as a trophy into their tribe.

"Pardon me thy death, and remember me in the country of spirits." All the French who affisted at this tragic event were moved to tears, and admired the heroic conftancy of this venerable old man, whofe virtue is equal to that celebrated Roman orator, who, in the time of of the triumvirate, was hidden by his fon. The latter was cruelly tormented, in order to extort from him the place where his father was concealed, who, being no longer able to bear that fo tender and fo virtuous a fon fhould fuffer fo much, came to prefent himfelf to the murderers, and begged the foldiers to kill him, and to fave his fon's life; the fon conjured them to kill him, but to fpare his father; the foldiers, more barbarous than the favage Indians, killed them both together, at the fame time, and in the fame place.

M. *Ferrand*, my fellow-traveller in my laft voyage to the *Illinois*, fell into the *Miſſiſippi* in the fevereft feafon; whilft his foldiers were exercifing; and, at the very moment that the rapidity of this river carried him into an abyfs, an *Akanza* hunter, who was happily on board his boat, faved him from the precipice. The officer told him, that he hoped to recompenfe him generoufly for this piece of fervice; but the Indian

dian immediately anfwered, that he had only done the duty of a brother, who ought to fuccour the unhappy in time of danger; that, as the *Great Spirit* had taught him to fwim like a fifh, he could not employ his fkill better than to fave the life of his fellow-creature.

All the Indians, both men and women, learn to fwim from their infancy. I have often feen the mothers put their little children into pools of frefh water, and I took great delight in feeing the little creatures fwim naturally. Would not fuch an education be better than thofe methods which people are fo fond of in Europe? The queftion I fpeak of here is of the utmoft confequence, efpecially in a country where almoft every body goes by water, and on fea-voyages. I fhall not enter into thefe details, which might prove tirefome: I fhall only fay, that, according to found reafon, the firft thing which it is neceffary to know in nature, is how to preferve one's exiftence; and that it is to be wifhed, that the European mothers would imitate the Americans in that particular, and likewife in fuckling their own children. This action, which is dictated by nature, would prevent many accidents with regard to children fuppofed to be legitimate; and, without quoting many facts to this purpofe from the *Caufes Celebres*, I have a recent example before my eyes of the confufion often caufed in families by thofe mercenary nurfes. A gentleman, who was an officer of the fame detachment which I was in, had long been fuppofed to be loft by his nurfe. As foon as he was born, he was fent down into the midft of *Normandy*; and his relations have only found him out, when he was twenty-two years old, through mere chance, after he had gone through a feries of miferies and dangers during that time.

I remember, that, in 1749, upon the road between *Paris* and *Arpajon*, I was witnefs of an accident which happened to one of the little victims which parents put from them, in order not to be importuned by their cries. The nurfe who was trufted with this child, had put it in her apron; as fhe was ftepping into one of thofe carriages deftined for thefe journies, her apron, which was tied behind, got untied, and the child fell upon the pavement, and expired.

Give me leave to fay, that there is an entire difference between the way of thinking of the European and the Indian women. The latter would think themfelves abufed, if they were to

leave

leave their children to the care of a woman far from their own infpection: they are not afraid, as fome European women, that their hufband's tendernefs will diminifh, becaufe they have borne the tokens of their mutual affection; on the contrary, the flame increafes on both parts, and the pleafure of feeing their race perpetuated, and to fee another felf grow up in a little creature which they brought into the world, amply repays the trouble they have of fupporting them.

The white women, whom we call *Creoles*, follow in *America* the European cuftom, difdaining to fuckle their own children; they give them, as foon as they are born, to a tawny or red flave, without reflecting, that her blood may be corrupted. Many able phyficians have demonftrated, that the milk has an influence on the inclinations of the children. I have often feen many an innocent fall a victim to the irregular life of their nurfes in *America*; which is a circumftance fatal to the propagation of the human fpecies. I leave this fubject to the gentlemen of the faculty, who will certainly handle it better than myfelf.

I conclude, by affuring you that I am, &c.

P. S. An

P. S. An Indian courier has juft brought us the agreeable news of the taking of *Choaguen,* and the places dependent on it, upon the famous lake *Ontario.*

The garrifon of that place, to the number of fifteen hundred regular troops, have furrendered prifoners of war; and have accepted the articles of capitulation which M. *de Montcalm* has granted them; that general immediately fent the five pair of regimental colours which he found in the place to *Quebec.*

M. *Rigaud**, the governor of *Trois Rivieres,* commanded the Canadians and Indians; he had taken poffeffion of an advantageous poft, in order to oppofe all fuccours, and cut off the retreat of the enemy.

The land troops, thofe of the colonies, the Canadians, and the Indians, have all equally diftinguifhed themfelves: we know not yet the number of men which the enemies have loft; all we have heard is, that their general was killed

at

---

* Brother of the Marquis of *Vaudreuil,* who returned into *America* with the title of Governor-General of *Canada* and *New France.*

at the beginning of the attack: we, on our side, have loft but three foldiers. M. *de Bourlamaque*, a colonel of foot, has been flightly wounded, together with feven or eight Canadians; but unhappily M. *Decomble*, the engineer, was fhot by one of our own Indians, who took him for an Englifhman, on account of his uniform, which was different from that of the other French officers.

The Marquis *de Montcalm* is now employed in deftroying the forts of *Choaguen*, and in fending the provifions and ammunition, and a hundred pieces of cannon which have been found there, to *Frontenac*.

At the Illinois, the 21*ft of July* 1756.

LETTER IX.

To the same.

The Author sets outs from the Koakias for Fort Chartres. His Observations on the Population. Account of a Caravan of Elephants arrived in the Neighbourhood of the Ohio.

SIR,

According to all appearances, this is the last letter I shall write to you from the Illinois; I prepare to set out by order of the physicians, who have judged it necessary that I should return to France, to use the baths of *Bourbon*, in order to prevent the bad consequences of a shot I received, many years ago, at the assault of *Chateau Dauphin* [*].

Yester-

---

[*] This is a fort in Piedmont, at the top of a mountain of

the

Yesterday an express arrived here from Fort *du Quêne* to our commander, who informs us, that the English make great preparations to come to attack that post again. M. *de Macarty* has sent provisions to victual the fort. The Chevalier *de Villiers* commands it in my stead, my bad state of health not allowing me to undertake that voyage; it would have enabled me to examine the place on the road, where an Indian found some elephant's teeth, of which he gave me a grinder, weighing about six pounds and a half.

In 1735, the Canadians who came to make war upon the *Tchicachas* (Chickfaws) found, near the *fine river* or *Ohio*, the skeletons of seven elephants; which makes me believe, that *Louisiana* * joins to Asia, and that these elephants came from the latter continent by the western part, which we are not acquainted with:

---

the Alps. It was taken the 19th of July 1744, under the command of the Prince of Conti.

The brigade of Poitou, commanded by the brave M. *de Chevert*, distinguished itself in this action by an uncommon valour, which has been admired by all Europe.

* The French set no bounds to the westward to Louisiana. F.

with: a herd of these animals having lost their way, probably entered the new continent, and having always gone on main land and in forests, the Indians of that time not having the use of fire arms, have not been able to destroy them entirely; it is possible that seven arrived at the place near the *Ohio*, which, in our maps of *Louisiana*, is marked with a cross. The elephants, according to all appearance, were in a swampy ground, where they sunk in by the enormous weight of their bodies, and could not get out again, but were forced to stay there *.

In 1752, the Baron *Porneuf*, who commanded Fort *François* in the country of the *Missouris*, received the skin of an animal from the Indians, which was hitherto unknown in *America*. That officer sent it to the Marchioness de *Vaudreuil*, who made a muff of it: this creature was about twice as big as an European fox, and its hair as

fine

---

* It appears from modern geographical observations, that our author's supposition of a migration of elephants is improbable and it is further confirmed by the examination of the teeth of these animals, which are very different from those of the common elephant, and consequently they cannot be of the same species. See Kalm's Travels, vol. I. p. 135. Philosoph. Transf. vol. LVIII. and Pennant's Synopsis of Quadrupeds, p. 91. F.

fine and soft as velvet, mottled with black and pearly white.

Many authors pretend, that it is possible that people went through *Nova Zembla*, (situated northward of the ancient continent) over the ice to *Greenland*; they think, that this is the track on which those went who first peopled *America*, and that the streights which separate it from the continent, has high mountains of ice on its eastern shore: but all those who have tried to go to India through this northern part, have been eaten by white bears, or have perished amidst the ice.

This is my observation on the subject: if men did go through those parts to inhabit *North America*, they probably would have preferred *Canada*, *New England*, and *Louisiana*, the northern parts of which are analogous to their country; whereas it is known, that when the French and English discovered *North America*, there were but few inhabitants in it; but, on the contrary, the Spaniards who conquered *Peru* and *Mexico*, found kings and emperors, who set on foot great armies, and who annually sacrificed twenty thousand captives to their false deities. Therefore there is reason to believe, that men went from the weſt to *Mexico* and *Louſiana* *. The elephants who came thither are a proof which confirms my obſervations †. Further, when I aſked the Indians called *Sioux des prairies*, who are a nomadic nation, they told me, that they had heard other Indians ſay, that, to the weſtward of their country, there lived a nation of clothed people, who navigated on great ſalt-water lakes with great piraguas ‡; that they inhabited great villages built with white ſtones; that the inhabitants obeyed one deſpotic grand chief, who ſent great armies into the field.

The *Mexicans* adore idols as the Indians do; the *Natches* Indians had a temple, and a kind of ſervice; in their language intelligent people have found Chineſe words. Some Indians cut off their hair, leaving only a tuft as the crown

of

---

* *Louiſiana* formerly touched *Canada* on the north-eaſt, *Florida* and the *Engliſh colonies* on the eaſt, and *New Mexico* on the weſt ſide. Its north-weſt boundaries were not determined. See more on this ſubject in a note to Kalm's Travels, vol. III. p. 125. F.

† But this proof does not hold good. See the note on p. 180.

‡ The Indians call the ſea a great lake, and the ſhips great piraguas.

LOUISIANA.

of a friar, to which they faſten feathers of various colours. They never cut their nails; and among the Chineſe it is a mark of nobility to let the nails grow very long.

If we ſuppoſe that men went over from our continent to *America*, they would have kept their white colour, ſince we ſee, that, during two centuries and a half after *Columbus* diſcovered this new world, the Europeans who ſettled in it preſerve their white complexion from generation to generation. The animals which have been found there are entirely different from ours, and neither *Pliny* nor any other old naturaliſt ſpeak of them. We muſt be contented with admiring the works of the Creator, without deſiring to dive into his myſteries *.

I ſhall

---

* This way of arguing is very ſtrange, and greatly promotes barbariſm. Man has got reaſon for the purpoſe, that truth ſhould be the object of his enquiries; and if he ſhould carry them no further, out of fear to dive too deep into the myſteries of the Creator, this would patronize ignorance and barbariſm. Many a thing, which ſeemed too abſtruſe, has been diſcovered by an indefatigable application. The way in which America was peopled, and the manner in which the ſkeletons of great bulky animals approaching to the kind of elephants came to the river *Ohio*, are now a myſtery, but may one day or other be diſcovered by a lucky accident, or a great and original genius. F.

I shall add here, by the way, that when the Spaniards discovered the isles of *St. Domingo* and *Cuba*, they found them well peopled with Indians, whom they murdered under pretence of a religious principle, but really in order to get their gold. Therefore a Cacique or petty king of the island, escaping from the Spaniards, gave his people to understand, that gold was the deity of their enemies, since they came so far, and exposed themselves to so many dangers, in order to get possession of it; and that it was necessary they should abandon every thing, in order to be left in quiet. Another Cacique being condemned to be burnt by the inquisition, was solicited by a Jesuit to become a Christian, in order to go to Paradise; but he openly declared he would not go there, if there were any Spaniards in it. These unhappy Indians abhorred the Spaniards so much, that they did not even converse with their wives for fear of begetting slaves to such masters: and whenever they eat of their flesh, it was more through revenge than any appetite; for they plainly said, that the flesh of a Spaniard was good for nothing.

I forgot to tell you in my last, that I have been invited to the feast of war, given by the grand chief of the *Illinois*, in order to raise warriors,

LOUISIANA.

riors, and march with the Chevalier *Villiers*. This gentleman obtained leave from the governor to raise a party of French and Indians, and to go with them to avenge the death of his brother, M. *de Jumonville*, who was killed by the English before the war broke out.

The grand chief of the *Illinois* is called *Papapé-changouhias*; he is related to several Frenchmen of distinction, settled among these people. This Cacique succeeded Prince *Tamaroas* surnamed *Chikagou*, who died in 1754. He wears the medal of the late Cacique: this *Illinois* prince has convinced the French, that he is worthy of wearing it, by his friendship for our nation. The detachment of the Chevalier *de Villiers* * being ready to set out, *Papapé-changouhias*

---

* The Chevalier *de Villiers*, who commanded this detachment, must not be confounded with M. *de Villiers*, called the *Great Villiers*, who went to avenge the death of *Jumonville* immediately after his murder in 1753. See the poem which the famous M. *Thomas* wrote on this subject.

Of the seven brothers who composed this family of *Villiers*, six were killed in Canada in defence of their country. The Chevalier *de Villiers* is the last; he was taken prisoner in the action at *Niagara* in 1759, being in the party of M. *Aubry*: this officer had defeated a body of English troops at Fort *du*

hias defired to ferve him as a guide with his warriors. They left Fort *Chartres* on the firft of April 1756, and arrived, towards the end of May, on the boundaries of *Virginia*, where the Englifh had a little fort furrounded with great pales. The Indians came near it in the nighttime, each having a fafcine of refinous combuftible wood, which they fet on fire clofe to the pales of the fort. The Englifh commanding officer, appearing to give orders for putting out the fire, was aimed at by an Indian, who killed him on the fpot. The fame Indian called out in their language: " Surrender, you Eng-
" lifh dogs, or elfe you fhall be burnt or eaten."
The foldiers, intimated by his threats, and being without a commander, furrendered at difcretion the next morning; the Indians then bound them two by two, like captives, except the ferjeant, whom one of the Indians found out to be the perfon who had beaten him with a ftick in time of peace. The poor ferjeant became the victim of the refentment of thefe barbarians, who burnt him without any mercy. I have already faid, that the Indians never forgive, and that they think themfelves free and independent: therefore one muft take care not to ftrike them, for they revenge themfelves fooner or later.

The

The Englifh prifoners, to the number of forty, taken in the fort, were divided among the French and Indians, who ftripped them according to their cuftom, plucked out their beards and hair, and, at the requeft of the French, they only made them flaves. But the French officers, and the humaneft among the French inhabitants of the *Illinois*, joined together, and releafed them, by making a prefent to that nation who treated their prifoners like dogs, only becaufe they were our enemies, and becaufe they thought of making themfelves great with us *.

From the village of the *Koakias* we arrived at the *Peorias*, allies of the *Illinois*, through a fine large meadow, which is twenty-five leagues long. The favages who were with me, killed fome little birds with fticks, and called them ftrawberry-bills. Thefe birds, whofe plumage is varied with many colours, are as good to eat as the *beccafigos* in Provence. The Indians told me, that they are birds of flight or of paffage, and that they affemble in flocks every year like fparrows,

---

* From a natural kind of antipathy between the two nations, the French take every opportunity to deprefs the Englifh, and to raife themfelves above them, fometimes at the expence of truth. F.

sparrows, to feed on the strawberries in this meadow, which is red all over with them in the season. The village of the *Peorias* is situated on the banks of a little river, and fortified after the American manner, that is surrounded with great pales and posts.

When we were arrrived there, I enquired for the hut of the grand chief; they brought me to a great hut, where the whole nation was assembled, on account of a party of their warriors, who had been beaten by the *Foxes*, their mortal enemies.

I was well received by the Cacique and his first warriors, who came one after another to squeeze me by the hand in sign of friendship, saying, *hau, hau!* which signifies, *you are welcome*, or *I am glad to see you*. A young Indian or a slave, lighted the calumet of peace, and the chief gave it to me to smoke out of, according to the common custom.

After the first ceremonies were over, they brought me a calebash full of the vegetable juice of the maple tree. The Indians extract it in January, making a hole at the bottom of it, and apply a little tube to that. At the first thaw,

they

they get a little barrel full of this juice, which they boil to a syrup: and being boiled over again, it changes into a reddish sugar, looking like *Calabrian manna*; the apothecaries justly prefer it to the sugar which is made of sugar canes. The French who are settled at the *Illinois* have learnt from the Indians to make this syrup, which is an exceeding good remedy for colds, and rheumatisms.

At the end of the session of this assembly, they brought a kind of bread which they call *Pliakmine*, bears paws, and beavers tails; I likewise eat of the dog's flesh through complaisance, for I have made it a rule to conform occasionally to the genius of the people, with whom I am obliged to live, and to affect their manners, in order to gain their friendship: they likewise brought in a dish of boiled gruel, of maize flour, called *Sagamité*, sweetened with syrup of the maple tree; it is an Indian dish which is tolerably good and refreshing. At the end of the repast, they served a desert of a kind of dry fruits which our Frenchmen call *bluets*, and which are as good as Corinth raisins; they are very common in the *Illinois* country.

The

The next day I saw a great croud in the plain this assembly was for making a dance in favou of their new *Manitou*; the priests were dresse(in a remarkable manner: their bodies were co vered with a clay in which they had mad(burlesque drawings, and their faces were painte(red, blue, white, yellow, green and black. Th(high priest had a bonnet of feathers, like ; crown on his head, and a pair of horns of ; wild goat, * to set the feathers off. I own th(appearance of this prelate tempted me to laugh but as these ceremonies are serious, one muſ(take care, not to burst out, because it would b(reckoned a want of religion, and an indecen action amongst them: nor do the Indians eve interrupt the Roman Catholics, in the exerciſ(of religion. But what a sight presented itſel: to my eyes; I saw a living monster conſidere(as a divinity: I was at the door of the templ(of this false deity; the master of the ceremo nies begged me to go in; I was not yet ſuffici ently acquainted with their customs, and shewec some reluctance, but one of the Indians who ac companied me, perceiving it, told me, that if I did not go in, the people would take it as an of fence,

---

* These animals are found at the *Mi/ouris*, their horns ar(of a fine black, and bent backwards.

fence, or at leaſt as a contempt. This diſcourſe determined me and I went in * : this is the picture of their *Manitou* ; his head hung upon his ſtomach, and looked like a goat's, his ears were like a lynx's ears, with the ſame kind of hair, his feet, hands, thighs and legs were in form like thoſe of a man: this falſe divinity ſeemed to be about ſix months old, the Indians found it in the woods at the foot of a ridge of mountains, called the mountains of *Sainte Barbe*, which communicate to the rich mines of *Santa Fé* in *Mexico*. The general aſſembly was called together on purpoſe to invoke the protection of this monſter againſt their enemies.

I let theſe poor people know, that their *Manitou* was an evil genius, as a proof of it, I added, that he had permitted the nation of *Foxes*, who were their moſt cruel enemies, to gain a victory over ſome of their countrymen ; that they ought to quit him as ſoon as poſſible,

and

---

* The maſter of the ceremonies, or prieſt, that is appointed to guard the temple, before he made his offerings, anointed his body with roſin ; he then ſtrewed the ſoft feathers of a ſwan, or the hair of a beaver all over this melted gum, and in that ridiculous plight he danced in honour of the falſe deity.

and be revenged on him. They anfwered, *tika-labé, houé nigué*, i. e. we believe thee, thou art in the right. They then voted that he fhould be burnt, and the great prieft pronounced his fentence, which, according to the interpreter's explanation, was conceived in thefe terms: " Mon-
" fter, arifen from the excrements of the evil
" fpirit, to be fatal to our nation, who has
" wrongfully taken thee for her *Manitou*; thou
" haft paid no regard to the offerings which we
" have made thee, and haft allowed our enemies,
" whom thou doft plainly protect, to overcome
" a party of our countrymen, and to make
" them flaves: therefore our old men affembled
" in council have unanimoufly decreed and with
" the advice of the chief of the white warriors,
" that to expiate thy ingratitude towards us,
" thou fhalt be burnt alive." At the end of this fentence all the affembly faid, *hou, hou, hou, hou.*

As I wifhed to get this monfter, becaufe I could not get that fnake I fpoke to you of before, I took the following method: I went to the prieft, made him a fmall prefent, and bid my interpreter tell him, that he fhould perfuade his countrymen, that if they burnt this evil genius, there might arife one from his afhes which would

could prove fatal to them; and that I would go on purpofe a-crofs the great lake in order to deliver them of it. He found my reafons good, and by means of the little prefent I gave him, he got the fentence changed, and he was ordered to be killed with clubs: As I defired to have the monfter, without being mutilated, I informed them that they muft deliver it to my people, who would ftrangle it; for if any of their nation killed it, fome misfortune or other might happen to him from it. They ftill approved my reafons, and delivered the animal to me, on condition that I fhould carry it far from their country. It was accordingly ftrangled; but having neither fpirits of wine nor brandy to preferve it in, I was obliged to get it diffected, in order to be able to bring it to France, to fatisfy your curiofity in regard to fubjects of natural hiftory *.

I fhall finifh this letter by another account of the fuperftition of thefe people, and of the divine fervice they give to horrid animals. In

---

* The fkeleton of this monfter, or falfe divinity, is now in the natural hiftory cabinet of M. *de Fayolles*, clerk of the office of the American colonies belonging to the French.

1756 there arrived a deputation of Indians at Fort *Chartres*, of the nation of *Miſſouris*.* ; there was an old woman among them, who paſſed for a magician ; ſhe wore round her naked body, a living rattle ſnake, whoſe bite is mortal, if the remedy is not applied the moment after.

This prieſteſs of the devil, ſpoke to the ſerpent, which ſeemed to underſtand what ſhe ſaid : I ſee, ſaid ſhe, thou art weary of ſtaying here ; go, then, return home, I ſhall find thee at my return : the reptile immediately ran into the woods, and took the road of the *Miſſouris*. If I had been inclined to be ſuperſtitious, I ſhould have told you that I had ſeen the devil appear to theſe nations under the figure of a ſnake. Many Miſſionaries have been willing to perſuade us in their relations and edifying letters, that the devil appears to theſe people, in order to be adored by them, but it is eaſy to ſee, that there is nothing preternatural in it, and that it is a mere juggle.

You

---

* A nation living to the weſtward of *Louiſiana*, on a river which bears their name, and falls into the *Miſſiſippi*.

You know besides, that all animals, even the most ferocious, are tamed by man, I do not pretend to say that the snake of the pretended witch went into her country. All I can tell you is, that I always had a very great antipathy against these animals, and that when I meet with them, I take a pleasure in crushing their heads.

I remember, that in the village of the *Péanguichias*, a nation allied to the *Illinois*, one of our soldiers was very near getting into a very bad scrape. He went into an Indian hut and found a live snake, which he killed with a hatchet, not knowing that the master of the hut had made his *Manitou* of it. The Indian arrived at the same time in a terrible passion to find his deity dead; he asserted that it was the soul of his father, who died about a year before; he having shot two serpents which were pairing upon the point of a rock, fell sick and died soon after.

The imagination of the old man being troubled by the height of the fever, he thought he saw the two snakes coming to reproach him with their death; he therefore recommended it to his son in dying, never to kill any of these animals,

mals, fearing that they would likewife b
the caufe of his death*. Knowing th
genius of thefe people, I advifed the fol
dier, whom the Indian looked upon as on
who had flain a deity, to pretend to b
drunk, and to do as if he would kill m
and his comrades. The Indians, not know
ing that it was only a farce, were th
firft to cry out, that the white warrior † ha
loft his wits. I afked for cords to tie him
and as I feemed very angry with him, th
chiefs and the warriors came to intercede fc
him, faying that it was a man who had lo
his fenfes by drinking; that the fame ofte
happened to the red men: in order to giv
more colour to the impofture, I waited yet fi
the Cacique's wife to beg me, and appear
pacified in deference to her fex, which I r
fpected very much.

I prefented the mafter of the fnake wi
a bottle of brandy, to drown his grief. T
India

---

* I have feen a peafant in France, who had killed an (
on his neighbour's roof; and his father dying fome time
ter, he believed that his death was caufed by that bird of
prefage.

† So they call our foldiers.

Indians are exceſſively fond of this liquor, and grow furious when they have drank too much of it. After their drunkenneſs is over, they ſay that they have neither ſpoken nor done any thing, and attribute all their follies to the brandy believing to juſtify their conduct by acknowledging that they had loſt their wits. When a drunken Indian kills another, the death is not revenged. But theſe people take care ſeldom or never to drink all at once, thoſe who are ſober keep in bounds the reſt, and the women hide both offenſive and defenſive weapons. Brandy may be reckoned among the pernicious things which have contributed towards the depopulation of North America: this liquor makes men brutes, and often kills them. I have ſometimes ſeen drunken Indians kill each other with hatchets and clubs.

I am now ready to leave the *Illinois*, and expect to be in *New Orleans* in January 1757. This letter ſets out in a piragua, which M. *de Macarty* ſends with diſpatches to the governor.
I am, &c.

At the Illinois, the 10*th November* 1756.

LETTER X.

To the fame.

The Author leaves the Illinois: His Navigation down the Miſſiſippi: he encamps in an Iſland formed by that River. His Soldiers make him Governor of it.

SIR,

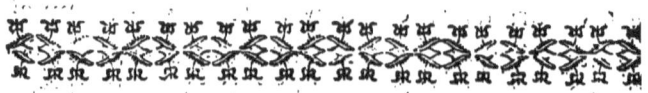OU inquire, whether the Indians have captains amongſt them, and whether they are governed by a king? The time I have ſpent among them procures me the pleaſure of ſatisfying your curioſity on that head You muſt know, then, that they are divided in to tribes or nations, each of which is governed by a petty king or Cacique, who only depend on the *Great Spirit*, or Supreme Being; theſe Caciques reign deſpotically, without making their authority odious, and know how to make them

ſelves

selves respected and beloved. They likewise have the satisfaction of being regarded by their subjects almost as demi-gods; born for the happiness of this world; for they have the tenderness of fathers for the people of their tribe; and that name flatters them much more than all the pompous titles of the *Grand Signior* or the *Great Mogul*. Those Asiatic emperors are often exposed in their extensive dominions to revolutions, by which their life is endangered; for often tributary kings rebel against them, and kill them with their whole family.

The crime of high treason is unknown among the *Americans*; the chiefs and Caciques go every where without fear. If any one should be bold enough to attempt any thing against their lives, he would be punished as a horrible monster, and the whole family of the murderer would be exterminated without mercy.

As to the captains or chiefs of war, who command their armies against their enemies, this post is occupied only by such as have given signal proofs of courage in defence of their country in several combats; and as the generals go naked, as well as the other Indians, the marks of wounds they bear upon their body are sufficient to diftinguifh them from the reft, and ferve inftead of teftimonials to them.

The old men, who cannot go to war any more, are not ufelefs to the nation. They hold fpeeches, and the people hear them as oracles. Every thing is done as they advife it; and the young men fay, that they having lived longer than themfelves, muft of courfe have more experience and knowledge. When I admired the countenance which thefe old men enjoyed, they told me, that fince they could no longer fight for their country, they taught others to defend it. The warriors, when they return from an expedition, never fail to throw part of the booty into the huts of thofe old men, who have exhorted them, and excited their courage. The prifoners of war are always given to the oldeft people in the nation, who make them their flaves. The old warriors who cannot go to war any more, harangue the foldiers. The orator begins with ftriking againft the poft with a club, and mentions all the fine actions he has done in war; that is, how many fcalps he has taken from different nations. The hearers anfwer, *hau, hau*, *i. e.* that is true. The Indians abhor lying, and fay that a liar is not a true man.

"The old speaker begins his discourse, and says: "If I were younger and more vigorous, "to conduct you against our enemies, as I have "formerly done, you should see me go on the "tips of my toes. Go my comrades, as men "of courage, and with the heart of a lion *; "never shut your ears, sleep like hares, go "like the roe-buck, do not fear the cold, nor "hesitate to go into the water like ducks; "when you are pursued, hide well your retreat. "Above all, do not fear the arrows of your ene- "mies, shew them that you are true warriors "and men. Lastly, when you find an oppor- "tunity, use all your arrows on the enemy, and "after that break in upon them with your clubs "in hand; strike, slay, and extirpate; it is "better to die fighting than to be taken and "burnt."

At the end of this harangue, the old warrior presents the calumet to the *Tacha-Mingo*, that is, the general or chief of war, and to all his offi- cers, who smoke it, each after their rank; and all those who have not yet been to war come to

smoke

---

* An hyperbole no Indian in America would make use of, not knowing that creature, which is not to be met with in that country. F.

smoke it, by way of enlisting themselves; they dance the dance of war, and, after that ceremony, they distribute dog's flesh, which, as I have already observed, is a dish principally appropriated to warriors *.

M. *du Tissenet* told me of an accident that happened to his father, who was one of the first officers that came to *Louisiana* with M. *de Bienville*. M. *du Tissenet* being at an Indian nation, together with some Frenchmen who came to barter goods; the Indians wanted to scalp them; M. *du Tissenet* had learnt their language, and heard their discourse, and as he wore a wig, he took it from his head, and threw it on the ground, saying from time to time, You will have my scalp, take it up, if you dare to do it. The astonishment of these people was inexpressible, for M. *du Tissenet* had got his head shaved a little before this happened; he told them afterwards, that they were very much in the wrong to attempt to hurt him, for he only came to make

an

---

* It is very remarkable, that, when the ancient kings of *Macedonia* performed the lustration of their armies, a dog was killed, and divided into two parts, and the whole army with the king at their head, went through the two halves of the dog. F.

an alliance with them; that, if they compelled him, he would burn the water in their lakes and rivers, to hinder them from failing, and set fire to their forests; he got a little pot, and put some brandy in it, and set it on fire with a match; the Indians, who were not yet acquainted with brandy, were amazed; at the same time he took out of his pocket a convex glass, and set fire to a rotten tree by means of the sun. These people really believed, that the officer had the power of burning their rivers and their woods; they caressed him, loaded him with presents, and sent him home well escorted, that no one might do him any harm. Since that time M. *de Bienville* has made use of M. *du Tissenet* in several negociations towards making alliances with the Indians.

M. *du Tissenet*'s adventure puts me in mind of that of an Italian, who was in the suite of M. *Tonty*, the then governor of Fort *Louis* among the *Illinois*. This Italian set out from thence by land, to join M. *de la Salle*, to whom he could have been very useful, by teaching him the road which he was to take in order to come to the *Missisippi*, if he could have been with him in time; he likewise saved his life by a singular stratagem. Some Indians being willing to kill him,

him, he told them they were much in the wrong in attempting to deftroy a man that bore them all in his heart. This difcourfe amazed the Barbarians; he affured them, that, if they would give him time till the next morning, he would convince them of the truth of what he had afferted; adding, that if he deceived them, they fhould do what they pleafed with him. Then, fixing a little mirror on his breaft, the Indians, who were much fuprifed to fee themfelves, as they imagined, in the heart of this man, granted him his life.

I have commanded the convoy in defcending the river, which M. *Aubri* brought up: M. *de Macarty* trufted the Englifh prifoners to my care to bring them to *New Orleans*; they are the fame which the Chevalier *de Villiers* and the Indian chief *Papéchangouhia* took. I have made hafte to come to the capital before the thawing of the ice, which breaks loofe in the northern rivers, and follows the current; I ran the rifk of being ftopt by it, if I had not given orders for rowing as hard as poffible; I even made ufe of the Englifh prifoners to relieve my foldiers: as every one has an equal right to his life on such occafions, the officers likewife lent a helping hand, to encourage the crew.

After

LOUISIANA. 205

After paſſing the rocks at *Prudhomme* *, there are no others in the *Miſſiſippi*; and when there are ſeveral boats, they are faſtened together, and go down with the current day and night. There is only one man at the helm, and one at the head of every boat, to take care of the floating trees. It is a pleaſure to go down this fine river: the ſame diſtance which, in going up, takes three months and a half, in deſcending is performed in ten or twelve days, when the water is high in the river.

I muſt not forget to mention, that on the firſt of January the ſoldiers come in the morning to wiſh their officers a happy new year, who generally return the civility by a preſent of brandy. I was juſt encamped on a little iſland about two leagues in circuit, ſituated on one of the branches of the *Miſſiſippi*, which I was deſcending. This iſle was ſurrounded with very tall trees. A facetious gaſcoon ſoldier, as thoſe of this nation generally are, gave his comrades to

under-

---

* Theſe rocks form the ſhores of the *Miſſiſippi*, which are on both ſides like walls of five hundred feet high. Formerly there was the Fort *Prudhomme* in this place, ſo named from a fellow-traveller of M. *de la Salle*, who died there, and occaſioned the fort to be called after him.

understand that they might get an extraordinary new year's gift if they would perform the ceremony of receiving me governor of the island. The ferjeant approved this droll thought, and immediately gave his orders for it. He began with graving my name on the bark of a tree, ordered the fwivels to be charged with powder, and made the troops appear in arms. The drummer beat a whirl, and the ferjeant as mafter of the ceremonies, taking off his hat, faid " in the king's name *, ye tygers, wolves, bears, " oxen, ftags, roe-bucks, and other animals of " this ifland, fhall acknowledge our commander " as your governor, and obey him in all that he " he fhall command you for his fervice ;" one of the foldiers then fired the fwivels of the boats, which were accompanied with a general falute from the fmall arms. The fudden explofion of thefe fire arms, frightened the wild oxen, who went into the river in order to fwim through it and to gain the continent: the foldiers went after them in a piragua and killed four of them, together with two roe-bucks that juft reached the fhore, and prefented them to me as my property, which obliged me to ftay here in order to dry the flefh for confumption,

during

---

* De par le Roi.

during the remaining part of our voyage. In order to take advantage of the fun of my foldiers, which I took good care to reward immediately, I had a mind to vifit the interior parts of my government: but I was hardly gone half a league, when I faw a bear, who was quietly eating acorns under a great oak: I fired my piece at him, but the ball only went into the lard of the animal, which was monftroufly fat; as foon as he felt the wound, he wanted to come up to me, but he was too heavy to run; then feigning to run from him, I drew him towards my foldiers, who foon furrounded and killed him as guilty of felony and rebellion. They held a court martial, where the ferjeant prefided. The corporal, who acted as the king's attorney-general, gave it as his opinion, that in order not to ruin the fine coat of the bear, who had revolted againft his mafter, he fhould only be fhot in the head, which was punctually executed.

He was then flayed, and I have taken his fkin, which is a very black one, and which I fhall not relinquifh, any more than Hercules did that of the *Nemean* lion which he conquered.

The

The soldiers melted the fat, and got above one hundred and twenty pots of oil from it*, you must know that the bears come out of their ... as soon as the fruits begin to ripen, and they do not go in again till they are all eaten up. They then stay in their retreats till the next season, and neither eat nor drink during that interval; their grease is the only thing they feed upon, by sucking their paws. It is dangerous to meet a lean one without company. The Indians make a great trade with bears' skins, and treat their friends with their paws and tongues; they have often regaled me with them on my voyages, and I found them extremely good.

I direct this letter to *Campeach*, to M. *de Arragory*, the agent of the French marine, who will send it to *Cadiz*, from whence it will come safer to you than by our vessels, as Spain is not at war with England: I do not write duplicates of this letter, besides, I hope to set out for Europe next April.

     I am, S I R, &c. &c.

At New Orleans, the 25th
of February 1757.

---

* *Bears oil* is very good to eat, in *Louisiana* they make use of it for sallad, for frying, and for sauces, and prefer it to hog's lard. The pot holds about two quarts English.

LETTER XI.

To the Same.

The Author sets out for Europe. He fights an English Privateer. He embarks at Cape François on a Vessel belonging to a Fleet of twenty-six Merchantmen, which were almost all taken in his Sight by Privateers. Taking of a little Vessel from the Enemy. Arrival at Brest.

SIR,

HAVING found no vessel here to return to *France*, I was obliged to go on board the brigantine *Union* fitted out as a sloop of war, and commanded by captain *Gau-Jean* who is well know for having taken five English ships during the war, on his voyage from France to *Louisiana*.

We set sail from the *Balise* on the first of April 1757, for Cape *François*. On the 20th of April being in sight of *Turk's* island [*], we perceived a ship, which we supposed to belong to the enemy; she chased us at night, and being a prime sailer, came up with us in three hours' time: the English privateer saluted us with a bullet from his cannon, and called out to us to surrender to the king of England; to which we returned a broadside, and a volley of the small arms; after which I haled him to strike his colours for the king of France, or else he should be sunk; the privateer finding that he had to meddle with a dealer in bullets, made off, and got among the rocks near Turk's island, hoping to draw us nearer to the shore, where we might have been lost. But our captain, who was very prudent, and a good mariner at the same time, saw the snare which was laid for him; therefore, instead of following the privateer, he continued his voyage, and we happily arrived in the harbour of Cape *François* on the first of May. There we found the squadron of M. *de Beaufremont*, destined for the succours of *Canada*, having on board M. *de Bart*, whom the king had appointed governor and lieutenant-general

---

[*] L'isle *Turque*.

neral on the iſle of *St. Domingo*. My firſt care on going on ſhore was to pay my reſpects to him. That general, who is always ready to ſerve unfortunate officers, prevented my cares, by diſpatching me four days after my arrival, and ſparing me the expence I ſhould have been at if I had ſtayed on this iſland, he procured me a free paſſage at the king's expence, as a fleet of twenty-ſix merchantmen were ready to ſail for France, under the convoy of M. *de Beaufremont*, who brought them as far as the *Cayques* iſlands, where he left them, in order to proceed on his deſtination according to the orders of the court.

I muſt tell you that I preferably choſe a *Bor-'eaux* veſſel, called the *Sun*, captain *Odouoir*; imitating the Indians, who indeed make a divity of the ſun). But the event has ſhewn that was very happy in my choice; for almoſt all the veſſels which compoſed the fleet have been taken in my ſight. Only four arrived in France, the *Sun* was the firſt: ſhe came to *Breſt* in forty-five days, after taking an Engliſh ſhip in the latude of the *Newfoundland* bank. I landed at *reſt* the fifteenth of June 1757, and immedi-:ely waited on the Count *du Guai*, commander f the marines in this port; I then paid a viſit to

P 2 M.

M. *Hocquart*, the counsellor of state, and in tendant of the marine in this department, who I informed of the death of M. *Auberville*, wh had succeeded for a time to M. *Michael de Rouvilliere*, as commissary general of the marin and regulator of the provisions of * *Louisian* M. *Hocquart* was known for his probity when was intendant of *New France*; it is certain th he came back from thence indebted forty-tho sand livres, which the king, contented with his se vices, has made him a present of; a fine examp for M. *Bigot*, his successor; but if he has n brought back treasures from his administratio he has at least the satisfaction of passing for o of the gallantest men of his rank: he has been 1 gretted by all the Canadians, and even by t Indians, who, as I have already said, know ho to distinguish merit.

On owning to this gentleman, that I had money to go to court with, he was so kind as order M. *Gaucher*, clerk of the treasurer of the c lonies to give me some. He likewise offered 1 his table during my stay in this town, whi I intend to leave the twenty-second of this mont

Y

---

* *Ordonnateur.*

LOUISIANA.

You will, perhaps, be amazed to hear, that in the space of eight months, I have seen two winters, two summers, and two springs; I shall now explain it to you. I wrote to you, that I left the *Illinois* at the end of December, 1756, when the *Missisippi* began to freeze, and descending that great river, I came to *New Orleans* in January 1757, the climate of which is comparable to that of the *Hierian* islands, where our regiment was in 1744. That is, it was the season of gardening or spring. I left *Louisiana* the first of April 1757, and came to Cape *François* the first of May, and found summer there: I embarked for Europe on the fourth, and after coming out of the *Bahama Channel* we met with spring; continuing our voyage to the great sands of *Newfoundland*, we saw on the twenty-second, at sun-rising, a floating mountain of ice, which at first we took to be a sail; but the keen air coming from it convinced us at last that it was a piece of ice from the frozen ocean. On the fifteenth of June 1757, we came to *Brest*, where we found summer. This therefore is a pretty extraordinary case.

I am, SIR, &c.

At Brest, the 18th of June 1757.

LETTER XII.

To the Same,

The Author arrives at Court, receives a Gratification from the King, and an Order to go to Rochefort. He embarks there for Louisiana.

SIR,

I AM now once more at *Rochefort* from whence I failed for *Louisiana*, eight years ago. I come from the court, where I prefented to the comptroller general and minifter of the marine, M. *de Moras*, the governor's letter, which explains the motives of my voyage. He was fo kind as to fpeak with me in his cabinet, in prefence of M. *de la Porte*, chief of

the

the board of plantations. He queftioned me on the prefent ftate of *Louifiana*. I affured the minifter that I had left in our intereft all the nations of that vaft continent, which I had vifited, and that the *Cherokees* were come to treat of peace with the French. He likewife afked me, whether I thought the colony could be attacked. I anfwered that there was little probability of the Englifh attempting to attack it, on account of the difficulty of coming in through the mouth of the *Miffifippi* at the fort of *Balife*; and that the colony wanted no other fortifications, than thofe which nature had provided it with.

M. *de Moras* obtained for me from the king a gratification of a thoufand livres in order to enable me to go to the waters which my health required I fhould take; after which I received an order from his majefty to go back to *Louifiana*, and continue my fervices there; therefore I came hither without lofs of time in order to embark; we intend to fet fail as foon as the convoy will be fitted out for *Cape Breton*.

M. *Druis Imbuto* fucceeds M. *Normant de Méfi*, as *Intendant* of the marine. The king could

could not choose a better person both on account of his abilities, and of his integrity, and likewise on account of his zeal for the king's interest in this important place. This intendant made me the same offer as his predecessor.

I am, SIR, &c.

*At Rochefort, the 12th
of September* 1757.

LOUISIANA. 217

LETTER XIII.

To the same.

The Author leaves Rochefort; *he meets with three English Merchant-Ships, taken by M. de* Place, *of which one was burnt and another sunk. He stops at the Isle of* Grenada. *Navigation along* Jamaica.

SIR,

I Wrote to you from *Rochefort*, that we intended to set out in December 1757; but the convoy destined to succour *Cape Breton* having in part been taken by the English fleet, we were obliged to fit out another. During that time a squadron of ten great English men of war having alarmed the coast of *Aunis*, that has retarded us till the month of *May*. This squadron disappearing, we set sail on the tenth of the same month.

I was

I was on board the King's frigate *La Fortune*, together with M. *de Rochemore*, commiffary-general of the marine, and *ordonnateur* of the province of *Louifiana*. M. *de Place*, a captain of a man of war, commanded the *Eopalme* frigate of thirty guns, deftined for our convoy: we met with three Englifh veffels on our voyage, which only coft us three cannon-fhot. M. *de Place* funk one of them, and burnt the other, after taking the crew and the goods out of them. As to the third, it came from the coaft of *Guinea*, was richly laden, and had on board four hundred and forty negroes, who were in part fold to the ifle of *Grenada*. The Baron *de Bonvouft*, who has juft been appointed governor of this ifland, entertained us very generoufly and politely during our ftay there. We remained there till the twenty-fecond of July, when we failed for *Louifiana*, keeping alongfide of *Jamaica*, to avoid the great fhips of the enemy, which never come to thofe fhores: we took that courfe in order to deceive the fpy, and we arrived happily at the mouth of the *Miffifippi* on the twelfth of Auguft.

M. *de Rochemore* [*], an honeft *ordonnateur*, who is very zealous for the intereft of the King, will have

---

[*] The brother of a M. *Rochmore* who is now commodore.

have a great deal of trouble in reforming the abufes that have crept into the management of the colony's affairs, fince the war; and during our voyage, I foretold him, that he would be much difturbed in his adminiftration: what I forefaw really happened; and by the fame fhips which brought us hither, the court has been prejudiced againft him, with a view to deprive him of his place. I was but juft arrived at *New Orleans*, when the governor gave me orders to prepare to go with a detachment to the *Allibamons*, an Indian nation two hundred and fifty leagues from the capital. I take advantage of the opportunity of the King's fhips, which will fail for France at the end of the year; and I write to you by duplicates, that if one fhip be taken, you may get the letter by the other. When I fhall be informed of the manners of the nations which I fhall pafs through, and which are fituated to the eaft of *New Orleans*, I fhall defcribe that country to you, which is reckoned very fine and very good.

*At New Orleans, the 10th
of November* 1758.

LETTER XIV.

To the same.

The Author departs from New Orleans *for the* Allibamons. *His Navigation on the Lake* Pontchartrain. *Short Description of* Mobile.

SIR,

I Left *New Orleans* on the fourteenth of December, according to M. *de Kerlerec*'s orders, and set out for the *Allibamons*. I sailed from the little creek of *St. Jean*, which is situated in the lake *Pontchartrain*. There is a portage of about a quarter of a mile from *New Orleans* to this creek *, which is about two leagues long; the winds were favourable to us, and on the twentieth of December I arrived
at

---

* *Bayouc*, a small inlet where the tide goes up.

at the bay and fort of *Mobile*, which is fifty leagues diftant from the capital.

The *Mobile* was formerly the chief fettlement in *Loufiana*, and the refidence of the governor, *ordonnateur*, and of the chief officers. The fu-perior council held its fittings there likewife.

There is a pretty regular fort, capable of re-fifting a whole army of Indians; but European troops could foon take it. It is fituated on a bay where the tide comes up; and between two rivers, one of which is fmall, and is called the river of the *Chaétaws*, the other is more confi-derable than the *Seine* before *Rouen*, is called *Mobile* river, and rifes in the *Apalachian* moun-tains; it is the rendez-vous of all the Indians who live to the eaftward. They come there to receive the prefents which the King annually dif-tributes to them by his governor. The foil about *Mobile* is gravelly; however, the cattle fucceeds exceedingly well there, and multiplies very much. The inhabitants are very laborious, and trade with the Spaniards; they go to the fort of *Penfacola*, which is near *Mobile*, and get falt beef, wild fowl, maize, rice, and other eat-ables from thence. The inhabitants of *Mobile* likewife carry on a trade with tar. As to the

fur-

fur-trade with the Indians, the officers carry it on exclusively of all others, contrary to the King's intention.

About this place, there are white and red bays * and wild cherry-trees †. There are likewise white and red cedars ‡; the latter is very fine, and very good for inlaid work; its smell expels insects, and the wood indeed is incorruptible. There are several sorts of trees in the forests hereabouts, which are unknown in Europe, and some which abound with a gum like turpentine. There are likewise cypresses § of such a size, that the Indians make piraguas out of one piece, which can contain sixty men.

Before the French came into *Louisiana*, the Indians constructed their boats in the following manner.

---

* The bays are probably the *Laurus æstivalis Linn.* which have white flowers; and the *Laurus Borbonia Linn.* which has red flower-cups, and black or purple berries. F.

† The wild cherries of this country grow in clusters, and there are chiefly three kinds of them growing in America, viz. *Prunus Virginiana, Canadensis,* and *Lusitanica,* Linn.

‡ The red cedar is the *Juniperus Virginiana Linn.* and the white cedar is the *Cupressus Thyoides Linn.*

§ Or *cedars.*

manner. They went to the banks of some rivers, which are very numerous in this vast region, and which by their rapidity tear up by the roots the trees which stand on their banks. They took their dimensions for length and breadth, and accordingly chose such a tree as they wanted; after which they set fire to it, and as the tree burnt on they scraped away the live coals with a flint or an arrow; and having sufficiently hollowed it out, they set it afloat. They are very well skilled in conducting these little vessels upon their lakes and rivers. They employ them in time of war, and likewise load them with the furs and dried flesh which they bring back from their hunts.

Their instruments and their weapons were made in the following manner: they chose a young tree for that purpose, in which they made an incision with a flint, or pebble as sharp as a razor, and they put a stone cut in form of a hatchet into the incision; therefore, as the tree grew up, it enchased the stone, which by that means became inseparable from it, and they afterwards cut it off in order to make use of it; their lances and their darts were made in the same manner. They had clubs of a very hard wood.

As

As to their inftruments of agriculture, they only made ufe of the bones of animals, or of fpades of a very hard wood. The ground throughout *America* is very fruitful; the grafs there grows high and clofe; and after the froft has dried it up, the Indians fet fire to it; then they dig the ground with their fpades, fow it, and reap three months after their crops.

They plant maize, millet, beans, and other leguminous plants, potatoes, piftachios, and water-melons; gourds are likewife very common there, and the French inhabitants call them *giromonds*.

Their kitchen-utenfils were difhes and pots of earthen ware, and deep wooden difhes. They made cups of calebafhes, and fpoons * of the horns of wild oxen, which they cut through the middle, and form into the proper fhape by means of fire.

As foon as we fhall have got ready the provifions for our voyage, and for the garrifon of the fort, we fhall fet out, M. *Aubert* and myfelf in a boat armed with foldiers and *Mobile* Indians, whom

---

* Which they call *Micouens*.

whom we have hired to row during the voyage.

M. *Aubert*, though he is adjutant of the fort at *Mobile*, has been appointed, by M. *de Kerlerec*, to command Fort *Touloufe* at the *Allibamons*, which is contrary to the King's order, forbidding all majors and adjutants to do other functions than thofe of the place they belong to.

If any fhips arrive from Europe, I fhall perhaps receive letters from you. M. *de Velle*, who commands here, will be fo kind as to fend them to me with the firft convoy.

I am, SIR, &c.

*At Mobile, the 6th of
January* 1759.

LETTER XV.

To the same.

The Author sets out from Mobile *for the* Allibamons. *Description of the Manners of this Nation. Their Way of punishing Adultery.*

SIR,

I AM at last arrived at Fort *Toulouſ*
among the *Allibamons.* I have beeı
fifty days a-coming; becauſe, takinɡ
boat in the rainy ſeaſon, the water in the rive
was often ſwelled to twelve or fifteen feet; thi
ſudden increaſe was cauſed by the heavy rains
which are frequent hereabouts, and by the higl
hills that run along this river.

We have been obliged to work hard againſ
the rapidity of the current, and there wer
days during which we ſcarcely advanced
league

league. It is impossible to fail, on account of the woods, the hills, and turnings of the river; and therefore we could do no otherwise than go along the shores. One day I had the misfortune to see my boat hemmed in by the branches of a tree * that was set under water: we were benighted in this disagreeable situation, and obliged to wait for the break of day. But as this river rises and falls by the floods, I found myself now quite in the air in my boat. We were twenty-five leagues from the mouth of the river, and the *Mobilian* savages that accompanied me, comforted me by the hope that the next tide would set me a-float again; and really the tide mounting up the river from *Mobile* bay delivered us from our uncomfortable situation. You see by this, dear Sir, what a difference it makes in navigating an *European* and an *American* river.

M. *Aubert* fell sick on the way, and I prevailed on him to stay at *Mobile* for the recovery of his health; and so he came from thence hither on horseback, by crossing the fir-woods, which

are

---

* There are hereabouts cedar-trees of so prodigious a size, that ten men can scarcely clasp them; which easily accounts for the goodness and fertility of the country, and besides this its climate is one of the most healthy.

are very thin. M. *de Montberaut* is to give him up the command of this poft by order of the governor, after having inftructed him during three months, of its fituation, environs, and many other articles. This latter gentleman* has a high reputation among the Indians of this country, who call him the *man of valour*, i. e. the *hero*. He was remarkable for the fpirited fpeeches which he delivered, in a manner analogous to the way of thinking of thefe nations. This officer had a quarrel with the Jefuits, and therefore afked to be recalled; and was fucceeded by M. *Aubert*, the brother of Father *Aubert*, a Jefuit miffionary in *Louifiana*. M. *Montberaut* is a declared enemy to thefe miffionaries. Whilft Father *Le Roi* was at *Allibamons*, he wrote to the governor to difcredit this officer, to whom the foldier who was to carry the letter delivered it. The commander faw after this the Jefuit, who fhewed him many civilities, according to the political principles of thefe good fathers: The officer afked him, whether he had written fomething againft him. The Jefuit, not fufpecting his letter to be in the officer's hand, affured him by all that was facred he had not. Then M.
Montberaut

---

* He is the brother of the Count *de Montaut*, who belonged to the houfehold of the Dauphin.

Montberaut called Father *Le Roi* an impoſtor and a cheat, produced the letter, and fixed it at the gate of the fort, giving it in charge to the ſentinel to take care of it; and ſince that time there were no Jeſuits among the *Allibamons*.

Whilſt I am here going to ſpeak of the *Allibamons*, I ſhall have an opportunity to treat likewiſe of the *Taſkikis*, the *Octaſhepas*, the *Tonicas*, the *Kawuytas*, the *Abekas*, the *Talapoaſhas*, the *Conſhakis*, and the *Pakanas*, whoſe manners are all nearly related to one another. All theſe nations put together can raiſe about four thouſand warriors. They are all well-ſhaped men, live commonly along the river ſides, and no ſooner are you arrived among theſe well-behaved men, whoſe women are of the ſame character, and for the greater part beautiful, but they come to receive you at the landing-place, ſhaking hands with you, and preſenting you with the calumet. After having ſmoaked, they aſk from you the cauſe of your coming, and the time you ſpent on the road; what ſtay you intend to make among them, whether you have a wife and children *.

They

---

* The politeneſs of the Indians goes even ſo far as to offer o the Europeans their girls, and for that purpoſe the chiefs

They likewise inquire the particulars of the war in *Canada*, and ask how the King their father does. They then bring you a dish made of maize or Indian corn, which they coarsely pound, and boil in water, generally together with some venison *. They likewise serve up bread made of the flour of the same corn, baked in hot ashes, roasted young turkies, broiled venison, pancakes baked with nut-oil, chesnuts when in season, boiled with bears grease or oil, roebucks tongues, together with hen and turtle † eggs.

The soil of *Louisiana* resembles, in the lower parts of the colony, that of *Egypt* after the Nile has overflown the country; it is excellent, and chiefly so in the country of the nations I now speak of.

The melons are here prodigiously large, ful of juice, and in great plenty: the water-melon:

ar(

---

speak the next morning in the following manner in the vi lage: Young men and warriors, do not be foolish, love th master of life; hunt for the support of the French, wh bring us our wants: and you young girls, do not be harc hearted, nor ungrateful with your body in respect to th white warriors, for to get their blood; by this alliance w shall get wit like them, and be respected by our enemies,

* This is called *Sagamité*. † Sea-tortoise.

are so delicious, that they are given to the sick to quench their thirst during the burning fits of the fever. Potatoes are plentiful here; and the Europeans are very fond of this kind of root, which tastes like chesnuts roasted in hot ashes.

The Indians are generally contented with one wife, of whom they are jealous to excess. When an Indian lies at a village where he has no wife, he hires a girl for a night or two, as he pleases, and her parents never have any objection to it; they concern themselves very little about their girls, saying their bodies are free: the Indian girls do not abuse this liberty; and they find it their interest to keep up an appearance of modesty, in order to engage their lovers to ask them in marriage: but in regard to wives the Indians maintain, that they have sold their liberty by marrying, and that they must not be served by other men than their husbands. The men keep the privilege of having several wives, and they can leave them whenever they please; but this seldom happens. When a woman is caught in adultery, the least punishment is being repudiated. The husband then leaves the hut; and if they have any children, he takes the boys, and the wife the girls; she must remain a widow for one year; but he can marry again immediately.

He can likewife take his wife again, therefore fhe muft not enter on a fecond marriage till a whole year be paft.

The marriage of the Indians is quite fimple, as I have already obferved; the mutual confent of the parties is the only tie which joins them. The future hufband makes fome prefents of furs and victuals in the hut of his bride's father; if they be received, a feftival is made, to which the whole village is invited; after the meal, the exploits of the new hufband's anceftors are fung, and a dance enfues. The next day one of the oldeft men in the village prefents the bride to the relations of her hufband; and thus the whole ceremony of marriage is concluded. All the Indians deduce their lineage from the women, alledging that they may be fure of their origin on that fide, and accordingly of their having their mother's blood in their veins; but that claiming their defcent from the men was uncertain. The great warriors and the beft huntfmen chufe the prettieft girls; the others have only their refufe, and all the ugly ones left. The girls, knowing that they cannot be miftreffes of their hearts after they are married, know how to difpofe of them to the greateft advantage: for when once they have a hufband, all coquetry muft ceafe;

they

they muſt apply themſelves to their duties in their houſes, ſuch as preparing their huſbands meals, dreſſing the ſkins, making ſhoes, ſpinning the wool of the wild oxen, and making little baſkets in which they are very well ſkilled and induſtrious.

The manner of puniſhing the infidelity of their wives is as follows: the huſband muſt firſt be perfectly convinced of his wife's miſbehaviour by his own eyes, and then ſhe is watched by his relations and her own. The huſband is then no longer allowed to keep his wife, though he ſhould wiſh it; becauſe the Indians ſay, that it is unworthy and beneath a true man to live with a wife who has failed ſo eſſentially in her duty to him. In this caſe, the huſband goes to the *Cacique*, and tells him his ſtory. The chief immediately orders ſome people to go and cut little ſwitches, and all keep a profound ſecret. The chief then gives orders for a grand dance, which every man, woman, boy, and girl in the village is obliged to attend, unleſs they will expoſe themſeves to be fined; but there are hardly ever any abſent: in the midſt of the dance the guilty woman is extended on the floor, and beaten on the back and ſtomach without mercy, and her ſeducer undergoes the ſame ceremony.

When

When thefe wretches have been well flogged, a relation on each fide comes and lays a ftick a crofs the criminals and the executioners. That moment they ceafe to beat; but then the hufband comes and cuts off all his wife's hair clofe to her head *, and reproaches her in prefence of all the people, that is, he reprefents to her how much fhe has done wrong to act as fhe had done with him, that he had let her want for nothing, but that fince fhe had however tranfgreffed, fhe might now go with her feducer; whofe hair they likewife cut on his forehead, and tell him, pointing to his paramour, There, that is thy wife. He is at liberty to marry her that inftant, but he muft go to fettle in another village.

When a married woman debauches a married man, the women meet together among themfelves each with a ftick of an arm's length, and go to the criminal woman, whom they beat without mercy, which creates great mirth and laughter amongft the young people; the women would kill the guilty wretch, if the men did not fnatch away the fticks.

Phyfic,

---

* The Indian women have long hair in treffes.

Phyfic, war, hunting and fifhing are the only arts which the Indians are ambitious of knowing. They educate their children very hardy, and make them bathe and fwim in winter time at day-break; which done the young men come of their own accord before their chief warrior, who holds a fpeech to them, telling them never to fear the water; that they may be purfued by their enemies; and that if they are taken they are burnt alive; that they muft on this occafion prove that they are true men, by uttering no complaints *.

When the harangue is finifhed, the chief fcarifies their thighs, breaft and back, in order to ufe them to pain, and he then gives them great blows with leather ftraps †. The young men are then allowed to take place among the warriors; and when they have done fome great action in the wars, they are marked with needles,

in

---

* The Indians are obliged to fupport bad luck with heroic conftancy, in order that their valour may defcend to their pofterity.

† Thefe leather ftraps are of the breadth of three fingers. The Indians ufe them for carrying their bundles when they fet out on a journey.

in the manner I have explained to you when I spoke of the *Illinois*.

Their children whilft they fuck their mother's milk, are daily bathed in cold water during winter; and when they grow up, the earth is their bed. As the Indians love their children very much, they accuftom them very early to fatigue; and indeed as their whole body is naked, it is no more fenfible to the cold than the face and hands.

The old men, that cannot follow them, whenever they make a retreat, defire to be killed with clubs, both to fpare them the wretchednefs of a decrepit condition, and to avoid falling into the hands of their enemies, who would certainly burn or eat them; for the Indians in their wars kill men, women and infants at the breaft, which together with the ravages of the fmall pox, is a caufe of the depopulation of America.

It will not be amifs Sir, to obferve that it is merely an act of humanity on certain occafions when a fon puts an end to his father's life. The Indians have a great veneration for their old men; they regulate their conduct by their advice, for they undertake nothing

LOUISIANA. 237

ithout their confent. They likewife take great re of the old men, and I have feen their chiefs 1 their return from a hunting party, before they ared the game, lay afide the fhare of the old ople, which is likewife appropriated to the ufe ʾ widows and orphans, whofe hufbands and fa-ers have been killed in defence of their country. he Indians are very hofpitable towards ftrangers ith whom they are in peace, and kind to their lies and friends, but cruel and unmerciful to eir enemies. They are furprifed and even andalized to fee a number of Englifhmen at *ew Orleans*, drawn thither in time of war, r the fake of trading under the fpecious pre-nce of coming to exchange prifoners[*]. A cique lately returned from *New Orleans* freely rned to me, that he had a great mind to eak their heads for killing the *French* in ? north, that is, during the fiege of Quebec, d that he was tempted to take his revenge on thofe that were at *New Orleans*. He added,

---

Here our author inferts a long invective againft the Eng- who come in veffels to *New Orleans* with prifoners of on board, which they offer to exchange, and that under cloak, they get information of the ftrength and fitu- n of the colony, and buy up all the furs they can get. e allowance muft be made for national prejudice and ich pertnefs. F.

added, that in his country they spoke to the enemies with the club in their hands, as foon *the hatchet is dug up*; a phrafe which denote that nobody ought to have any commerce or co refpondence with the enemy, directly or i directly, under any pretence whatfoever, aft war is declared, unlefs he will prove a trait to his country, and be punifhed accordingly.

When peace is concluded they bury tl hatchet or the club under ground, fignifyir thereby that all their hatred towards their en mies is buried in oblivion, that the horrors war are at an end, and that friendfhip ar good underftanding are growing again betwee them and their friends, like the white flowers their tree of peace, (which is the white laure that ought to fpread its branches over the *whi* ground; which is a metaphorical expreffic which means the ground of peace.

The cacique I mentioned before, is call *Tamathlemingo*, and he is very warm in t French intereft. I know that he has fcornfu rejected the prefents which fome Englifhm would have loaded him with, and he had a gr mind to break their heads for making him fu a propofition. He wears a filver medal fafter round his neck by a leather thong. He often told me, he would be buried together with the image of his father (that is, the king's portrait) which he wears on his breaft; and having always been faithful to him he hoped to fhake hands with him in the land of the fouls, where he expected to fee him one day. After this worthy chief had fhewn me thefe fine fentiments which parted from his heart, I gave him a bottle of brandy to drink the health of his father and mine. Such little *douceurs* when given on proper occafions, have a great effect upon thefe people; thus they were greatly moved when I pulled off my fhirt and gave it them in the name of their father, telling them that he pitied them, becaufe he knew by means of the *fpeaking fubftance* * that his children were naked.

Thefe nations have no idea of the political fyftems which are known among the European powers. In their opinion, the allies of a nation muft affift them, when they are in war, and have no correfpondence with their enemies. I have had a long and ferious conference with one *Allexi Mingo*, who is a juggler and likewife the chief of a diftrict among them, and pretends to have

been

---

* Paper, or letters.

been abused by some *Spanish* soldiers of the garrison of *Pensacola*: this Indian owned that he had formed a design in order to be revenged of them, to make a general incursion with his warriors into *Florida*, to the very gates of *Pensacola*. This Indian would pay me a compliment, and make me approve of his design, by telling me, that he was partly drawn into it, because the Spaniards lay still upon their mats; i. e. they were at peace with the English, whom they received into their ports, though at that time, they were our enemies.

I answered this discourse of the Cacique in express terms and such as were most capable of making him desist from his enterprize, as I was willing to prevent a massacre of the Spaniards who were our allies and neighbours: accordingly I spoke to him in a manner analogous to the genius and character of the nation.

Alexi Mingo, said I, prepare thy heart, open thy ears to hear the force of my words, for it will bring back to thee thy wits, which thou hast lost to-day.

I tell thee, then that the grand chief sovereign of the *Spaniards*, who lives on the other
side

fide of the great falt-water lake, in the old world that fwarms with inhabitants is the brother * of the father of the red men, i. e. of the king of *France,* and accordingly, I muft fay, I difapprove very much of thy bold defign. I fairly declare to thee, that if thou perfifteft in it, thou canft do no better than to begin with breaking my head. The Cacique anfwered, " Thy blood is as dear to me " as my own; befides, the *French* have never done " me any harm, and I am ready to give my " life for them; thou canft affure our father of " that. Oh that I had the fpeaking fubftance " which thou haft, to let him know my words, " but no, I rather wifh I had a hundred mouths " which he might hear †."

After this proteftation of friendfhip he gave me his *Calumet,* and when I had fmoked a little I returned it to him, as having made peace for the *Spaniards,* by whom he pretended to have been ill-ufed; and as a ratification I gave him a bottle

Vol. I.   R

---

* The Indians call their allies brothers.

† Some time after the author's departure, the Indians of hefe parts maffacred feveral Englifhmen, that were come within two leagues of fort *Toulou/e,* where *M. de Grand-Maiin* then commanded, who is now Major of the troops at *New Orleans.*

tle of the fiery water, that is of brandy, saying, this I give thee to clean thy mouth, that it may not utter any more bad words againſt the Spaniards our allies: and to ſtrengthen my diſ- courſe I gave a great roll of tobacco, for his warriors to ſmoke out of the great *Calumet* of peace. After my harangue was at an end, the young people came one after another to ſqueeze me by the hand, as a mark of friendſhip, which is cuſtomary among them.

I wiſhed, however, to perſuade this Cacique who was piqued at the *Spaniards*, who receive Engliſh veſſels at *Penſacola*, becauſe they are a peace: for he ſaid they came to inform them ſelves of the ſituation and ſtrength of theſe coaſts.

By way of appeaſing the Indian, I told him that the governor daily waited for the arrival o a great piragua*, which ſhould bring him ſom of the ſpeaking ſubſtance, wherein the grea chief of the Spaniards ſhould order him to dig uj the hatchet of war, and to lift up his club againſt the Engliſh.

Thi

---

* An European ſhip.

This difcourfe fatisfied my Cacique; and as he had drank a good portion of brandy, he was very talkative, and I took the opportunity of queftioning him concerning the grudge he bore the *Spaniards* in *Florida*. He told me, that he had heard by tradition, that the firft *warriors of fire* * who came into this country had committed hoftilities in it, and violated the law of nations; and, that ever fince that period, the anceftors of his nation had always recommended it to their pofterity to revenge the blood which had been unjuftly fhed. I told the juggling Cacique, that the Lord of life had revenged them fufficiently, by the death of *Ferdinand Soto*, and almoft all his warriors.

I added, that they had no further reafon to hate the *Spaniards*; that *Philip* II. grand chief of the *Spaniards*, had difavowed all the mifchief which his generals had done in thefe climates, as being contrary to his intentions.

I told

---

* Hiftory inform us, that in 1544, *Ferdinand Soto* made incurfions into this country; the Indians there, who had never feen any Europeans, called the Spaniards warriors of fire, becaufe they were armed with guns and piftols: they faid, that the cannon was thunder, and that it caufed the earth to tremble, by killing people at a great diftance.

I told this American prince part of the story of *Don Francis de Toledo,* viceroy of *Peru*, who publicly hanged the presumptive heir to the crown, and ordered all the princes of the royal family of the *Yncas* to be killed, not even excepting the Spaniards, who from their mother's side were descended from *Atahualipa*. Don *Francis*, after such an execution, expected to be raised to the greatest dignities of the state on his return to Spain; but he was very ill received by the grand chief of the nation, who ordered him with a harsh voice to get out of his presence, saying, I have not appointed thee to be the executioner of princes but to serve me and assist the unhappy. These words struck the viceroy dumb, and caused him such an illness that he died a few days after. The same king caused the death of one of his ministers that had imposed upon him, merely by saying the word *Hoolab*, which in the Indian language, signifies *What, dost thou lye?* The Cacique very gravely replied, " But if the grand chief
" of the men of fire, appeared, as thou
" sayest, so angry at the viceroy, on account
" of the cruelties which he had com
" mitted against his will, why did he not pu
" hi

him in the frame *? or why did he not cut off his head, and fend it back to *Peru?* This example of feverity and juftice would in part have fatisfied the people whom this general had ill-treated, by hanging on a gibbet, like a thief, the heir of a great empire, who depended only from the *Lord of life*, or the Supreme Being. Thus we red men, whom the Europeans call favages and barbarians would act towards the wicked and the murderers, who ought to be treated like the fierceft beafts of the foreft."

I again replied to this Indian chief in the folwing terms, " Thou muft know that the grand chiefs of the white men that live in the old country, are defpotic and abfolute, and that when they drive from their preſence their generals or warriors, who have abuſed their fubects without cauſe, this affront is much more enfibly felt by thofe proud chiefs, who are ated by the *Great Spirit*, or by God, on acount of their mifdeeds, than the punifhment

" of

---

* A punifhment which the Indians adjudge to thofe that committed cruelties, and are taken at war: they are put a kind of frame, compofed of two pofts, and a pole acrofs them, and burnt alive.

" of the frame, or a hundred blows with t[he]
" club upon the head, would be by a r[e]
" man."

At laſt I ſucceeded in ſoftening the h[a]tred which theſe people had conceived agai[nſt] the *Spaniards*, and I imagine every hoſtile inte[n]tion is ſuppreſſed now; for my explication w[as] very ſatisfactory to my juggler.

I believe I have already obſerved to you, t[hat] the Indians are very ſenſible of injuries, and t[hat] they generally remember thoſe that have o[ut]raged them when they are in liquor. I have [of]ten been the mediator in order to terminate [the] quarrels between two Indians; I told th[em] that they ought to live together as good b[ro]thers, forget the paſt, and employ their cour[age] in the common defence of their country only. [I] further aſſured them that if they did not g[ive] ear to my words, the *Great Spirit* would be [diſ]pleaſed with them, and make their crops [of] maize fail. The Indian women ran quickly [to] me, whenever any two were ready to fi[ght] that I might judge between them, and I alw[ays] did all I could to reconcile the parties; wh[ich] pleaſed the women very much, who have noth[ing] wild about them, but the name which peo[ple] give them, and whofe features are very regular. In a word, in this new world, as well as in the old, that lovely fex is born to populate and not to deftroy.

What I have ftill to fay of this nation is fo ample, that I am obliged to divide it; I fhall, therefore referve their mourning and their funeral cuftoms for another letter.

I am, SIR, &c. &c.

Among the Allibamons the 28th of April 1759.

LETTER XVI.

To the same.

Mourning and Manner of burying the Dead among the Allibamons; Justice done to the Chevalier d'Erneville, for a Soldier killed by a young Indian: their Religion; their Means of catching the Roebuck and the wild Turkies.

SIR,

THE day before yesterday I received one of your letters, which informs me that you are in good health, and that you continue to give me marks of your remembrance of me. In my preceding letter, I spoke to you of the marriage of the Indians; I shall now proceed to describe their mourning. When a grand chief of the nation dies, this mourning consists in not washing nor combing themselves; the men daub their whole body with soot, mixed

up

up with bear's oil; and in a word, they renounce all forts of diverfions. When a woman lofes her hufband, fhe is obliged to be in mourning for a whole year, and to lay afide all her ornaments.

All the *Allibamons* drink the *Caffine* *; this is the leaf of a little tree, which is very fhady; the leaf is about the fize of a farthing, but dentated on its margins. They toaft thefe leaves as we do coffee, and drink the infufion of them, with great ceremony. When this direutic potion is prepared, the young people go to prefent it in calebafhes formed into cups, to the chiefs and warriors, that is the honourables, and afterwards to the other warriors, according to their rank and degree. The fame order is obferved when they prefent the Calumet to fmoke out of: whilft you drink they howl as loud as they can, and diminifh the found gradually; when you have ceafed drinking, they take their breath, and when you drink again, they fet up their howls again. Thefe forts of orgies fometimes laft from fix in the morning to two o'clock

in

---

* This is the *Prinos glaber* of Linnæus. Sp. pl. p. 471. and *Caffena vera Floridanorum*. Catefby's Carol. 2. t. 57.

in the afternoon. The Indians find no inconveniencies from this potion, to which they attribute many virtues, and return it without any effort.

The women never drink of this beverage, which is only made for the warriors. In such assemblies, where they are never admitted, the Indians tell their news and deliberate on political affairs, concerning peace or war. However the Chevalier *d'Erneville*, says that he saw a woman, who was the grand chief's wife, go in, because she was a female warrior, and had a quick, penetrating mind. Her opinion sometimes prevailed in the conclusion of treaties.

The *Allibamons* love the French very much; there is an agreement on both sides, that if a *Frenchman* kills one of the *Indians*, he must die, and the same if an *Indian* kills a *Frenchman*; the last accident happened whilst the Chevalier *d'Erneville* commanded the fort at the *Allibamons*; a young Indian shot a soldier of the garrison, and disappeared immediately. As the officer did not know where the criminal was, he applied to the chiefs of the nation, saying, they must do him justice. They answered, that the young man had taken refuge with another nation; the *Chevalier*

valier d'Ernville did not put up with this excufe; he told them that the dead man called for vengeance, and that blood ought to be avenged by blood, as is their expreffion; that the murderer had a mother, and that fhe ought to fuffer in his ftead. They anfwered, that fhe had not killed the man; but the officer replied, that he fpoke like the red man, who when fomebody killed a perfon of their nation, and they had not juftice done them for it, were revenged upon fome perfon of the nation of the murderer. He laftly reprefented it to them, that in order to keep the good underftanding between the white and the red men, they ought not to oppofe the punifhment of the criminal. They offered him a great quantity of furs, and even horfes loaded with booty. This officer who is known for his zeal in preferring the king's intereft to his own, and the honour of the nation to his fortune, refufed all thefe prefents. He added, that he had not been able to fleep fince the death of his warrior, who called every night to him, *avenge my blood*. The poor Indians, feeing they could not move him, held a council and fent out eight men, conducted by a young chief of the warriors. He went immediately with his men to the murderer's mother, and told her that fince her fon was not to be found, fhe muft die in his
ftead.

ftead. The poor woman fuffered herfelf to be led away, and was all in tears; her relations followed her with very fad countenances; one of them feeing there was no pardon to be hoped for, faid to the chief of the troop, " *My mother-in-law dies through courage, as fhe has not ftruck the blow.*" He propofed they fhould wait whilft he went to fetch the murderer; he actually brought him into the affembly, where the Chevalier *d'Erneville* was, and faid, See, there is the guilty man, do what you pleafe with him. The officer anfwered, that they ought to do him juftice; and they immediately killed him †.

Juftice

---

* Thus the Indians execute juftice; there is no need of drawing up cafes; all thefe forms are unknown; the law is, that he who has killed muft be killed again; unlefs it be by accident, as in a drunkennefs, in a fit of madnefs, or in their exercifes.

† The relation of this ftory, is by no means favourable to the French. They acted upon a barbarous and cruel principle, by bringing the mother of the guilty man to a punifhment which fhe did not deferve; and had not her fon on this occafion preferred filial duty to felf-prefervation, the French Chevalier would have committed an inhuman action; by inflicting death on an innocent perfon. The *Indians*

Juftice being thus done, the chief harangued the young people, and recommended it very ftrongly to them, to keep their hands from the *French,*

---

dians act upon principle, by avenging the death of their countrymen upon any other perfon of the nation to which the murderer belongs; for, on account of their confined ideas, and ignorance, they think the fame conftitution and manners take place among the Europeans, as are ufual among themfelves; and as they look upon their whole nation as a body of brethren, and a fingle family, they are, therefore, of opinion that all the Europeans muft be anfwerable for the death of one of their brethren. But as the Europeans boaft to be civilized, inftructed and Chriftians, they ought to act according to the principles of their religion, the knowledge and inftruction they enjoy, and their own conftitution; all thefe oblige them to fhew the Indians, by their example, the fuperiority of their religion, knowledge and conftitution; make them fenfible, that if they acted like Indians they would commit an open injuftice; and to enforce the return of fuch actions in fimilar cafes. The Europeans inftead of inftilling principles of humanity into the minds of the poor Indians, very frequently fcandalize them by their uncharitable and barbarous manners; and thus the high refinements of our manners, our boafted civilization, our pride, founded upon the fuperiority of our knowledge, and that real great advantage of being inftructed in a religion founded upon reafon and charity, inftead of bringing our immortal minds to that pitch of excellence they are capable of, according to the true intention of thefe advantages, prove only our deep corruption, and the wilful depravity of our hearts, and I may fay, the barbarity of our manners. F.

French; and added, that as often as they should lose their senses and kill our people, they would do us the same justice again.

The Chevalier *d'Erneville* held a speech to the assembly in his turn, and made the nation a present which the governor had sent him. The Indians gave him the great calumet of peace to smoke, all the soldiers and *French* inhabitants likewise smoked it, in sign of a general amnesty; afterwards they drank the *Cassine*, which is the potion of the *white word*, i. e. the potion of oblivion and peace.

Since that time this nation has never offended us. The *Allibamons* offered, in 1714, to build upon their ground, and at their expence, a fort, which was afterwards called Fort *Touloufe*, and they introduced the *French* into it. M. de *Bienville*, who was then governor, went to take possession of it in the King's name[*].

They

---

[*] This governor is in such great esteem with them, that they always mention him in their harangues. His name is so deeply graved in the hearts of these good Indians, that his memory will always be dear to them. As soon as they saw me they inquired after him; I answered, that he was at the great village, or *Paris*, in good health, with which they were highly pleased.

They never would permit the *English* to do the like; they pay no regard to the menaces of the King of *England*; every Cacique or chief of a village thinks himself a sovereign, who only depends upon the *Master of life,* or the *Great Spirit.*

The *Allibamons* have called their country the *white country*, or land of peace; and repose on their mats, that is, *they attack no body*; which is a kind of allegory by which they seem to tell all the nations on earth, that the murdering hatchet is buried, and that they may come to trade with them in safety.

The following is an harangue which I heard one of the chiefs of this nation hold: " Young
" men and warriors, do not disregard the *Ma-*
" *ster of life*; the sky is blue, the sun is with-
" out spots, the weather is fair, the ground is
" white, every thing is quiet on the face of the
" earth, and the blood of men ought not to be
" spilt on it. We must beg the spirit of peace
" to preserve it pure and spotless among the na-
" tions that surround us. We ought only to
" spend our time in making war with tygers,
" bears, wolves, stags, and roe-bucks, in order
" to have their skins, with which we may trade
" with

"with the Europeans, who will bring us what
"we want, in order to maintain our women and
"children."

The Americans in general have no knowledge of letters. The art of writing is unknown to them. They are furprifed to fee that one can converfe with another at a great diftance by a paper; and they look upon the miffive letters with admiration. When they are trufted with letters, they bring them very exactly to the perfons they are directed to; and though it fhould rain ever fo hard, and they had a great many rivers to pafs, thofe letters are never wetted. The *Allibamons* trade with the *French*, *Englijh*, and *Spaniards*, but they do not love the latter much; they make war upon them fooner than upon any other nation, on account of their cruelties towards the *Mexicans*; their memory is admirable, they always remember the wrong which is done to them.

Thofe whom I fpeak of here acknowledge a Supreme Being, whom they call *Soulbieche*. I afked them what they thought of the other world; and they anfwered, that if they have not taken another man's wife, or if they have not robbed nor killed any one during their life, they

they shall go after their death into a very fertile country, where they shall want neither wives nor proper places for hunting, and that every thing will be eaſy to them there; but that on the contrary, if they have behaved themſelves fooliſhly, and diſregarded the great Spirit, they will come into a barren land full of thorns and briars, where there will be no hunting, and no wives. This is all I have been able to learn concerning the belief of theſe people of another life.

The *Allibamons* bury their dead in a ſitting poſture; in order to juſtify this cuſtom they ſay, that man is upright, and has his head turned towards heaven, which is to be his habitation. They give to them a calumet, and ſome tobacco to ſmoke, that they may make peace with the inhabitants of the other world. If the corpſe be of a warrior, he is buried with his arms, which are a muſket, ſome powder and bullets, a quiver full of arrows, a bow, and an hatchet or club; and beſides theſe a mirror[*], and ſome vermilion with which they may dreſs themſelves in the other world.

[*] The young Indians are never without a little hatchet or a mirror hung on their wriſt.

When a man kills himself, either in despair or in a sickness, he is deprived of burial, and thrown into the river, because he is looked upon as a coward.

I have already said, that the Indians must support misfortunes with heroic constancy. Their enthusiasm prompts them to make songs of death when they are taken prisoners, and destined to be burnt; on such an occasion an Indian says: " I fear neither death nor fire, make me suffer " ever so much, because my nation will revenge " my death." This occasions his enemies either to accelerate his fate, or sometimes adopt him, saying he is a man of courage.

When there is a disturber of public peace amongst them, the old men speak to him thus: " Thou art at liberty to go away; but remem- " ber, that if thou art killed, the nation shal " disown thee; we shall not weep for thee, no " avenge thy death." So irregular a life is pu nished with the greatest contempt among thes people, as among all others *.

Th

---

* The young Indians sometimes ramble into the neigh bouring villages, and carry off the women; these kinds

The Indians generally set out a hunting towards the end of October. The *Allibamons* go sixty, eighty, and sometimes an hundred leagues from their villages, and they take their whole families with them into their piraguas: they do not return till March, which is the time of sowing their corn-grounds. They bring back many furs, and a great quantity of dried flesh. When they are returned into their villages, they regale their friends, and make presents to the old men, who have not been able to go with them, and have kept in the huts during the time of the great hunt.

These nations have singular methods of catching the roe-deer; an Indian takes the head of a roe-buck, and dries it; he then carries it with him into the woods, where he covers his back with the skin of this animal; he puts his hand into the neck of the dried head, taking care to put little hoops under the skin to keep it firm on the hand; he then kneels down, and in that attitude,

---

rapes occasion the wars among the different tribes; for they fight not for land, having more of that than they can cultivate. It is a capital crime among the Indians to carry off another man's wife; if it is the Cacique's wife, the whole nation is obliged to avenge the affront offered to their chief.

titude, mimicking the voice of thefe creatures, he fhews the head; the roe-deer are deceived by it, and come very near the hunters, who are fure to kill them.

There are Indians who, by means of this ftratagem, have deftroyed four hundred roe-deer in one winter's hunting. They employ very nigh the fame trick to get the wild turkies in the woods; fome of them put the fkins of thefe birds on their fhoulders, and on the heads a bit of fcarlet or other red cloth, which is agitated by the wind, and whilft the birds look at them, their comrades kill them with arrows; they do not ufe fire-arms, for fear of frightening them, and whilft there are any turkies on a tree, they continue to fhoot them with great dexterity; thefe birds are commonly foolifh enough to expect the return of their fellows who fell down; the Indians have often treated me with thefe birds, and I found them excellent during autumn.

The Indians are likewife very dextrous fifhermen; they neither employ hooks nor nets; they take reeds, which are very common along the fides of rivers, dry them near the fire, or in the fun-fhine, fharpen one end like a dart, and faften en a cord made of the bark of a tree, to the other end; when they are upon the lakes in their canoes, they throw this dart or harpoon into the water at the fish, and draw it up again by means of the cord; others shoot the fish with a bow and arrows, and when they have wounded a fish, it comes to the surface of the water.

Before I have done with the *Allibamons*, I should not forget to tell you, that in July, when their harvest begins, they have a great feast. That solemn day they pass without eating; they light a new fire for physic, as they call it, or juggling, after which they take a purge, and offer to their *Manitou* the firstlings of their fruit: they finish the day in religious dances.

This nation has likewise jugglers or quacks; I shall relate to you a very droll adventure which happened to me with one of them. As I was going up the river of *Allibamons*, a quack and juggler came to see me with several Indians, men and women. He asked for some brandy, I gave him a bottle full of it, which he drank with his companions. He asked me for some more, but I told him I had no more; he would not believe me, and seeing that he could not get any thing, he thought he would intimidate me, me, by telling me he was a magician, and would *practise physic* * againſt me, if I gave him no brandy; *i. e.* he would enchant my boat, ſo that it could not proceed. I told him I feared him not; that I was a phyſician myſelf. This word aſtoniſhed my adverſary.

This pretended magician told me to ſhew him the effects of my art; I anſwered, that he ought to begin, but he replied that I ſhould do it being a ſtranger; at laſt, after many debates, I began to make ridiculous geſtures, and looked into a book which the juggler underſtood nothing of; I bid him retire, and leave me alone, it being the cuſtom of the jugglers, by which means they conceal their impoſtures from the other Indians. I had the ſkin of a tyger-cat, the fleſh and bones of which had been extracted through an inciſion in the neck; I gave this ſkin to the Indian quack, telling him to reſtore its ſight, and make the creature go about. He anſwered, that he could not do it; I ſee, ſaid I, thou art a mere novice in this art, I ſhall perform it.

I muſt

---

* This is an expreſſion which the Indians make uſe of, denoting the application of their ſlight-of-hand tricks, and grimaces intended for to make their countrymen believe that they are magicians or conjurors.

I muſt previouſly inform you, that, in my laſt voyage, I brought with me from France enamelled eyes, which perfectly imitated the natural eyes; a thing which the Indians here had never ſeen; I faſtened them with the reſin of firs, in the place of thoſe which were wanting in the ſkin, into which I afterwards put and confined a living ſquirrel, with its head towards the neck of the tyger-cat; a ſoldier whom I had inſtructed was quite ready with a club; every thing being thus prepared, I opened the door of the cabin, and the Indians advanced, with the juggler or quack doctor at their head. I held the cat in my arms, and the ſquirrel jumped about in it, which immediately ſurpriſed my pretended magician; he cried out that I was a true *phyſician* or ſorcerer, becauſe I had brought to life, reſtored to ſight, and made dead cats walk. When the other Indians had well conſidered it in my arms, I let it go on the ground, pricking the ſquirrel with a pin, which made it run with the cat's ſkin towards the ſpectators, who thought it would devour them; they went backwards, and the women, through a natural fear, ran from my boat, declaring that I was a ſorcerer. I then ran to my tyger-cat, ſeeming to be very angry with it, I quickly took out the ſquirrel and the glaſs-eyes, then preſſing the teeth in the cat's head againſt my ſtomach, I cried out as if the creature had bit me, flinging it on the ground immediately; the ſoldier whom I had armed with a club, ſtrikes at the revived tyger-cat, in order to kill it for having revolted againſt its maſter, and for having been willing to attack red men, who were our friends and allies.

After this comic ſcene, I gave the ſkin to the Indian juggler, and deſired him to make it revive as I had done. He owned, that my art was above the reach of his. I then bid him enchant my boat to prevent its going on; but he anſwered, that one phyſician againſt another could do nothing; that I was his maſter in the art, and he an ignorant fellow *. All the ſavages

---

* The Indians repoſe a great confidence in their doctors; the juggler's hut is covered with furs, with which he covers and dreſſes himſelf. He goes in quite naked, and begins with pronouncing ſome words which no body underſtands; they are, as he ſays, to invoke the Spirit; after that he riſes, cries, agitates himſelf, appears quite frantic, and gets into a profound ſweat †.

The hut ſhakes, and the ſpectators believe it is done through the preſence of the Spirit; the language which he ſpeaks on this occaſion, has nothing in common with the ordinary Indian language; it is nothing but the ravings of a

hot

vages who were out upon the winter hunt along the river, brought me provisions of roe-deer and turkies, that I might begin again to play off my trick; but for fear of being discovered, and to preserve my reputation, I said I could

not

---

hot imagination, which these quacks have imposed upon their countrymen as a divine language; thus the most cunning people have always deceived the rest.

† The heathen nations in the Russian empire have exactly such jugglers or conjurors as are here described. In the government of *Cazan* are the *Tcheremisses*, the *Tchuwashes*, and the *Wotiaks*, three nations; the first of which call their conjurors *Mushan*, the second *Yommas* or *Yymmas*, and the third *Tona* or *Tuno*; they are of both sexes, and make the same grimaces as these American jugglers. In *Siberia* the *Tungusi*, the *Yakuti*, and the *Byrati*, call their conjurors *Shamans*, and they perform the same tricks, and make many antic gestures at their pretended conjurations. Their dress is on these occasions likewise very remarkable, sometimes ornamented with the fangs and talons of beasts and birds of prey, sometimes hung with such a terrible quantity of several pieces of iron, as will both make the robe very heavy, and cause a great rattling noise at the least motion of the conjuror's body. The more we go east in *Siberia*, the more common is this kind of conjurors, and the more striking is the likeness between the savage inhabitants of *North America*, and the savage Nomadic nations of the north-east parts of *Asia*. Some more hints of this similarity are pointed out in a note to *Kalm's Travels into North America*, vol. III. p. 126. F.

not do it over again, left some one of them
should be devoured by the revived creature, and
the better to convince them, I shewed them the
marks of the animal's teeth on my stomach.
They then approved very much of what I had
said, and thanked me for interesting myself so
much for them, as to expose myself generously
to prevent the furious revived tyger-cat from
killing their women and children; they added,
that I had done well to reduce it to its lifeless
state, in order to make it an example to others,
because it was an evil spirit; these poor people
regard the French as supernatural men.

It is sometimes dangerous to be a doctor; for
if some one dies among the Indians, they attribute his death to the physic, and not to the in-
curable disposition of the patient; therefore I
would never advise any body to abuse the cre-
dulity of these people. I likewise told them, that
since I had been bitten I had abjurated the office
of a magician, and that I knew no other physician than the *Master of life*, whose aid they ought
to implore; that he was as much the father of
the red men as of the white men, who are their
elder brothers.

The

The pretended resurrection of my tyger-cat, however, gave me great reputation among the quacks or jugglers of this country, and even among those of Spanish *Florida*, whose natural curiosity led them to pay me a visit; they joined the *Allibamons* doctors, and begged me to perform the same piece of legerdemain which I had done on my voyage: I told them, I was sorry that I could not satisfy their curiosity, because I had struck the post*; however, that I might not send them away discontented, I told them, that their presence was very agreeable to me, that the *Grand Chief* of the French and the father of the Indians was contented with their nation, and with them in particular; that the doctors having more knowledge than the others, both in the art of curing the sick, and in their zeal towards inspiring their countrymen with fidelity and friendship for the French, it was on that consideration I come on purpose to bring them a present, which was the word of their father, and that M. *Aubert* had orders from the governor to divide it among them.

I further told them, that as I was glad to get acquainted with them, and to converse with them,

---

* The Indian manner of swearing is to strike against a post with a club.

them, I wished they would tell me their proper names. As these people are neither baptised nor circumcised, they commonly take the name of some animal, such as bear, wolf, fox, &c. The gravity which I affected, in order to command the respect of these Indian doctors, made them ask me, whether I wrote their names in order to give an account of them to their father, by means of the speaking paper? to which I answered, that it was for that very purpose.

When I had written down their names, I sometimes made use of them in order to pass for a fortune-teller.

I shut myself up in the hut of one of the doctors, and a soldier, to whom I had told the number of letters which composed each name, put his hand on the shoulder of the juggler, and with a little rod struck him as many times as there were letters in his name; I being within easily guessed what man my soldier laid his hands upon; and so on with all the rest. They could not comprehend how I could guess so well without seeing them, and they owned that it went beyond their imagination.

The

LOUISIANA. 269

The Sieur *Godeau*, chief surgeon and keeper of the magazine at the fort of *Allibamons*, had already before me practised phyſic in the preſence of the Indians, who were looking at a little phial full of mercury; after looking at it with attention, they told him they wiſhed to have it. He ſaid he would give it them, but that he wanted the phial; he poured out the quickſilver immediately on the ground, and bid them take it up; they could never do it, for it rolled away on all ſides; the aſtoniſhed ſavages called it a ſpirit which divided itſelf into ſeveral parts, which being collected together formed only one body; but their aſtoniſhment was much greater when the Sieur *Godeau* took up all the mercury with a card, and put in the phial again, in their preſence, which none of them had been able to do. This ſurgeon did more, he poured *aquafortis* upon it, which diſſolved it, and made it diſappear entirely; ſince that time the Indians have revered him as a great doctor.

M. *de Montberaut* has put the command of the fort of the *Allibamons* into the hands of M. *Aubert*, who is adjutant of the fort *Mobile*. I take the liberty to write to the governor, in order to repreſent it to him with all reſpect, that being the ſenior officer of that gentleman, I could not

ſtand

stand here under his orders; that he might not be further obliged to do any services foreign to his function *, the King's order concerning that particular being very explicit; that as our institution is founded upon honour, I should think I would derogate from that which I had acquired in the King's service, if I did not make the observations of a soldier, whose zeal for the service he knows; that it was very natural for me to think, that by this consideration he would think himself obliged to let me enjoy the emoluments annexed to my place, otherwise I should beg him to recall me to *New Orleans*, that I might seize the first opportunity of setting out for Europe, where I should have the pleasure of assuring you that I am, S I R, &c.

*At the Allibamons, the 2d
of May* 1759.

P. S. I

---

* I must, however, do M. *Aubert* justice; he has had the command of the fort at the *Allibamons* to my prejudice, but I must praise the regard he has had for me, in offering to divide the authority, and to live upon the footing of a friend with me.

P. S. I have forgot to mention to you a vifit which the emperor of the *Kawytas* has paid us fome time after M. *de Montberaut*'s departure. As we had advice of it by a courier, I went to meet his Indian majefty in order to receive him at fome diftance from the fort. I had pofted fome foldiers, who fired their mufkets by way of fignal to the gunners to fire the cannon at the moment, when the prince fhould put his hand in mine * : he was mounted on a Spanifh horfe, with an Englifh faddle, and with a houfing of a tyger's fkin †.

This emperor marched gravely at the head of his attendants; I could hardly keep from laughing, on feeing tall well made naked men, painted with all kinds of colours, follow each other in a file, according to their rank, like fo many Capuchin friars.

The Indian prince appeared enraptured with the honours that were fhewn him; he had
never

---

* The Indians are without compliments and ceremonies, they laugh at our bows, or method of faluting with the body bent, and the foot advanced forwards or retreated backwards.

† American leopard.

never seen cannons, and called them great muskets.

He wore on his head a crest of black plumes; his coat was scarlet, with *English* cuffs on it, and beset with tinsel lace; he had neither waistcoat nor breeches, but only an apron made of a bit of scarlet cloth, which was taken up between the thighs and fastened to his girdle. Under his coat he had a white linen shirt; his feet were covered with a kind of buskins, of tanned roe-deer skins, which were died yellow. As he was a young man, of eighteen or nineteen years old, his nation had appointed a noble and wise old man as a regent; he held a speech in his sovereign's name, and he presented the calumet of peace to M. *Aubert*, who told him after the first compliments were over, that he should go to rest, it being the custom among the Indians, not to speak of political affairs till the next day, in order to have time to make reflections.

The Sieur *Laubéne*, the king's interpreter, translated the discourse of the regent, who likewise acted as the emperor's chancellor,; he did not fail to call to mind the great services which his late father had done to the French, and that

the

the fon had always been willing to come to fee them, in order to renew the friendſhip, which had never ceaſed to exiſt between his nation and ours, and to ſmoke the ſame calumet with them.

It is true, his predeceſſor always was inviolably attached to M. *de Bienville*, and the latter granted that Cacique the title of emperor on that account.

The governor likewiſe defired to bring all the tribes of *Allibamons* to acknowledge the emperor as their grand chief; but they refuſed it ſaying, that it was quite ſufficient that every village was ſubjected to a chief: in a word, they would change nothing in their form of government.

The emperor, his regent, his chief of war or general, his doctor or juggler, and his hired ſervant appeared at ten o'clock in the morning before our commander, where we all were dreſſed in our uniforms in order to compoſe a kind of court for him. As to the emperor, his imperial habit was no better this day than that of his attendants, for they all were

Vol. I.   T   dreſſed

dreſſed as Adam was in the terreſtrial paradiſe *.

This young prince had a noble ſhape, and a handſome appearance; he was ſprightly and graceful; during his ſtay here he has been treated at the king's expence. As he was of my ſize, the governor of the fort begged me to give him a blue coat, and a gold laced waiſtcoat, a hat with plumes, and a ſhirt with laced ruffles.

M. *Aubert* likewiſe made ſome trifling preſents to this American prince, and to the officers of his court, at the king's expence, and ſent them home very well ſatisfied.

Their country is ſituated between *Carolina* and *Eaſt Florida*, eaſtward of *Mobile*; theſe people have never been conquered by the *Spaniards*, who are become their declared enemies. The emperor always dined at M. *Aubert*'s table, with his regent. The others had not the ſame honour done

---

* The coat which the emperor had on when he arrived at the Allibamons, had been given him by a captain in the king of Great-Britain's army. He laid it by on this public day, through political views, and in order to get one from the French.

lone them, in order to infpire them with a
greater regard for the *French* officers. I muft
tell you, that the fon of that noble *Kawytas*
whom the French had honoured with the pompous title of emperor, was very much at a lofs
the firft time he dined with us; for he had never made ufe of a fork before; therefore he
looked at us very attentively, in order to ini-
ate our way of eating. His regent had not the
fame patience, he took the breaft and back bone
of a turkey and broke it with his fingers, faying, that the *Mafter of life* had made them before the knives and forks were made.

Towards the end of the repaft we had a
little farce with the hired fervant of the Emperor, who ftood behind his Indian majefty during dinner; this fellow obferving that we eat
muftard with our boiled meat, afked M. *de Bou-
lin* what it was that we feemed to relifh fo
much; as this officer fpeaks the language of the
nation, having lived forty years among them,
he anfwered, that the French were by no means
covetous of what they poffeffed; the Indian
immediately took a fpoonful of muftard, which
being very ftrong, forced him to make many
ridiculous contortions, which made his mafter
burft out laughing; his fervant was far from
laughing

laughing; for he thought he was poisoned; M. *Aubert* ordered a bottle of brandy to be brought and bid him take a good draught, assuring him that he would be cured immediately.

The *Kawytas* are very reserved towards strangers in matters of religion; they never speak in public till they have reflected sufficiently on what they are going to say.

These people annually hold a general assembly in the principal village of their nation; there is a great hut for that purpose, in which every one takes place according to his rank, and has a right to speak in his turn *, according to his age, abilities, wisdom, and the services he has done his country.

The grand chief of the tribe opens the session by a speech, which concerns the history or tradition of their country; he tells the military exploits of his ancestors, who have distinguished themselves in defence of their country, exhorting his subjects to imitate their virtues, in supporting the wants and miseries of human life

wit

---

* The Indians disapprove of the European habit of speaking all together in an assembly.

with patience, and above all, without complaining againſt the *Great Spirit, who is the Lord of the life of every being here on earth*; and in enduring adverſity with courage, and laſtly in ſacrificing every thing to the love of their country and of liberty; it being a thouſand times more glorious to die as a man, than to live as a vile ſlave.

The chief having ceaſed ſpeaking, the oldeſt among the nobles riſes, ſalutes his ſovereign, and harangues with his body naked to his girdle; he is all over in a ſweat, on account of the heat which his action and declamation throws him into; his geſtures are natural, and his metaphors explain his mind: he perſuades his audience into a belief of all that he ſays, by his eloquence, and the excellence of his diſcourſe. Nothing is more edifying than theſe aſſemblies; you hear no prattling, no indecency, no ill-timed applauſe and no immoderate laughter there. The young men are very reſerved and attentive to hear the words of the old men, being perſuaded that it is for their good.

T 3 LET-

LETTER XVII.

To the same.

The Author leaves the Allibamons. *His Navi[gation] tion in the River of* Tombekbé. *How he [es]capes the voraciousness of an Alligator. He m[eets] with a Party of revolted* Chactaws, *and bri[ngs] them to their Duty again. He returns [to]* Mobile.

SIR,

NSTEAD of an answer to the le[tter] which I had wrote to the governor [I] received an order at the *Allibamons* [to] go to Mobile, and serve there under the or[ders] of M. *de Velle*, the king's lieutenant in [that] place; thus in stead of going to *France* as I told you, I have got orders to command a c[on]voy of provisions and ammunition to the

Tombekbé, which is fituated on a river of the fame name, this ftation is about ten legues from the nation of *Chactaws*, I have followed my inftructions with the greateft exactnefs, and to the entire fatisfaction of my fuperiors; the letters and certificate which I can fhew up, are proofs of it.

I left *Mobile* on the 20th of Auguft 1759, with three boats, in which were foldiers and *Mobile* Indians : the latter offer themfelves to help the French in rowing, for fome trifle or other which is given them.

You embark in the river *Mobile*, and after going up about fifteen leagues, you come to a place called la *Fourche* (i. e. the fork) that is the juncture of two rivers which fall into the *Mobile*, viz. the river of *Allibamons* and the river *Tombekbé*; I entered into the laft on the 27th of Auguft, in order to go up to the fort; we were in the fine feafon, and I had chofen a very proper place for a camp on the banks of a river; the Indians having had good fuccefs in fifhing thereabouts, made me a prefent of a *barbel*, a fifh of about four feet long, which they commonly dry. The weather being fair, I did not chufe to pitch my tent, but only fat down by myfelf upon a kind of plat-form covered with green fods, which overlooked the river, thinking that place the moſt convenient for reſting : I ſpread the bear's ſkin taken in my pretended government, and wrapped myſelf up in my tent, covering my face with it, becauſe the vapours at night are dangerous in this ſeaſon; this little nicety was near coſting very dear to me as you ſhall ſee.

I had put my fiſh at my feet, leſt it ſhould be ſtolen; but it happened worſe. I had already ſlept for a whole hour very quietly, for the inhabitants of theſe parts are our allies and friends, when all of a ſudden, I found myſelf carried away by an extraordinary force, I awoke immediately, believing ſome one was playing me a trick; I aſſure you I never was more frightened, and I believe that a thing of leſs conſequence will often have the ſame effect; I thought the devil was carrying me off. I called for help, and the people believed that I was dreaming, or a viſionary; but how great was my ſurpriſe when I awoke. I ſaw an alligator (crocodile) of above twenty feet long * ; he was

come

---

* His ſize frightened me, and I was likewiſe infected with the bad ſmell of muſk which that animal carries with it.

come out of the river in the calm of night, and voracious as thefe creatures are, being attracted by the barbel which lay at my feet, he greedily fell upon it, and carrying it to the river he took me along by the corner of the tent in which I had wrapt myfelf up. I had time enough left to get out of it, at the border of the precipice, and fo efcaped with the fright. I only faved the bear's fkin, which I never leave now. This ftory, plain as it is, may pafs for a prodigy among thofe who love the marvellous.

The *Collapiſſas* and *Wanchas*, two little Indian nations, which live above *New Orleans*, fight with the crocodiles, or alligators, in the water in the following manner.

One takes a piece of hard wood, or of iron, and fharpens it at both ends; he takes hold of it in the middle, and fwims with that one arm extended. The alligator advances with his mouth open, in order to devour the arm of the Indian, who thrufts in his hand in which he holds the piece of wood, and the alligator pierces both his jaws through with it, can neither open nor fhut his mouth again, and is brought on fhore, by the Indian; they often take this diverfion;

and

and the negroes of *Guinea* or of *Senegal* do the fame.

After going up about fixty leagues between forefts and mountains which confine the river, we met with fuch low water, that we were obliged to unload all the goods, and hide them in the woods; I only left the provifions and ammunition in the boat, and gave them all my attention. I never was in a more difagreeable fituation; we were obliged to draw the boats for upwards of fifteen leagues; I put myfelf at the head of the foldiers and Indians, and drew at the cord, in order to fet them an example. You may judge of my uneafinefs, if you will confider that during this piece of work, it would have been eafy to defeat and to plunder us. I met a party of revolted *Chaétaws*, going to the Englifh; I exhorted them to return; they croffed the river in a place, called in their language *Tafkalouffas*, which fignifies the white mountain *; their chief, whofe name is *Mingo Howmas*, had the infolence to pretend he could oblige me to give him brandy; he even was audacious enough to lift his hatchet over my head.

On

---

* It is a kind of marle or chalk which would be of great value in Europe.

On this occafion, I told him I was a *true man*, that I feared not death, that I had given up my body *, and was willing to die, being perfuaded that if he killed me and my warriors, who were but few, the grand chief of the French, beyond the great lake, would revenge my blood on their nation, by fending as many warriors there, as there are leaves on the trees.

Thefe men were furprifed at my refolution; they faid, " That I was a *man of valour*; that I " made them recover their wits which they had " loft in forming the deteftable defign of leaving " their father's hand, but that they hoped I " would forget what was paft, becaufe I was " very good." At the end of this harangue, they prefented the calumet of peace to me, which I accepted on condition that I fhould fmoke with a new fire out of it, to fignify an eternal oblivion of what had paft, and a renovation of the alliance with the *Chaƈtaws*, children of the grand chief of the French. To convince them that I would forget the paft, I told them that the fire would be produced of itfelf.

In

---

* That is, devoted myfelf to die for my country.

In my laſt voyage from France I took with me a little phial of phoſphorus; I put ſome of this powder into the calumet of peace, and looked up to the ſky in pronouncing ſome words addreſſed to the Great Spirit; in the mean time the phoſphorus being expoſed to the air, ſet fire to the tobacco, which ſurpriſed, not only the Indians, but even the Frenchmen who were with me, becauſe they had never ſeen the experiment tried with this powder.

After this myſterious ceremony, I made theſe people preſents of ſome European trifles, and gave their chief a bottle of brandy, for it is cuſtomary among the Indians, that when you treat with them, you muſt give ſomething to confirm your words. Then they all ſhook hands with me, and went back to their village. They told me, they were aſhamed of their fooliſh conduct, and we ſeparated, ſatisfied with each other.

Some time after this adventure, the rains were ſo frequent, that they ſwelled the water in the river very much,

As I had diſpatched an Indian to M. *de Cha-bert*, governor of Fort *Tombekbé*, he ſent me a
detachment

detachment commanded by M. *de Cabaret*, a very fkilful officer, who was of great fervice to me on this occafion, by bringing me refrefhments for my foldiers, who had hardly any provifions left.

Our European coxcombs, who carry mirrors, toilets, night-gowns, &c. with them, would be looked upon as women by the Indians, and not as chiefs of the warriors: they would not diftinguifh themfelves in thofe campaigns, where they muft endure the exceffive heats of the fummer, and the rigours of winter, lie on the bare ground, and expofe themfelves to all the changes of weather, in order not to be furprifed by the Indians. Mr. *Braddock*, general of *New England* in 1755, made the fatal experiment, when he came to take Fort du *Quêne*; he was maffacred with his whole army at fome diftance from that place, by a fmall number of French, and fome faithful Indians, led by brave *Canadian* and European officers, who did wonders of bravery in this action.

At laft I happily arrived at Fort *Tombekbé* on the 25th of September, after going a hundred leagues by water, without feeing a fingle habitation. Every night we are obliged to camp in the woods

woods upon the banks of the river; but the greateft inconvenience are the *Mufkitoes* or *Maringoins*, a kind of gnats which are infupportable in *Louifiana*. In order to be free from them, we put great reeds into the ground, and bent them over like arches; we then covered them with a linen cloth, and laid down a bear's fkin as a matrafs. All the voyages made by people of the colony are done in the fame manner by water.

After going on fhore to camp, the commanding officer fhould always take care to appoint a guard, and to place fentinels in the woods to prevent furprifes. The officer ought always to be very careful in chufing an advantageous fituation for his camp, fuch as an ifle or a cape.

If the Sieur *D**** had taken thefe precautions, when he was fent to the *Illinois* by M. *de Bienville*, in 1735, with a boat laden with gunpowder, in order to carry on the war with the *Chickfaws*, he would not have been furprifed, as he was, by a party of warriors of that nation. It may be afferted, that the neglect of that officer has been no lefs fatal to us, than the meannefs, ignorance, and avidity of the governor of the fort of the *Natches*; this boat laden with powder,

powder, being taken by the *Chickſaws*, ſerved them to carry on the war againſt us for above thirty years, and cauſed the death of many brave men, and the loſs of many millions of money to the king.

The following is, in a few words, the manner in which M. D * * * was ſurpriſed and taken priſoner. One day when it blew a north wind, he was obliged to bring his boat to the ſhore, and ſo encamped thereon, in order to wait for better winds. He went out hunting, and his ſoldiers did the ſame in imitation of their chief; but the *Chickſaws*, who had followed and watched them for a long while, took the boat with the gun-powder, and made all the ſoldiers in it priſoners. When M. D * * * returned from hunting, he was inveſted and taken as his ſoldiers had been; but the Indians, contented with their capture, and having loſt none of their people, granted them their lives; M. D * * * had the good luck to eſcape, and returned to *New Orleans*.

When one is on a journey, he ſhould always have an Indian ſcout to go before him, both for the ſake of reconnoitring the enemy or preventing ſurpriſes, and likewiſe for finding out game. It

It happened to me as I was going up the river of *Tombekbé*, that I was in want of provisions, but Providence supplied it visibly. The Indians, who are like ferrets in the woods, came to give me advice that they had made a good discovery; they found the nest of a great eagle, called the *royal eagle* *; as the tree on which this

nest

---

* The eagle here called the *royal*, is called in English the *Golden Eagle*, Penn. Br. Zool. p. 61. tab. A. and in 8vo vol. i. p. 121. Falco chryfaëtos, Linn. and Le grand aigle royal, *Planches enluminées*, tab. 410. Mr. Permant relates, from *Smith*'s history of Kerry, "That a poor man in that county " got a comfortable fubfistence for his family, during a fum-" mer of famine, out of an eagle's nest, by robbing the ea-" glets of the food the old ones brought." This in some measure confirms our author's account. M. *Buffon*, in his *Hift. naturelle des oifeaux*, 12mo. edit. vol. i. p. 117. attacks M. *Salerne*, for having related the account he got from a friend, *who found three strong eaglets of this kind in a nest, fixed between two rocks*. M. *de Buffon*, though a great natural historian, is frequently subject to have his peculiar opinions, which he defends against all facts proving the contrary: and, by his eloquence, he explains away the strongest arguments; and invalidates even facts, in so much, that their strength in proving against him dwindles quite away. Our author had no peculiar opinion to favour; he must have known the bird, which is not uncommon in France, and may be seen in the menageries of the King and the nobility, and in various cabinets; and therefore I think our author's

account

nest was placed, was a very tall one; they came for hatchets to cut it down; they were indeed well paid for their trouble, for they found a great quantity of game of all kinds in the nest; such as fawns, rabbets, wild turkies, grous, partridges, and wood-pigeons, there were four eaglets in it, already pretty strong; these the Indians took for themselves, to the great sorrow of their parents, who would have picked out their eyes, if the Indians had not been armed with muskets; the poor birds were quite furious, and the eagle is very justly called the king of the birds on account of his intrepidity; but the balls did not spare their feathered majesties, who

account a strong proof against M. *Buffon*'s opinion, that the golden eagle has no more than two eaglets, seldom three, ever four. This will be a warning to all naturalists, not so much to rely upon the assertions of that French natural historian, who, with all his abilities, indulges too much his opinions; in spite of facts that are against him. I now and acknowledge the merit of this able zoologist; but his fine language, the fine prints, the vanity of the French nation, and the present fashionable taste, have procured him a high reputation, it is no more than natural that his authority should be decisive with many, who like rather *light summer-reading*, than the heaviness of a critical discussion in natural history. I therefore thought, that such a hint might be serviceable to those whom M. *de Buffon* would carry a-stray by his florid style. F.

fell the victims of parental love. The Indians told me, that the great Spirit sent us thefe provisions; indeed it was to be looked upon as a *manna* fent by Providence, which favoured us in thefe defarts.

I have received news here from *New Orleans*, from whence my friends write; that every thing is in great confufion there, on account of an Englifh fhip which is arrived from *Jamaica* as a fmuggling veffel, commonly called there an *interloper*.

This fhip is called the *Texel*, commanded by Captain *Dias-Arias*, a Jew, born an Englifh fubject. The *Ordonnateur* having found, that it ought to be confifcated according to the order: of the marine, has feized it for the King's ac count; M. *de Belleifle*, who is fort *major*, and the governor's *locum tenens*, has been requefted t(affift with the military for that purpofe; but M *de Kerlerec* returning from *Mobile*, has fufpende(M. *de Belleifle* in the performance of his func tions; that governor afterwards has had M. *d Rochemore*'s fecretary taken up at three o'clocl in the morning, by a detachment of foldier: who, after breaking the doors and window: dragged him out of bed, and put him on boar(a vef a veffel, the deftination of which remains unknown: upon this M. *de Rochemore* has fent to the minifter, Monfieur *de Fontenelle*, counfellor in the fuperior council.

When I fhall be better informed of all that has happened there, I fhall impart it to you; I write to the governor to grant me my recall to *New Orleans*.

I am, SIR, &c.

At Tombekbé, the 19th of September 1759.

LETTER XVIII.

To the Same,

Description of the Country of the Chactaws. *Their Wars; their Way of treating their Sick; their Superstition; their Commerce; their Plays of Exercise. Country of the* Tchicachas *or* Chickfaws, *our Enemies.*

SIR,

Thought of setting out from hence in two days, but the desire of knowing the most warlike and most numerous nation of *Louisiana* made me change my mind; I employ my leisure hours to describe what I have seen and heard of them. The *Chactaws* are entirely the friends of the *French*; they have given proofs of it under the government of M. *Perrier*, when they were made use of to punish the *Nat-*

ches

ches who maffacred the *French* that were fettled among them. The court likewife annually makes them prefents to keep them in our intereft. This nation can bring four thoufand warriors into the field, who would march with pleafure. It would be very eafy, if it was managed as carefully as it ought to be, to make them fing their fongs of war, and ftir them up to revenge us againft the *Englifh*, who are committing hoftilities in our poffeffions in *Canada*; thefe people might on occafion ferve us to great advantage, if they made incurfions into the Britifh colonies, efpecially the provinces of *Georgia* and *Carolina*, which are quite empty, all their troops and the national militia having been fent to the fiege of *Quebec*. Many brave officers of this colony, who fpeak the language of the Indians, fuch as M. *de Rouville*, *du Tiffenet*, and others, are eager to head fome parties of this nation, who could deftroy the crops of our enemies, would pillage and burn their habitations, and give the alarm even to the walls of *Charles-town*, which might make a diverfion in favour of *Canada*.

The *Chactaws* love war, and are acquainted with ftratagems. They never fight in order, or ftand their ground, they only harrafs and teaze their enemies much, without being cowards;

for when they come to close engagement, they fight very coolly. Some of their women are so fond of their husbands as to go into the wars with them. They stand by their sides in the battle, with a quiver full of arrows, and encourage them continually by telling them, they ought not to fear their enemies, but die as *true men*.

The *Chactaws* are very superstitious; when they go to war they consult their *Manitou*, who is carried by the chief. They always expose him to that side where they are to go towards the enemy, and place some warriors as sentinels round him. They have such a veneration for him, that they do not eat till the chief has given him first his share.

During the continuance of the war, they obey their chief very exactly; but as soon as they return, they only consider him according to the liberality with which he disposes of his property.

It is a custom among them, that when the chief of a party of warriors has got booty from the enemy, he must distribute it to the warriors, and to the relations of those who have been killed ed in battle, in order, as they say, *to dry up their tears*. The chief keeps nothing for himself, except the honour of being the support of the nation.

Interest, which is the cause of so many crimes in the old world, is unknown in the new world; it is not without reason that the *Cuba* Indians said, Gold is the true God of the Spaniards, and we must give it them in order to have peace. In *America* we do not see any of those men, whom we call *savages*, kill their brothers in cool blood, or make use of false witnesses to undo them, in order to get their estates. Those intrigues are unknown there, which are made use of to acquire riches, by means unworthy of a human being. No wife poisons her husband there, as is done in Europe, in order to marry again. There are no women lascivious or audacious enough publicly to declare the impotence of their husbands, as the European women do; nor does any Cacique's wife get her husband strangled, as that Neapolitan princess did with her's, because he would not satisfy her brutal passion; no girls there destroy their own offspring, in order to appear chaste in the eyes of men. The Indian women abhor the Christian girls who fall into that case; they oppose the fiercest fierceft wild beafts to them, becaufe they take great care of their young.

If the chief of a party of *Chaflaws* does not fucceed in the war which he has undertaken, he lofes all his credit; nobody has any truft in his command, and he is obliged to come down to the rank of a mere warrior. However, admire the variety of opinions among the different nations. It is no fhame, if, among thefe warlike people, a man turns his back upon the enemy. This defertion is attributed to a bad dream; if the chief of a great party, having dreamt that he will lofe fome men, tells his warriors that he has had a bad dream, they return immediately to their village; as foon as they arrive there, they have recourfe to phyfic, *i. e.* to juggler's tricks, which they employ on all occafions; then they march towards the enemy; and if they meet him, they kill five or fix of his men, and come home as content as if they had fubdued a great empire.

A general who fhould gain a victory with the lofs of many of his men, would be ill received by them; becaufe they do not value a victory when it is bought with the blood of their friends and relations: their chiefs are always careful to
preferve

preserve their warriors, and never attack the enemy unless they are sure of an easy victory, either on account of their numbers, or their advantageous situation; but as their adversaries are likewise cunning, and evade all the snares that are laid for them, it depends then upon superior finesse; therefore they hide themselves in the woods in day-time, and only walk at night; if they are not discovered, they attack by break of day. As they are generally in a woody country, he that goes first sometimes carries a very thick bush before him, and as they all follow each other in a file, the last hides the marks of their feet, by putting the leaves on the ground on which they went in order again, so as to leave no vestiges that might betray them.

The chief things by which they discover their enemies are the smoke of their fires, which they can smell to a very great distance, and their tracks or footsteps, which they can distinguish in an incredible manner. One day an Indian shewed me, in a place where I had seen nothing, the footsteps of some *Frenchmen*, *Indians*, and *Negroes*, and the time when they had gone that way; I own that this knowledge is amazing: it may well be said, that when the *Indians* apply to any single thing, they excel in it.

Their

Their art of war confifts, as you fee, in vigilance, attention to prevent furprife, and to attack the enemy unprepared, in patience and ftrength to fupport hunger, thirft, the rigours of the weather, and the labours and fatigues infeparable from war.

He that has done a fine action carries the fcalp of his dead enemy as a trophy, and gets the mark of it made on his body, then he mourns for him, and during that time, which lafts a month, he muft not comb himfelf; and when his head itches, he is only allowed to fcratch it with a little rod, which he ties to his wrift for that purpofe.

The *Chactaws* and their wives are very uncleanly, living chiefly in places at a diftance from rivers. They have no kind of religious fervice, they live without troubling their heads with futurity, and however believe that they have an immortal foul. They have a great veneration for their dead, whom they do not bury. When a *Chactaw* dies, his corpfe is expofed upon a bier, made on purpofe, of cyprefs bark, and placed on four pofts fifteen feet high. When the worms have confumed all the flefh, the whole family affembles; fome one difmembers the fkeleton,

leton, and plucks off all the mufcles, nerves and tendons that ftill remain; they bury them and depofit the bones in a cheft, after colouring the head with vermillion. The relations weep during this ceremony, which is followed by a feaft, with which thofe friends are treated who come to pay their compliments of condolence; after that, the remains of their late relation are brought to the common burying ground, and put in the place where his anceftor's bones were depofited. During the performance of thefe fad ceremonies, a deep filence is obferved, they neither fing nor dance, and every one goes home weeping.

In the firft days of November they celebrate a great feaft, which they call the feaft of the dead, or of the fouls; all the families then go to the burying-ground, and with tears in their eyes vifit the chefts which contain the relics of relations, and when they return, they give a great treat, which finifhes the feaft.

It may be faid in praife of thefe *Americans*, that the friendfhip fubfifting among the relations, a thing uncommon in *Europe*, is worthy of imitation. I have mentioned fome inftances of it which exceed thofe of antiquity. The mutual

love

love of the *Indians* towards each other, inclines them to aſſiſt each other when they are infirm. This ſincere love particularly ſhews itſelf in the laſt duties which they pay to their friends and relations by their tears and grief, even then, when they exiſt no more.

The *Indians* in general have a great veneration for their doctors or jugglers, who are real quacks, that impoſe upon the people, and live handſomely at their expence. They have a great authority among the *Indians*, and the latter go to them upon every occaſion for their advice; they conſult them as oracles. When a *Chactaw* is ſick, he gives all he has in order to be cured by them; but if the patient dies, his relations attribute his death to the phyſic, and not to his indiſpoſition; and can conſequently kill the doctor if they have a mind to do it *; however, this caſe ſcarce ever happens, as they generally have an excuſe at hand. Theſe doctors are, however, acquainted with ſeveral excellent plants for curing the diſeaſes common in their country;

---

* There are, likewiſe, people in *France*, who lay the death of their relations to the charge of the phyſician, and reſemble the Indians very much in their thoughts on this ſubject.

LOUISIANA. 301

country; they know a certain remedy for the bite of rattle snakes, and other poisonous animals.

When the *Indians* are wounded with a bullet or an arrow, the doctors or jugglers begin with sucking the wound of the patient, and spitting out the blood: they never employ lint, or tents, in their chirugical operations; but they have the powder of a root, which they blow into the wound, to accelerate its suppuration, and they make use of another which dries and heals it; they preserve wounds from mortification, by bathing them with a decoction of some roots, which they know *.

When they are tired and excessively fatigued, after returning from a war, or from a hunt, they use sweating in stoves †, as a restorative.

In

---

* M. *de Bossu* would have very much obliged all the world, by making use of his influence over the Indians, which he repeatedly mentions, in order to get from them the knowledge of such plants as they employ in their several diseases and aliments: this would have been really useful, and a proof of his humanity and curious inquiries. F.

† These stoves are round huts, built like ovens in the middle.

In these baths they boil all sorts of medicinal and odoriferous herbs, whose essences and salts rising with the steam of the water, enter into the body of the afflicted person, and restores his lost forces. This remedy is equally good for abating and destroying all kinds of pains; of course you see no Indian affected with the gout, the gravel, and other distempers which we are subject to in Europe; but this may likewise be attributed to their frequent bodily exercises. You see no great Dutch bellies there, nor any great tumours under the chin, such as the Piedmontese wens.

The Chactaws put a firm belief in enchanters and magicians, and when they meet with one such pretended sorcerer, they cut off his head * without any ceremony.

I saw an Indian of the nation of *Chactaws*, who had lately been baptized: as he had no luck

---

middle of the villages; they are kept in order by an *Alexis*, or public doctor.

* In 1752, when I was at *Mobile*, I saw an Indian whom the others killed with a hatchet, because he pretended to be a sorcerer. The other Indians attributed to him all the misfortunes that happen to their nation.

luck in hunting like his companions, he imagined he was bewitched; he went immediately to Father *Lefèvre* the Jesuit * who had converted him, and told him that his *medicine* or trick was good for nothing, becaufe fince he had practifed it upon him, he could kill no ftags or roe-deer; he therefore defired he would take off his enchantment again. The Jefuit, in order to avoid the refentment of this Indian, did as if he annihilated the baptifmal ceremony. Some time after, this Indian killed a roe-deer, either by accident, or by his own fkill, and thus thought himfelf freed from the enchantment, and was content.

The mind of this nation in general, is very rough and unpolifhed. Though one tells them ever fo much of the myfteries of our religion, they always anfwer, that what we fay is above their underftanding. They have, befides, very bad morals, moft of them being addicted to fodomy. Thofe defiled men, wear long hair, and a little petticoat like the women, who defpife them very much.

The

---

* The Indians call the Jefuits the men with the black robe; they fay that they are not like other men, and call them women, in derifion.

The *Chaëtaws* are very active and merry; they have a play at ball, at which they are very expert; they invite the inhabitants of the neighbouring villages to it, exciting them by many smart sayings. The men and women assemble in their best ornaments, they pass the whole day in singing and dancing; they even dance all the night to the sound of the drum and *chichikois*.

The inhabitants of each village are distinguished by a separate fire, which they light in the middle of a great meadow. The next day is that appointed for the match; they agree upon a mark or aim about sixty yards off, and distinguished by two great poles, between which, the ball is to pass. They generally count sixteen till the game is up. They are forty on each side, and every one has a battledoor in his hand, about two feet and a half long, made very nearly in the form of ours, of walnut or chesnut wood, and covered with roe-skins.

An old man stands in the middle of the place appropriated to the play, and throws up into the air a ball of roe-skins, rolled about each other. The players then run, and endeavour to strike the ball with their battledoors; it is a pleasure to

LOUISIANA.

see them run naked, painted with various colours, having a tyger's tail faftened behind, and feathers on their heads and arms, which move as they run, and have a very odd effect: they pufh and throw each other down; he that has been expert enough to get the ball, fends it to his party; thofe of the oppofite party run at him who has feized the ball, and fend it back to their fide; and thus they difpute it to each other reciprocally, with fuch an ardour, that they fometimes diflocate their fhoulders by it. The players are never difpleafed; fome old men, who affift at the play, become mediators, and determine, that the play is only intended as a recreation, and not as an opportunity of quarelling. The wagers are confiderable; the wonen bet among themfelves.

When the players have given over, the wonen affemble among themfelves to revenge their hufbands who have loft the game. The battleloor they make ufe of, differs from that of the nen, in being bent; they all are very active, and run againft each other with extreme fwiftnefs, pufhing each other like the men, they having the fame drefs, except on thofe parts which modefty teaches them to cover. They only put

rouge

rouge on their cheeks, and vermillion, inftea
of powder, in their hair.

After playing well on both fides all the da
long, every one retires with his glory or fham
but without rancour, promifing to play aga
another time as well as they can: thus the I
dians both men and women, exercife themfelv
in running; they are likewife very fwift, fo1
have feen fome run as faft as ftags.

The children exercife themfelves in fhootin
with a bow and arrows for prizes; he that fhoc
beft, gets the prize of praife from an old ma
who calls him an apprentice warrior; thus th
are formed by emulation, without corporal p
nifhment; they are very expert in fhooting wi
an inftrument made of reeds about feven fe
long, into which they put a little arrow, fe
thered with the wool of a thiftle, and in ai
ing at an object, they blow into the tube, a
often hit the aim, and frequently kill little bi
with it.

Almoft all the affemblies of the *Chactaws*
held in night-time. Though they are barbar
and ferocious, it is neceffary, in order to g
their confidence, to take great care to keep y

prom

LOUISIANA. 307

promises to them, without which, they treat you with the greatest contempt, proudly telling you that you are a liar; an epithet which the *Indians* have given to the present governor, whom they call *Oulabé Mingo*, i. e. the lying chief.

When the women are with child, their husbands abstain from salt, and from pork, for fear those aliments might do harm to their children. The women never lie-in in their huts; they go into the woods to be delivered, without receiving any assistance.

As soon as they are delivered, they wash their infants. The mothers apply a mass of earth to the foreheads of their children, to make them have flat heads, and as they get more strength they increase the bulk, it being a beauty among these people to have a flat head. They never swaddle their children.

They never wean their children till they are disgusted with their mother's milk. I have seen some children grown up so as to be able to tell the mother, *set down, that I may suckle,* and the mother immediately sat down. Their cradle is made of reeds, they put their children into it so
that

that their head lies three or four inches lower than the reſt of the body, therefore you never ſee any contracted or hump-backed people amongſt them. The women leave the huts in their catamenia, which the Indians call marks of valour. During that time, they are obliged to prepare their own meat and drink, and they do not return among men, till they are thoroughly purified. The Indians believe, that if they come near a woman in that ſtate, they would fall ſick, and that if they went to war after it, they would have bad luck.

Though the *Indians* only value themſelves upon their origin from the ſide of the women, yet the latter are not allowed to correct the boys; they have only an authority over their daughters. If a mother ſhould ſtrike her ſon, ſhe would be reprimanded and ſtruck again; but if the boy diſobeys her, ſhe muſt bring him to an old man, who inflicts a puniſhment on him, and then throws ſome freſh water over his body.

If a woman commits an infidelity, ſhe muſt *paſs through the meadow*, i. e. all the young men, and ſometimes even the old ones, ſatisfy their brutality on her, by turns. Such is the puniſhment

ment of adultery among the *Chaâaws*. Sometimes the guilty woman, has the good luck, after this infamy, to find a mean fellow, who takes her as his wife, under the pretence that she muft be difgufted with a criminal conduct, that has drawn fuch a punifhment on her, and that fhe will confequently behave better for the future. Be this as it will, fhe is always looked upon as a depraved and immoral woman.

Before I finifh my letter I muft fay a word of the *Tchicachas*, or *Chickfaws*. This nation is not fo numerous as the *Chaâaws*, but more terrible, on account of their intrepidity. All the northern and fouthern *Indian nations*, and even the *French*, have attacked them, without ever being able to drive them out of their country, which is the fineft and moft fruitful on the continent. The *Chickfaws* are tall, well made, and of an unparalleled courage. In 1752 and 1753, they attacked Meff. *Benoift* and *de Reggio*, who commanded the convoys from the *Illinois* tation, defcending the river *Miffifippi*: thefe *Indians* always choofe fome advantageous fituation, to make an attack in, their moft common poft is at the rocks of *Prudhomme*, the river being

ing narrow there, they can annoy the boats, which have no decks.

It is believed that the *Chickſaws* killed Meſſ. *Bouſſelet* and *de la Morliere*; theſe two officers, though they were very brave, fell into an ambuſcade for want of experience, not knowing the topography of the country they were in any more than general *Braddock*. An officer ought, therefore, always to apply to that, in order to avoid ſurpriſes, or elſe he ſhould always be on the defenſive and prepared.

The *Engliſh* have always been in alliance with theſe valiant warriors; they have always traded with them, and ſupplied all their wants.

The *Indians* of this nation ride well on horſe back: they leave the care of cultivating and ſow ing their grounds to their women, who are hand ſome and cleanly. When a *Chickſaw* has killed roe-deer, he tells his wife whereabouts it lies ſhe goes to fetch it, dreſſes it, and ſerves it u to her huſband: the women never eat with th men, who ſeem very indifferent about them, bu really love them better than any other nation.

The *Tchicachas*, or *Chickſaws*, only puniſh adultery with whipping the two offenders who have been caught in the fact, making them run naked through the village; after which the huſband repudiates his wife.

As theſe *Indians* gave ſhelter to the *Natches*, after the maſſacre of the *French*, the latter armed in 1736 againſt, and attacked them, with the united forces of the whole colony, but without ſucceſs.

M. *d'Artaguette* major and governor for the king, in the country of the *Illinois*, came to join M. *de Bienville* the governor of *Louiſiana*; he brought him the troops of the *Illinois*, and from the frontiers of *Canada*, but the army which that officer commanded, was ſurpriſed and defeated, becauſe he had been abandoned by the *Indians*, who were our allies. M. *d'Artaguette* was taken, with ſeven officers, and about twenty-ſix ſoldiers and inhabitants, by the *Chickſaws*, who burnt them alive; among them was the Father *Senat* a Jeſuit, who went with M. *d'Artaguette* in the quality of chaplain. The detail of this tragic ſcene has been related by a ſerjeant, called *Louis Gamot*, who was a ſpectator of the ſad fate which his companions underwent; he reserved to be burnt last, but he escaped by an odd stratagem. As he was acquainted with the language of the *Indians*, he employed it on this occasion to utter invectives against them; and getting loose, he threw all he found near him at their heads, saying, you are dogs, because you have burnt my chiefs; I will be burnt too, I fear neither fire nor death, for I am a true man; make me suffer much, because I desire it. The *Chicksaws*, seeing his resolution, looked upon him as an extraordinary fellow, and granted him his life; he was afterwards ransomed by an *Englishman* from *Carolina*, and is now at *Charlestown* the capital of that colony.

In another expedition against the *Tchicachas*, which was undertaken on the 26th of May in the same year, and commanded by M. *de Bienville*, we had not any more success; many brave officers lost their lives in it, and the major-general of the army, and the adjutant received such dangerous wounds, that the last died of them. I have heard from the Chevalier *de Lucer*, who is of a Swiss offspring, that his father, who served as captain in our troops, had been in this unlucky expedition; this officer has likewise told me the story of the Chevalier *de Grondel*, who now belongs to the garrison of *Mobile*, and

commands

commands the Swifs troop of the regiment of *Halwill*, belonging to the fervice of the marines; he had then the command of a detachment of grenadiers of the regiment of *Karrer*, in M. *de Bienville*'s army againſt the *Chickſaws*.

In order to abridge the account of this affair, I fhall only fay, that this officer, joining fidelity and bravery natural to his nation, to the impetuofity of youth, received five fhot in his body during the attack. As he remained on the field of battle after the retreat, he was juſt going to become the object of the enemy's vengeance and fury, if feveral foldiers of his troop had not generoufly expofed their lives to fave his, notwithſtanding the balls and arrows which were fent at them from the fort of the *Chickſaws*, killed five of them one after another.

However, one, without fearing the danger, returned to the field, and happily arrived in his troop carrying his officer on his fhoulders. The chief furgeon of the army tried all he knew to cure him, and the general, who values military merit, did not fail to give in an account of the officer's behaviour at court; and M. *de Maurepas*, in confideration of the wounds M. *de Grondel* had received, granted him an extraordinary

grati-

gratification, till he could get the crofs of *St. Louis*.

The foldier *who faved him at the peril of his life, was immediately made ferjeant at the head of his troop. You fee, Sir, by this fhort account, how worthy of admiration that well-eftablifhed fubordination is, among the troops of the *Helvetic* body, that are fo inviolably attached to the fervice of our King, and how much thofe that keep it in force feel the happy effects of it.

The action of thefe foldiers, which was really an heroic one, well deferves that their names fhould be tranfmitted to pofterity.

In 1754, the Baron *de Porneuf* imparted to me his intention of going upon a difcovery into the weft of *Louifiana*, up the *Miffifippi* and the river *Miffouris*, the fources of which are unknown to us. This officer, who is a *Canadian*, has the proper qualities for undertaking fuch an expedition; but the war which arofe between *France* and *England*, on account of the boundaries

---

* His name was *Regniffe*.

ries of these countries, has been an obstacle to the execution of this project.

I can assure you, that I should have been very happy to accompany him, both for the honour of my King and for my own satisfaction; for, notwithstanding the fatigues and dangers I have undergone in my voyages, I have never been disgusted or tired out of patience. Misfortunes pass like dreams, and I see nothing so happy as the life of a traveller; he constantly sees new objects, which instruct and amuse him at the same time. His mind is cultivated in an agreeable manner, he learns to read the great book of the universe, which cannot be read in a library, where there are as many systems, opinions, and contradictions, as authors. If you were in my place, you would have room to make philosophical reflections. I am, S I R, &c.

At the fort of Tombekbé, the
30th of September 1759.

P. S. As I may perhaps not meet with an opportunity of writing to you this good while, on account of the war, I shall add here an abstract concerning the differences which have arisen between

tween us and the *Chaƈtaws*. Some time after the war with the *Tchikachas* or *Chickſaws*, the *French* had ſome quarrels with a party of *Chac-taws*, who followed the intereſt of a prince of their nation called the *Red Shoe*, who was inſolent, and committed ſeveral hoſtilities againſt the *French*. M. *de Vaudreuil*, then governor of *Louiſiana*, having heard of this action, and what gave occaſion to it, immediately forbid all the *French* to go to that nation, and commanded them not to ſell them any arms or ammunition, in order to ſtop theſe commotions ſoon, and without bloodſhed.

The Marquis *de Vaudreuil*, after theſe precautions, ſent to the ſovereign of the nation, to inquire whether he was angry with the *French*, as the *Red Shoe*; the ſovereign anſwered, by means of the interpreter, that he was the friend of the *French*; that his general, meaning Prince *Red Shoe*, had loſt his ſenſes.

After this anſwer, he got a preſent, but was much ſurpriſed to find neither arms nor powder and ſhot in it, at a time when he was our friend as before. This proceeding, together with the prohibition of ſelling them arms, which they knew had been iſſued out, redoubled their aſtoniſhment, nifhment, and brought them to an explication with the governor, who told them, that our people would not treat with them concerning arms and ammunition, as long as the *Red Shoe* had not found his wits again; becaufe, if they got powder, they could not help, being all brothers, to give a fhare of it to the warriors of captain or chief *Red Shoe*. This anfwer determined them to fpeak to the tribes that infulted us; they told them, if they did not foon go with the calumet to the *French*, they themfelves would go to war againft them as rebels. This threat made them afk peace, and offer a reparation to the *French*, who were not in a condition to fuftain a war againft fo numerous a nation.

Thus M. *de Vaudreuil*, as a wife politician, put a ftop to this war, without expences to the ftate, and without expofing a fingle man; it was M. *de Grand-pré*, a captain of our troops, who was charged with this important negociation; the Marquis could not pitch upon a fitter perfon. M. *de Grand-pré* is a *Canadian*, and ferves the King with zeal, bravery, and difintereftednefs. I was upon the point of going to ferve under him at Fort *Tombekbé* among the *Chaétaws*, when I firft arrived here in 1751.

LETTER XIX.

To the same.

The Author returns to Mobile. *Remarkable Events which happened in the* Cat's Isle. *Tragic Death of the Sieur* Duroux *governor of that isle.*

SIR,

I AM now returned from my voyage up the river of *Tombekbé*. I have fulfilled this important and troublesome mission, to the satisfaction of my superiors. In waiting for my recal to *New Orleans*, my curiosity led me to visit the little isles on the coast of *Louisiana*.

The isle of *Massacre* was the first where the *French* made any settlements. It got its name because the *French*, when they landed there found a great quantity of human skeletons

bu

but could not diftinguifh whether they were of *Spaniards* or *Indians*.

It has fince been called the *Dauphin* ifle *. It was peopled by degrees; they built magazines, a fort, and barracks there.

In

---

* It muft not be confounded with that which is mentioned in the relation of the firft voyage of the Eaft India company to the ifle of *Madagafcar*, which they called too precipitately the *Dauphin*'s ifland.

The author of this relation, who wrote in 1665, and had done that fame voyage, agrees that the *Englifh* and *Dutch*, who were already eftablifhed in *India*, were the models which M, *de Colbert* propofed to imitate, and afterwards to furpafs; but all the projects of that worthy minifter proved abortive, both by the imprudence and vanity peculiar to the nation, and by the mifmanagement of thofe who were at the head of affairs.

The fame author adds, that he only found there " violent " and unfkilful men, ill chofen officers, incapable of the oc- " cupation they were intended for; whereas they ought to " have been men above the coarfer paffions, with no other " inclinations than for the good of their country, which " ought to be the rule by which every one fhould be guided " who wifhes to acquit himfelf with honour."

It feems to me, that this ufeful leffon fhould be graved into the hearts of all thofe who go to our colonies with fome authority.

I have

In 1717, the entrance of the harbour was stopped up by a prodigious quantity of sand, collected together by a hurricane; the whole isle was almost overflowed, and great numbers of cattle were drowned; it was necessary to seek another port, and they chose the isle *Surgere*, which has since been called *Ship Island*; it has a pretty good harbour. In 1722 M. *de Bienville* transported every one from thence to *New Orleans*, and that place became the capital of *Louisiana*.

Six leagues from the *Ship Island* is the *Cats Isle*, so called on account of the number of wild cats which have been found there. This isle is only remarkable on account of the murders and robberies which have been committed there during the command of two officers, who were sent thither by M. *de Kerlerec*, governor of *Louisiana*.

In 1757, he appointed the Sieur *Duroux* chief commander of this isle, and gave him a detachment

---

I have chosen this piece of history as an example, which has a particular similarity with what is seen every day in our colonies. There are, however, governors and intendants, that must not be confounded with those who have got fortunes with rapidity, and in an odious manner, from the public miseries, and from the blood of many unhappy people.

ment of troops from the marines, and from the Swifs regiment of *Haluyl*.

The Sieur *Duroux* was no fooner come thither, than he looked upon himfelf as abfolute; he immediately affumed the right of having a garden made by the foldiers of the garrifon; he likewife employed them to make for him lime from fhells, and charcoal, but he never paid them; and thofe who refufed to fubmit to thefe vexations, were faftened quite naked to a tree, and expofed to the infupportable attacks of the *maringoins* or gnats. This was the punifhment which the officer made the foldiers of his garrifon undergo; an unworthy treatment, unexampled even among barbarians.

The Sieur *Duroux* obliged them to make their bread of the flour faved from the wreck of a Spanifh fhip, which was loft on the coaft; and fold for his own account the King's flour, intended for the ufe of the garrifon. This repeated bad ufage from this commander, determined fome foldiers to go to *New Orleans*, in order to complain to the governor, to whom they fhewed fome of the bad bread they were forced to eat; but M. *de Kerlerec* paid no regard to their juft remonftrances, and fent them back at the

VOL. I. Y difcretion

discretion of their commander. Then these wretches, fearing his resentment, resolved to make an example of him, which they executed in ceremony.

One day, when that officer was gone out a hunting in a neighbouring little isle, the revolted troop took their measures for executing their plot, which was to murder the Sieur *Duroux*. So strange a resolution could only be occasioned by their not having obtained the desired justice from the governor. If an officer superior to M. *Duroux* had been sent in his place, and the latter left to command as the second officer, this misfortune would have been avoided.

As he returned from hunting, the sentinel, perceiving the boat at sea, hoisted the *French* flag, upon which the garrison took to arms, and went out into the field. The rebellious soldiers advancing to the shore with their corporal at their head, called to the boat by means of a speaking trumpet, according to custom; the Sieur *Duroux* answered, "*Commander*;" he lands, and as he sets his foot on shore, the corporal gives the signal, and at the same instant the soldiers fire, and their commander falls, pierced with wounds;

wounds; the soldiers then stripped him, and threw his corpse into the sea. Such was the burial and the punishment of this petty tyrant, who was regretted by nobody, for he had no other recommendation than that of the Sieur *Thiton*, the governor's first secretary. The soldiers, become masters of the isle, set at liberty an inhabitant whose name was *Beaudrot*, who had been unjustly imprisoned by the late commander. The Sieur *Duroux* had assumed the privileges of an admiral of France, and pretended to share with the soldiers and inhabitants all that they should save of any vessel wrecked upon the *Cats Island*; and all that refused to pay him his share were severely punished, as if they had committed some great crime. This was the crime of *Beaudrot*; he was put in irons because he would not share some goods with the commander, which he had saved from the wreck of a *Spanish* ship called the *Situart*, which was wrecked on the isle in 1758.

The soldiers who had killed M. *Duroux*, having afterwards pillaged the effects belonging to the King in the *Cats Isle*, took the inhabitant whom they had set free, and obliged him to bring them into the road to the English colony of *Carolina*. When they arrived in the country of a great Indian chief, whom the Europeans have ſtiled Emperor of the *Kawytas*, they ſent back *Beaudrot* with a certificate, which proved that he had been obliged to ſerve them as a guide. Part of this troop went towards the *Engliſh*; but thoſe who remained among the Indians, were ſoon ſeized by order of M. *de Montberaut*, then governor of the fort at the *Allibamons*; among this laſt party was a corporal of the regiment of *Halwyl*, who, in order to avoid being ſawed aſunder, as is uſual among the Swiſs, killed himſelf with a knife, which he wore hung from his neck, as the Indians do.

M. *de Beaudin*, an officer of the garriſon, was ſent with a detachment, in order to conduct the criminals to *Mobile*. During this interval, the two ſons of *Beaudrot* arrived at *Mobile* from *New Orleans*, and brought, without knowing it, an order from the governor to M. *de Velle*, who commanded at *Mobile*, for arreſting their father; who was in his habitation with great ſecurity; he returned to priſon without reluctance, not knowing that the deſerters whom he had guided were taken. M. *de Velle* tranſmitted the criminals to *New Orleans*, where a court-martial was held to judge them.

Beaudrot

Beaudrot the inhabitant, for guiding the murderers of the governor of *Cats Isle*, was sentenced to be broke upon the wheel, and his corpse to be thrown into the river; which was accordingly executed; a soldier suffered the same punishment, and a Swifs was sawed alive through the middle of his body.

When one reflects upon the fate of the unhappy *Beaudrot*, it is easily perceived that he was judged contrary to form, and by military men, who were ignorant of civil and criminal laws, as he could not have deserved the cruel punishment which he underwent. If politics require that for preserving public safety, no crime should be left unpunished, justice demands in favour of humanity, that the judge should always be more afraid of punishing too much than too little, according to the axiom, *It is better to let an hundred guilty men escape, than to punish one single innocent man.*

If the man ought to be punished in order to serve as an example, according to this law, the punishment might have been mitigated in favour of his wife and four children, whom his death threw into the greatest desolation; among the four children was a girl of an admirable figure,

figure, who was admired in the whole colony for her beauty, and still more for her virtue; this charming Creole, and the rest of the family, are retired into an habitation far from the commerce of men, to lament the death of their unhappy father.

This unhappy man had been successfully employed in some important negociations with the *Indians*, with whom he was in high esteem. He spoke their language, and, from experience, he knew the situation of the country as well as themselves. He had likewise an extraordinary bodily strength. All these qualities had so far gained him the esteem and friendship of the *Chactaws*, who had adopted him into their nation, that they would certainly have revolted on his account, had not M. *de Velle* * wisely taken care to keep his imprisonment and execution from coming to their knowledge.

After the tragic death of the Sieur *Duroux*, M. *de Kerlerec* fixed upon the Sieur *de Cha——* to succeed to the command of the *Cats Island*.

That

---

* This officer knows that nation perfectly well, having been governor of *Tombekbé* for several years; the *Indians* esteemed him much on account of his bravery and disinterested behaviour.

That officer set out from *New Orleans* in 1758, with a garrison composed of soldiers and inhabitants of the capital; but the inhabitants were all vagrants, whom the magistrates sent in their own stead, with the governor's consent, for the service of the place.

These vagabonds stayed in the *Cats Isle* as long as those citizens paid them, whose business it was to guard the place. You may well imagine, that a body of such troops, who are not alternately relieved in their posts, according to the rule of service, take opportunities to lay schemes for deserting, as it has happened in many stations of *Louisiana*.

In March 1759 there appeared, in sight of this island, a three-masted ship, belonging to M. *St. Criq*, a merchant, who had bought her at the *Havannah*; her cargo consisted in sugar, coffee, taffias, cables, and some warlike stores. The crew were merely Spanish sailors, who abandoned Captain *St. Criq* upon the coast of *Louisiana* near *Balise*; this obliged him to embark in his long-boat, with a few men who remained with him. He arrived at *New Orleans*, and addressed himself to M. *de Belle-Isle*, fort-major and commander during the governor's absence;

absence; he begged this officer to give him people, in order to go out in search of his ship, which could only be lost on the coast of the *Cats Island*.

M. *de Belle-Isle* gave the Sieur *St. Criq* an intelligent serjeant and ten soldiers, to navigate his ship; at the same time he wrote to the Sieur C——: " That if this ship were lost near his
" station, he should immediately place a guard
" on her, and forbid, under pain of death, that
" nothing should be unloaded out of her, with-
" out the consent of the Sieur *St. Criq*, the pro-
" prietor; and lastly, that he should not fail
" to conform to the orders of the King's marine,
" specified under the title *Shipwreck*," &c. Unhappily for the Sieur *St. Criq* the advice of M. *de Belle-Isle* came too late; the Sieur *de* C—— had already taken care to have the cargo of the ship unloaded by the soldiers and inhabitants, who hid it in the neighbouring sands; they took all the necessary precautions to cover this trick. The Sieur *St. Criq* arrived at the *Cats Isle*, put the major's letter into the commander's hands, and then went into his ship with his people in order to search her; but perceiving that he had forgotten his pocket-book, in which he had the bill of lading, he left her immediately, and

went

LOUISIANA. 329

went on shore to fetch it: a happy accident of Providence! he was but just come on shore, when his ship suddenly took fire, and burnt with such fierceness, that three men who were in the hold were burnt to death: the others only escaped by throwing themselves into the sea, and swimming on shore *.

The Sieur *St. Criq* complained to M. *de Kerlerec*; but after a long delay, the governor *obliged* the captain to terminate his quarrel with the Sieur *de C—*, the latter giving the former the sum of 1500 livres. This commander being recalled to *New Orleans*, gave himself up to such debaucheries, that he scandalized the whole colony.

---

* At the time when the Sieur *St. Criq* reclaimed his ship with M. *de Bell-Isle*, and received his orders addressed to M. *de C——*, to take care of the preservation of the cargo, the governor of the *Cats Isle* wrote to M. *de Belle-Isle* himself:
" That, on such a day, a ship with three masts was lost in
" sight of his station, and he having made signs without re-
" ceiving any answer, he took it to belong to the enemy,
" who kept his men in close quarters; that he having arm-
" ed the boat belonging to his station, and going into it
" with all his people, after getting no answer upon a re-
" peated signal, came on board the ship, but found no living
" soul in her, and the cargo taken out of her; he only
" found a cut cable upon the deck, and saw that the ship
" was bored for twenty-six guns.

ny. When he had confumed all that he had gained by his iniquitous practices, he went on board a Dutch ship from *Curaçao*, a colony belonging to that republic. The opinions are divided upon the clandestine evasion of this officer; some believe, that he escaped in order to avoid the punishments which his crimes deserved; others think he was charged with papers to court from the governor: the event will determine this.

It is sufficiently proved by this restitution of 1500 livres on the part of the Sieur *de C----*, that this commander had pillaged the ship of Captain *St. Criq*, getting 60,000 livres by it, according to his own confession to the Sieur *la Perliere*, who succeeded him in the government of *Cats Island*. He has however escaped the capital punishment which this piracy deserved*. For the quoted order says, "That all who shall " endanger the life of shipwrecked persons, and " lay hands upon their goods, shall be punished " with death." This crime is so enormous, that, though one were not a Christian, natural religion

---

* The Sieur *de C----*, hoping to enjoy the fruits of his iniquity in France, died there as he had lived, that is, in a debauch, by a decree of Providence.

LOUISIANA. 331

religion engages us to affift the unhappy in time of danger. Such were the officers in whom the governor of *Louifiana* put confidence.

We have juft received advice, that a party of warriors of the nation of *Cherokees*, commanded by their chief of war called *Wolf*, have taken the fort *London* belonging to Great Britain, and that the Englifh governor of it, M. *Damery*, has been killed by the Indians, who have put earth in his mouth, faying, You dog, fince you are fo very greedy of earth, be fatisfied and gorged with it; they have done the fame to others.

If I do not fet out for *France*, I fhall write to you from *New Orleans*, concerning the difcord between the two chiefs of the colony, M. *de Kerlerec* the governor, and M. *de Rochemore* the *ordonnateur*. I am, S I R, &c.

At Fort Mobile, the 10th of January 1760.

LETTER XX.

To the same.

The Author goes to New Orleans. *Cause of the Troubles which agitate that Place. Moving Relation of M.* de Belle-Isle's *Captivity among the* Attakapas. *Curious Animals and salutary Simples to be met with in* Louisiana.

SIR,

I HAVE so much news to communicate to you, that I know not where to begin: I wrote to you from *Tombekbé*, that every thing was in confusion in the capital; indeed every body talks of quarrels and divisions; avidity and interest are every where lighting the torch of discord. As I neither have, nor will have, any part in all these quarrels, and as I cannot satisfy my zeal for the king's service in this colony, where every thing is in disorder,

I have

LOUISIANA. 333

I have not ceased to demand leave to return to *France*. The moſt faithful ſubjects, who will do their duty, are contradicted and diſgraced, and their zeal is rewarded with the moſt cruel perſecutions. But without enquiring minutely into the ſufferings of a number of brave officers, moſt of them ſtill alive, I ſhall only ſpeak of thoſe which M. *de Belle-Iſle* has undergone. This worthy officer, whoſe probity and unqueſtionable conduct have gained him the good will and eſteem of all worthy men, and eſpecially of the general officers, ſuch as M. *de Perier*, M. *de Bienville*, and the Marquis *de Vaucreuil*, &c. well deſerves that I ſhould tell his ſtory to you, having heard it from himſelf with all its circumſtances.

I ſhall give you an account of what has happened during the forty-five years which he ſerved the king in this colony *. I ſhall ſay nothing but truth,

---

* The hiſtory of M. *de Belle-Iſle*, Chevalier of the royal military order of *St. Louis*, Major of *New Orleans*, and who has formerly ſerved as Major General of the troops of the marine in *Louiſiana*, has been inſerted in a *Relation of Louiſiana* printed at Paris in 1758. The author of it left the colony in 1733, has forgotten the moſt intereſting circumſtances, and the facts he has mentioned, have been diſowned by M.

de

truth, though some circumstances may appear very wondrous.

As I know the goodness of your heart, I am sure you will pity the unhappy fate of this poor officer; great souls are not ashamed to shew that they are touched by the misfortunes of others: even the *Indians* say, that he who is not sensible to the sufferings of his brothers, is unworthy of bearing the name of a man, and that he ought to be avoided as the pest of society.

In 1719, M. *de Crozat* put *Louisiana* into the hands of the West India company, who sent a thousand men to people it. M. *de Belle-Isle* embarked in one of their ships at port *l'Orient*, with some other officers and volunteers, for the new colony. The winds and currents carried the ship to the bay of *St. Bernard* in the Mexican gulph. The captain sent his boat on shore in order to fetch water. M. *de Belle-Isle* and four of his companions went into the boat with the captains consent. Whilst the boat returned to the ship, the officers went a hunting: the boat came on shore again, and having taken

in

---

de Belle-Isle himself: my relation is an abstract of a manuscript memoir, written by that officer's own hand.

LOUISIANA.

in the neceſſary proviſion of freſh water, returned on board without the young officers, who were not yet returned.

The captain is impatient, weighs anchor and ſets ſail, leaving the five paſſengers on ſhore. Their agitation and anxiety, when they returned to the ſhore and found the boat and ſhip gone, may well be imagined. Thus being abandoned in an unknown country, they erred for a long time upon the deſart coaſt, having the ſea on one ſide, and a country inhabited by a nation of cannibals on the other. They did not venture to quit the marſhy ſhores of the ſea; they were in ſuch deſpair of finding a remedy for their misfortunes that they knew not what to do: this alone was capable to make them loſe their ſenſes; and then the thought of falling into the hands of cannibals, troubled the imagination of theſe young Europeans. They went along the ſhore in the miſtaken opinion, that the ſhip was gone to the weſt, imploring divine mercy, and complaining of their unhappy fate. They lived upon inſects and herbs, not knowing whether they were good or bad; what was moſt troubleſome to them was the abundance of gnats in that place, as they had nothing to defend themſelves againſt them. They continued ſe-

veral

veral days in this situation. M. *de Belle-Isle* had taken a young dog from the ship, which was very fond of him. His companions were often tempted to kill him; their hunger was extreme: M. *de Belle-Isle* gave the dog up to them, but would not kill it himself; one of his companions seized the dog; but he was so weak, that as he was going to strike with the knife, the dog escaped, ran into the woods, and was not seen again. The four unhappy officers died with hunger one after another, in sight of M. *de Belle-Isle*, who did all he could to dig them graves in the earth, or rather in the sand, with his own hands, to preserve their sad remains from the voraciousness of wild beasts: he paid this tribute to human nature in sighing over its miseries, nothing but the strength of his constitution could make him survive them. He was resolute enough, in order to subsist, to eat the worms which he found in rotten wood. Some days after the death of his comrades, he saw at a distance his dog holding something in his mouth; he called him, the creature came to him fawning, and with great demonstrations of joy, threw at his feet an *opossum*; the dog howled, as if he would say, I bring thee something to support life. The opossums are good eating, and of the size of a sucking pig. M.

de

de Belle-Ifle, having no other company than his dog, looked about for food every where. At night he always made a little intrenchment at the foot of a tree, in order to shelter himself against the wild beasts. One day a tyger,[*] came near the place, where he slept; his dog watched by his side, he saw the tyger, and ran at it with a prodigious howl. M. *de Belle-Ifle* awoke, and haftened to his affiftance; the tyger let the dog loofe, but had wounded him: his mafter was obliged to kill him, left he fhould turn mad, and afterwards he eat him. Then being left alone in this defart place, he fell on his knees, lifted up his hands to heaven, and thanked the Almighty for preferving him till now; and refigning himfelf to Providence he went into the country in order to feek for men. He foon found foot-fteps, and followed them to the banks of a river, where finding a *piragua*, he croffes the river in it. On the oppofite fhore were fome *Indians*, drying human flefh and fifh; they were of the nation of the *Attakapas*[†];

they

---

[*] By this muft always be underftood the *American* tyger, . e. the *brown cat* of P. *Synopfis of Quad.* p. 179, and the *Cagucuara* of *Pifo* and *Margrave* in their *Nat. Hift. Brafil.*

[†] This name fignifies men-eaters among the *American* nations.

they went towards M. *de Belle-Isle*, whom they took for a ghost, because he was lean; he pointed to his mouth, and made signs of being hungry. The Indians would not kill him because he was excessively lean; they offered him some human flesh, but he preferred fish, of which he eat greedily. The *Indians* looked at this cloathed man, stripped him naked and divided his cloaths among themselves; they then carried him to their village in order to fatten him. There he had the good fortune to become the *dog* * of an old widow. He recovered his strength gradually; but was extremely sad, constantly apprehending, that his hosts would sacrifice him to their false deities, and afterwards make a feast of his flesh; his imagination was always struck with the terrible sight of the feasts which those barbarians made of the flesh of their fattest prisoners of war, which I cannot help shuddering at, whilst I relate it. He always expected to receive a blow with the club, as soon as he should be fat. The Indians held a council

---

tions. When they take an enemy in the wars, they make great feast and eat his flesh. They commonly live upon fish and drink the *Cassine*. They can speak by signs, and hol long pantomime conversations.

* An expression which signifies *slave*.

cil, in which they refolved that it would be fhameful and cowardly to kill a man, that did not come to them to do any harm, but to demand their hofpitality; in confequence of this refolution, he remained a flave of the widow. The firft days of his flavery, though it was not a heavy one, were very difagreeable to him, becaufe he was obliged to take care of the little children of thefe men-eaters, and to carry them on his fhoulders, which was very troublefome to him; for he was naked like them, having no more cloaths than were fufficient to make his nakednefs lefs indecent; but the widow abovementioned, having taken him under her protection, he was better treated in the fequel.

As M. *de Bell-Ifle* was young and ftrong, he acquitted himfelf very well of his functions as a flave, and even gained the good graces of his miftrefs fo much, that fhe adopted him, and he was then fet at liberty, and looked upon as one belonging to the nation. He foon learnt the manner of converfing in pantomimes, and the art of ufing the bow and arrows as well as they could do it. They took him into the wars, where he fhewed them his dexterity, by killing one of their enemies with an arrow in their prefence, he was then acknowledged a true warrior.

Another *Indian* having killed a roebuck, they dried the flesh of the man and the roe, to make ufe of it as provifions on their expeditions. One day as they were walking, M. *de Belle-Ifle* being hungry, afked for fomething to eat. An *Indian* gave him fome human flesh, faying it was of the roe-buck. M. *de Belle-Ifle* eat of it without knowing the cheat; and the Indian afterwards faid to him: *Formerly thou didft make difficulty, but now thou canft eat man's flefh as well as ourfelves*: at thefe words M. *de Belle-Ifle* threw up all he had eaten.

About two years after his captivity, fome deputies arrived at the *Attakapas*, from a nation who fent them the calumet of peace. A kind providential care! This nation lived in *New Mexico*, and were the neighbours of the *Natchitoches*, where M. *de Hucheros de Saint Denis* commanded, who was beloved and refpected by the deputies of this nation, though they lived on Spanifh ground. After attentively confidering M. *de Belle-Ifle*, they told the *Attakapas*, that in the country from whence they came, there were white men like him : the *Attakapas* faid he was a *dog*, whom they had found towards the great lake, where his comrades were ftarved to death; that they had brought him to their habitations,

where

where a woman had made him her flave; that they had taken him to war againft a nation which they conquered in a battle, and that he had diftinguifhed himfelf on that occafion, and fhewed them his fkill in fending an arrow, which killed one of their adverfaries; that they had for that reafon adopted him, and received him as a warrior.

This officer, who heard their converfation, did as if he took no notice of it; and immediately conceived the idea of returning to his country: he took one of the Indian deputies apart; and queftioned him much about the white men he had feen. M. *de Belle-Ifle* had luckily preferved his commiffion in a box; he made fome ink with foot, and wrote with a crow-quill the following words: " *To the firft chief of the* " *white men*. I am fuch and fuch a perfon, aban- " doned at the bay of *St. Bernard*; my comrades " died of hunger and wretchednefs before my " face, and I am captive at the *Attakapas*." This unhappy officer gave his commiffion to the *Indian*, telling him it was fome fpeaking paper; that, by prefenting it to the chief of the *French* in his country, he would be well received. The *Indian* believed, that this letter had fomething divine in it, becaufe it was to fpeak for him to the *French*. His countrymen wanted to take it from him; but he efcaped by fwimming acrofs a river; and left he fhould wet the letter, he held it up in the air. This *Indian*, after a journey of one hundred and fifty leagues, arrived at the *Natchitoches* *, an Indian nation. The French commander there at that time being M. *Hucheros de St. Denis*, an officer of diftinction, known for having made the firft journey over land from *Louifiana* to *Mexico*, where he married the *Spanifh* governor's niece. The Indian gave him M. *de Belle-Ifle*'s letter, and M. *de St. Denis* received him very well, and made him many prefents; after which, this officer began to cry after the manner of the Indians, who afked what ailed him? He anfwered, he wept for his brother who was a captive among the *Attakapas*. As M. *de Saint Denis* was in great efteem with the nations about him, the *Indian* who brought the letter promifed to fetch M. *de Belle-Ifle*, and fome other Indians joined him.

M. *de Saint Denis* gave them fome fhirts and a hat for M. *de Belle-Ifle*, and they fet out immediately, ten in number, on horfeback, and armed

---

* A ftation near *Mexico*. There is a fettlement of Indians on the *Riviere Rouge*, or *Red-river*.

ed with guns; promising to M. *de Saint Denis* to return in two *moons* time with his brother upon a horse, which they led with them.

On arriving at the *Attakapas*, they discharged their fire-arms several times, the explosion of which the other Indians took to be thunder: they gave M. *de Belle Isle* the letter of M. *de Saint Denis*, which mentioned, that he had nothing to fear with those Indians, and that he rejoiced beforehand that he should see him. The joy which this letter gave to the officer is inexpressible; however he feared that the *Attakapas* would oppose his departure. But the chief of the deputation made him get quickly on horseback, and went off with his whole troop. The *Attakapas* being frightened with the report of the muskets, did not venture to say any thing, and the woman who had adopted M. *de Belle-Isle* shed tears. Thus this officer escaped from a captivity, which might otherwise have lasted as long as his life.

The *Indian* who carried off M. *de Belle-Isle* was as proud as *Hernando Cortez* when he conquered *Montezuma*, the last emperor of *Mexico*. They arrived at the *Natchitoches*, but did not find M. *de Saint Denis* there; for he was gone to *Biloxis*, which

which was then the chief place of *Louisiana*, *New Orleans* being not yet built.

M. *d'Orvilliers*, who commanded at the *Natchitoches* in M. *Saint Denis*'s absence, sent M. *de Belle-Isle* and his escort to M. *de Bienville*, then governor of *Louisiana*. That general embraced him, being happy to see him, and liberally rewarded his deliverers. Every one complimented him on his escape from this captivity; M. *de Bienville* gave him a suit of cloaths.

This officer has since been very useful to the governor, by his knowledge of the customs of the *Attakapas*, whom the Spaniards of *New Mexico* could never subdue, as they have done with the other nations of their empire.

M. *de Bienville* sent a present to the *Attakapas*, and another to the widow who had adopted and protected M. *de Belle-Isle*.

These people, who did not expect this generosity from the governor, sent ambassadors * to him to thank him, and to make an alliance with the *French*.

---

* The chief of the embassy addressed the following speech to M. de *Bienville*, which M. de *Belle-Isle* interpreted; " My
" father,

French. M. *de Belle-Isle*'s mistress attended in person; since this period the *French* have always been humanely treated by the *Attakapas*, who have at their desire left off the barbarous custom of eating human flesh.

When the *Attakapas* came to *New Orleans*, they were well received by all the *French*, in gratitude of the reception M. *de Belle-Isle* had met with among them; for without them, he would have undergone the unhappy fate of his companions.

M. *de Bienville* sometimes procured himself the diversion of a pantomime with these cannibals, by means of M. *de Belle-Isle*, who, as their pupil, conversed with them by gestures. The *Attakapas* are armed with bows and very great arrows; they cultivate maize, as the other *North American*

" father, the white man, whom thou seest here, is thy flesh
" and blood, he was united to us by adoption. His brothers
" were starved to death, if my nation had found them sooner,
" they would live still and enjoy the same prerogative."

The hospitality shewn to M. de *Belle-Isle* by the *Attakapas*, convinced us, that we must regard their cruelty only as a fault of education, and that nature has planted sentiments of humanity in their breast.

American nations do. This part of the world is of fuch an extent, that it has not yet been poffible to become acquainted with all the nations in it, nor with its limits.

In 1759, M. *de Marigni de Mandeville**, an officer of diftinction, formed the defign, with the confent of the governor of *Louifiana*, of making new difcoveries towards the ifle of *Barataria*, of which we know the coafts but very imperfectly: with this intent he made a general map of the colony. This officer has difcovered this unknown country at his own expence, with indefatigable zeal, which characterizes a worthy citizen, who is always occupied for the glory of his prince, and the enlargement of his poffeffions.

I have endeavoured, in my preceding letters, to give you an abridgment of the hiftory of the country, from the time of its difcovery till now, and an idea of the fituation of its commerce, and likewife of every thing that feemed inftructive and amufing to me. I do not believe I have omitted any thing material, I fhall now finifh

our

---

* See the Memoirs of this officer, printed at Paris, by *Guillaume Defprès*, in the ruë *S. Jacques* 1765.

our correspondence by some observations on the natural history of this colony, of which you could learn nothing from the special relations that are published. You must know then, Sir, that all the fruit-trees which have been transported thither from *Europe* succeed very well there. M. *Fazende*, one of the superior council of *Louisiana*, has brought a fig-tree from *Provence*, the figs of which are excellent; as this tree is propagated by layers, it richly supplies all the habitations with them. Among the fruit peculiar to this country, there is one called a battledoe, it has the figure and taste of a pickled cucumber. This fruit is very common about *Mobile*, and it is very refreshing.

The *piakmine* is a kind of medlar, called *ougouflé* by the Indians; this fruit, which is no bigger than the European medlar, is yellow and red like an apricot; it is a very good astringent, and an excellent remedy to stop the dysentery and bloody flux. The Indians make bread of it, in the form of ginger-bread, and dry it for their long voyages *.

The

---

* The piakmine has yet another virtue: take a quantity of its seeds, pound them, then infuse fresh water upon them,

which

The *Jasmine* fruit has the form and colour of a lemon; it is odoriferous, and tastes like Banian figs; it feeds resemble beans; they are a poison to hogs ‡.

Here are a number of orange and peach trees; and both the oranges and peaches are so common in this colony, that they are left under the trees to rot.

There are apple-trees and plum-trees; and whole forests of walnut-trees; of which there is a white kind or the *hiccory*, and another black; both kinds bear nuts; they are as in Europe of different goodness for eating; there are likewise some walnuts as big as the fist, but they are bitter, having very thick and hard shells. There is a tree which bears a fruit called *pacannes*; they are oblong like almonds, and more delicious:
the

---

which must stand upon them twenty-four hours: strain the water through a cloth and keep it in a bottle. When you are attacked with the gravel, drink a glass full of the infusion fasting, and continue to do it till you are cured †.

† This is perhaps the persimon, *diospyros Virginiana* Linn. F.

‡ This plant seems to be one of the various kinds of *anona*, which grow over all the warmer parts of *North-America*. F.

the Indians make an oil of it, to feafon their *fagamitty* with.

It is a circumftance worthy of admiration, to fee the providence of the Creator, who has planted fuch a number of fruit-trees of various kinds in this part of the new world. There are thoufands of curious animals, known before neither by their fhape nor by their name, and of which men of the preceding ages have not even had an idea.

There are red and likewife white bays; the latter bears a white flower like a tulip; it is an exceeding bufhy tree, and would be an ornament to the gardens of European monarchs: the Indians call it the tree of peace *.

Near the banks of rivers there are vines, which climb fo high along the trees, that when the grapes are taken off, they can often make a whole barrel full of wine from a fingle ftock. Thefe vines grow without cultivation, and the wine that is made of them is very harfh

---

* This is probably either the *tuliptree, liriodendron tulipifera.* Linn. or the *laurus æftivalis.* Linn. F.

harsh *. There are many mulberry-trees † in the woods, and their berries are very sweet; there are likewise some that always keep the figure of shrubs, and their berries are made use of for jellies.

There is a tree in the woods full of spines of six inches in length; its wood is so hard, that it makes the edge of the hatchets blunt, and sometimes breaks them. The Indians, by means of fire, make mortars of it to crush their maize in. This tree bears pods about a foot long like *caffia*; the fruit they contain is gummy and sticking, having several seeds like beans. It is an excellent laxative, and the Indians take it as a purge.

There are resinous trees (such as pines, &c.) in the woods, which produce resin and tar; there are likewise many trees, from which a kind of gum like turpentine runs down.

There

---

* The American forests have three kinds of vines; the *vitis labrusca*, *vulpina*, and *arborea*, Linn. And this, here mentioned, seems to be the last. F.

† The *morus rubra* Linn. is the mulberry-tree, known to grow in *North America*. F.

There is a shrub which we call *cirier*, or the wax-tree, and it resembles an olive-tree. It bears little berries like juniper, they are melted in water *, and give a kind of wax for candles; this wax is of a fine green, and has an aromatic smell. The Sieur *Alexandre*, a surgeon and chemist, is the first that discovered it here. The academy of sciences gave him a pension for this discovery. He has likewise found the method of bleaching it, as we do bees wax in *Europe*.

Whilst I was in *Louisiana*, the inhabitants got from *St. Domingo* plants of sugar-canes, in order to make plantations of them. M. *Dubreuil*, who commands the militia of citizens, was the first planter that built a sugar-mill at *New Orleans*.

It is known, that sugar is made of the juice of a reed or cane, which is propagated by layers; it grows tall and thick, in proportion to the goodness of the soil. The canes have joints at certain distances; when these are ripe, which is easily known by the yellow hue which they get, they are cut above the first joint, which has no juice; the leaves on both sides are plucked off;

the

---

* Boiling water. The tree is the candleberry myrtle, *myrica cerifera*. Linn. F.

the canes are made up into bundles, and brought to the mill, where they are crushed between two wooden cylinders, covered with steel. A negro puts the canes between the cylinders, which press all the juice out, which is received in a great hollow, from whence it goes through a leaden pipe into a reservoir, which leads it into the place where the ovens are, which are destined to boil it in great boilers. When the juice is refined, it is poured into another boiler; it must be continually stirred, and boiled till it has a proper consistency; and when the sugar is got to the first state of perfection, it is put into forms of earthen ware, in order to be refined; it acquires the second degree of perfection by the opening being covered with clay to prevent the air from acting upon the sugar, and that it may not harden too much before it is refined by the separation of syrups and melasses.

It is with the scum of sugar that they make taffia or kill-devil. This liquor is prepared as brandy is in *France*; and goes through the still. The *Europeans* in *America* prefer it to brandy for curing of wounds. They likewise make rum with it.

In

In the country of the *Illinois* there is a little shrub, about three feet high, which bears a fruit of the fize of a fmall apple, and of the tafte of citrons. The woods there likewife contain chefnuts, and hazel-nuts of the fame kind as in *France*.

Louifiana abounds with good fimples; among them is the *ginfeng*, the root of which is an excellent reftorative, *jalap*, *rhubarb*, *fnake-root*, *farfaparilla*, and *St. John's wort* *, of which they make an excellent oil for healing of wounds. The following is the Indian doctor's method of making the oil. They take an earthen pot, and put the flowers of St. John's wort in it, and fome bear's oil above it; the pot or vafe is well ftopped up, and expofed to

---

* *Ginfeng* is the plant fo much in requeft in China; it is *Panax quinquefolium*, Linn. See Ofbeck's Voy. to China, vol. i. p. 222. and Kalm's Travels into North America, vol. iii. p. 114. and Catefby's Nat. Hift. of Carolina, app. t. 16. ——*Jalap* is the *Mirabilis* of Linnæus, there are feveral fpecies of it.——*Rhubarb* is the *Rheum* Linn. but probably not the true one.——*Snake-root*, perhaps the *Polygala Senega*, Linn. or elfe an *Ariftolochia*.——Sarfaparilla, *Smilax farfaparilla*, Linn.——St. John's wort, *Hypericum*, Linn. there are many plants of this genus in *North America*; and it is among the *defiderata* of the botanift to know what fpecies are employed for medicinal ufes. F.

the morning fun; the heat concentrated in the vafe turns the oil of a red colour, and gives it an agreeable fmell, which cures and purifies all kinds of wounds. There are even plants which have the virtue of ferving as counter-poifons; but it is a rare and precious gift to man to know them, and to know how to make a proper ufe of them; the Creator has not granted this knowledge to all men. There are numerous fimples proper for cleanfing the mals of blood, and of which the Indians have a peculiar knowledge.

There are forefts of *faſſafras* trees *, the wood of which is ufed in phyfic, and for dying; there is likewife the *copal* tree †, whofe gum is an excellent balfam, equal in goodnefs to the balfam of Peru; the animals which are wounded by hunters, cure themfelves by rubbing againft the tree from which this balfam exfudes, which has an aromatic fmell. The *Indians* have in their huts bitter gourds and calabafhes, of which latter they make a pectoral fyrup; *maiden-hair*, which is a good pectoral medicine, and the *caſ-fine*,

---

* Saffafras-tree grows all over North America, it is *Laurus faſſafras,* Linn.

† *Copal* tree grows only in the fouthern part of Nortl America, *Rhus copallinum,* Linn.

fine, which is a good diuretic [*]. When the dose is strong, it excites a kind of convulsions; which, however, cease immediately. The *Allibamon* Indians call it the *liquor of valour*. The natives of *America* value their simples more than all the gold of *Mexico* and *Peru*.

You find several sorts of curious animals in *Louisiana*, which are unknown in *Europe*.

The wild ox is very large and strong; the French and the Indians make various uses of it; they eat its flesh, which they salt or dry; they make coverings of its hide. The wild bull is covered with a very fine wool, with which they make good matrasses; of its tallow they make candles, and its pizzles afford cords to the Indian bows. The Indians work its horns, and make them into *micouens* or spoons, and into powder-horns.

---

[*] Bitter gourds, *Coloquintes*, *Cucumis colocynthis*, Linn.—Calabashes, *Cucurbita lagenaria*, Linn.—Maiden-hair, *Adiantum pedatum*, Linn. grows all over *North America*, from *Canada* down to *Virginia*, and is much esteemed as a medicinal herb. See *Kalm*'s Trav. to North Amer. vol. iii. p. 113.—Cassine is the *Prinos glaber*, Linn. mentioned in Letter XVI. p. 249. F.

The wild ox has a bunch or hump on its back * like a camel. It has long hair on the head like a goat, and wool on its body like sheep, which the Indian women spin into threads.

On going towards the head of the river *Missouris*, you find all sorts of wild beasts. The wild goats and their young ones are very common at certain seasons †. These animals are very lively and pretty; the females have double furrows or ringlets to their horns, and are not so big as ours: the French that eat of them have assured me, that the young venison was as good

as

---

* The hump is situated on the shoulders. The animal has been described by *Linnæus* under the name of *Bos bison*, and drawn by *Catesby* in his *Nat. Hist. of Carolina*, app. t. 20. and in Mr. *Pennant's Synopsis of Quadrupeds*, p. 8. t. II. f. 2. F.

† This animal seems to be of the antelope kind, perhaps the *Temamaçama* of *Hernandez*, an animal which hitherto has not been noticed by our zoologists. It seems not to be an animal belonging to the goat kind, on account of the double ringlets or *cornichons* mentioned by the author. This would be perhaps a new animal; and however it be, it will deserve the attention of our natural historians. And as the English dominions now extend to the river Mississippi, it would certainly be worth while to describe the animals upon that river, and those that fall into it. F.

as the best mutton. As the *Indians* of these parts do not use our muskets, they kill them with arrows; for these animals feed in the mountains, and when they are wounded they cannot climb so easily, and by that means the *Indians* catch them.

The hunters have likewise told me, that they had found a large kind of eagle in the woods, of the species called the *royal eagle* *.

I think it my duty to mention to you the singular manner in which the Indians hunt and take these birds, which the northern nations esteem very much, because they adorn their calumets of peace with eagle's feathers, which they call *feathers of valour*.

This kind of hunting is reserved for the diversion of old warriors, as it requires no exercise. The old man who intends to take eagles, first of all examines the places which are most frequented by them; after that, he brings flesh, the entrails of animals or dead snakes to those spots, and fastens these baits to some fixed wood. The

first

---

* The royal eagle is the *Falco Chryfaëtos*, Linn. or *golden eagle*, Penn. Br. Zool. fol. 61. tab. A. & in 8vo vol. i. p. 121. F.

first eagle that comes there eats of it, grows familiar with the place, and attracts others of his species thither, that greedily dispute the prey with each other. Then the old man digs a kind of *niche* or hollow at the top of the hill; he makes a chimney or vent to it which he stops up with a bundle of fagots, on which he places the baits: he suffers the bird to eat its fill; then he puts his hands, which he has wrapt in a little sack of leather through some straw under the faggots; takes hold of the eagle's legs, pulls it down, wraps it in his ox-hide, and so kills it. If he is lucky enough to take five or six of them, he is content, because the feathers are an article of trade throughout *North-America*. This way of hunting is not very troublesome: the baits are taken together by the old man's children, and the women send him victuals.

You likewise see hares* and white bears whose skin is very fine and soft.† The *tygers* of Louisiana differ from those of Africa and South America

rica

---

* The American hares are already declared by *Prof. Kalm*, vol. p. 105. to differ from the European ones; so that is improper to think the American ones to be the same F.

† The white bear here mentioned, cannot be the great *Polar*

rica, because they have no spots.‡ They take the roe-deer as cats do mice. As to the *tyger-cats*,§ they kill the wild oxen in the following manner. They get upon a tree, in a little path where the oxen are used to go to the river; and as they come by, the tyger-cats fall upon the necks of the oxen, bite through their throats and

kill

---

lar bear, Penn. Synn. Quad. p. 192. to 20. f. 1. as this latter is only to be met with in the most frigid parts of our globe; and the soft hair here mentioned will not admit to think of the polar bear, whose hair is like bristles. The common black bear is sometimes found quite white in Siberia, and therefore it is not improbable that some of these white bears are found in the interior parts of *North America*. Besides this, I find it necessary, here to observe, that the *black Virginia bear* seems to me to be a species different from our European bears, my reasons for this opinion are these: *first*, the European bear has never so black a coat as the Virginian, *secondly*, the snout of the Virginian is longer, and the head smaller than in our European ones; *thirdly*, the European bear is more clumsy than the Virginian. F.

‡ The North American tyger is the *Cuguacara* of Marggrave, or the *brown Cat*. Penn. Syn. quad. p. 179. In South America it is immensely fierce on account of the heat of the climate, and mistakenly called a lion. F.

§ The American tyger-cat is the *pichou du sud* mentioned in *Kalm's Travels*, vol. 3. p. 275, and *Penn. Syn. quad. Cayenne Cat.* p. 182.

kill them; their strength and their horns are rendered useless by this treachery.

The *wood rat* or *Indian-rat* is of the size of an European cat; its head is like the head of a fox, it has feet like a monkey, and the tail of a rat.* This animal is very curious; I once killed a female that had seven young ones; what is most surprising is to see them all stick fast to the teats, where they grow, and continue till they are able to run about; then they drop into a membrane that forms a pouch: those young ones which I saw were as big as new-born mice; nature has furnished the female with this pouch under the belly, which is covered with hair, as a retreat for her young ones, when they are pursued, by means of which the mother can save them and carry them off. Their flesh tastes like that of a sucking pig; their hair is whitish, and they have likewise a down or wool like the beaver. This pretended rat, lives in the woods upon the seeds of beech-trees, upon chesnuts, walnuts, and acorns. I have often eaten of them on my voyages: their fat is very white and fine; a fine pomatum or unguent is made of it for the Hemorrhoids.

Here

---

* This is the Virginian *Opossum*. *Penn. Syn. quad.* p. 304. and *Didelphis marsupialis*. Linn.

LOUISIANA.

Here is likewife an animal, which they call the *wood-cat*; it is of the fize of a fox, and nothing but its tail is like that of a cat. This creature is very fond of oyfters; it refembles a marmot in its figure; and may be tamed like a dog, licking and fawning upon its mafter, whom it follows every where; it takes its food with its paws, like a monkey. I believe thefe were the *dumb dogs* which the Spaniards found, when they difcovered the Antilles or Caribee iflands.*

There are four forts of fquirrels in Louifiana; large, black, red, grey, and little ones of the fize of little rats; the latter are called flying fquirrels, on account of a membrane which joins their four legs, and which they extend in jumping from one tree to another.†

The *French* and the *Indians* have often told me that the fnakes have the power of fafcinating

fquir-

---

* This animal here called *wood-cat* is common all over the Britifh colonies in America, and known by the name of *Raccoon*, fee Penn Syn. quad. p. 199. *Urfus lufcus.* Linn. and Kalm's Travels into North America, vol. i. t. 2. p. 96, 208. F.

† Black fquirrel, *fciurus niger*. Linn.—red fquirrel *fciurus ftriatus*. Linn.—grey fquirrel, *fciurus cinereus.* Linn.—flying fquirrel, *fciurus volans.* Linn. F.

squirrels; this I wished to see with my own eyes. I cannot avoid communicating my observations on this subject to you. I was once hunting at the *Illinois*, in a wood which abounded with hazelnuts, which is a very nice food for squirrels; they were likewise very plentiful there; I heard upon a tree, under which I stood, the sad cry of a squirrel which seemed frightened; I did not know what ailed it; at last I perceived a snake hung over a branch of the tree, looking upwards. waiting for its prey; and the unhappy squirrel, after leaping from branch to branch, fell into the mouth of the snake, which swallowed it.

Without entering into a physical detail, I imagine the squirrel was fascinated by the snake in the following manner. The antipathy of the squirrel, makes it look upon the snake as fastened to the tree, when it sees it thus immoveable, and hung upon a branch; therefore instead of remarking that it is only a snare, laid by its adversary, it jumps from branch to branch, as it were to insult the snake; when by jumping round the reptile, the latter sees it near enough to dart upon, seize and swallow it.† Many authors pretend

---

† This is a very ingenious explication, but it supposes, that we must attribute to the squirrel nicer feelings, than animals

pretend that the snakes have an attractive power.

The cunnnig of snakes is admirable; I have seen some, which perceiving that I looked at them, did not stir at all, in order to make me believe they were not there, and always continued in the same attitude; but as soon as I went aside to get a stick or stone to crush their heads, the snakes made off and I did not find them again when I returned. This is an experiment I have often made in the desarts which I have gone through, and where these animals are common.

There are many sorts of them, of which the most remarkable is the *rattle-snake*, having four or five round bones, at the end of the tail, which make a kind of noise by rubbing against one another, similar to the noise of a child's rattle. The Indian women pound this rattle and swallow it when they are going to lye-in, because they pretend that they can by its assistance bring forth without pain. The fat of the rattle-snake makes an

mals in general and squirrels in particular have; another method to account for this pretended fascination, see in *Kalm's Travels* I. p. 319. note. F

an excellent unguent for the rheumatic pains; this unguent penetrates into the body, to the very bones.

It is generally believed that the number of *vertebræ* in the rattle encreafes with the age of the fnake; I have feen fome rattle-fnakes fo big, as to be able to eat a whole roe-deer, by fucking it little by little.

There is another kind of ferpent, which they call the whipper, *fouetteur*; it is red on the belly and black on the back; it is fometimes about twenty feet long, and when it finds any body in the water, it twines round him fo violently as to take away his breath, and drown him.*

That fnake which is called the *whiftler* is about two feet long; but is fo much more dangerous, becaufe it is not fo eafily feen, being very little; fo that the Indians and negroes often tread upon and are bitten by it: it has a prodigious wide mouth and when angry, it whiftles at a terrible rate,

---

* This fnake is reprefented by *Catefby nat. hift. of Carol.* II. 46. It might be called *coluber erythrogafter*, for Catefby call it the *copper-bellied-fnake*. The circumftance here mentioned, relative to its twifting round people in the water, and its enormous fize are both new. F.

rate, and therefore the Indians call him *ho-huy*, that is, *whistler*. During my voyage to *Tombekbé*, a whistler hidden under the leaves, bit a soldier of my detachment, who trod upon its tail; the soldier was barefoot, and the snake was so angry that it got hold of his big toe and would not let go its hold. I was very uneasy and sorry to see this soldier exposed to perish he being my interpreter; I applied to an Indian doctor who accidentally went by the place, where we were. He took a powder out of a little sack, and blew it through a tube upon the snake's head, which died instantly; he put another powder upon the wound, which prevented the poison from taking its effect; he likewise gave some of it in water to the patient, who was quite well after. I recompensed this juggler very handsomely; I wished likewise to know his secret, but he would not teach it me, and acted like a quack telling me haughtily that the master of life had communicated it to him alone.*

The

---

* It is highly probable that this powder, was of the root or whole plant of the *aristolochia anguicida* a Mexican plant, which probably grows likewise in *Louisiana*, and according to Dr. *Jacquin* is an infallible remedy against the snakes, for these animals are actually fascinated and even killed by it. In

Car-

There are very large and long *crocodiles* or *alligators* in some parts of the river *Miffifippi*; they are so carnivorous, that if they find a man asleep on the land, they carry him into the water and devour him, though they are else very cowardly, and run off as soon as one walks towards them; it seldom happens that they eat a man, because it is so easy to escape from them; they pursue those that fly from them, and are very formidable in the water. The alligator is the most horrid animal in nature and I cannot without horror remember that which had almost carried me into the river of *Tombekbé*; I thought I saw the devil just come out of hell, and I believe he could not be better represented than under that hideous form; its back is covered with impenetrable

---

Carthagena the Indians chew the root of this *Ariſtolochia*, and mix its juice with the ſaliva; if one drop of this mixture is put into the ſnake's mouth, it inebriates it, and you may handle the ſnake as you pleaſe; if two or three drops are forced in; and they reach the ſnake's ſtomach, convulſions immediatly enſue, and the reptile dies. The Indian who ſhewed Dr. Jacquin this method, likewiſe informed him that he had been thrice bit by ſnakes, and had always cured the wound by uſing the *Ariſtolochia* both internally and externally. The plant itſelf has ſo nauſeous a ſmell, that it is always avoided by ſnakes, and cauſes, when chewed, vomiting even to men. See Jacquin's Hiſt. Select. Stirp. American. p. 232. t. 144. F.

ble fcales, almoft as ftrong as oyfter-fhells, refifting the force of a ball from a mufket. It is difficult to hurt an alligator any where except in the eye. They are numerous in the *red river*: they are torpid during the cold weather, and lie in the mud* with their mouths open, into which the fifh enter as into a funnel, and can neither advance nor go back. The Indians then get upon their backs and kill them by ftriking their heads with hatchets, and this is a kind of diverfion for them.

Here are likewife frogs of an extraordinary fize, whofe croaking exceeds the roaring of a bull. On my voyage from Mobile to New Orleans, I touched at the Horn Ifland and found a fhell fifh there, which the Indians call *Naninatelé*, which means *Sea Spider*; it was petrified. Its outward covering confifted of a more fhining varnifh than the Chinefe; its eyes were petrified and hard as diamonds. This fhell fifh is of the fize

---

* This circumftance of the allegator's being torpid during winter, is quite new, and very remarkable for natural hiftorians. It feems almoft all the clafs of animals called *amphibia* by Dr. *Linnæus*, when found in cold climates, grow torpid during winter. F.

fize and figure of a barber's bafon turned upfide down, and has a very fharp tail about ten inches long, and they fay it is dangerous to be ftung by it *.

The higher parts of *Louifiana* contain beavers and others; the Indians fay that thefe beavers have been expelled by their brethren from *Canada*, becaufe they were too lazy to join with them in conftructing the habitations which thofe animals make in common, and the dikes, to alter the bed of rivers, all which they contrive and execute with great art and induftry.

The *Karancro*, a bird of prey, is of the fhape and fize of a turkey †, and the moft voracious

bird

---

* This fhell-fifh is now in the Marquis *de Marigny's* cabinet of Natural Curiofities.

This *rare* animal is nothing elfe than the king's crab, common in the feas all round *America* and the *Weft-Indies*; *monoculus Polyphemus.* Linn. Thefe animals are employed in New-York to feed pigs with, and the ingenious gentleman, who communicated this remark, adds, fometimes it is eaten even by the two legged pigs. F.

† Hence it is called *Turkey Buzzard* by Catefby, Carol. I. t. 6.----It is the *Carrion Vulture*, Forfter's N. Amer. Animals, p. 8. and *Vultur Aura*, Linn.

bird that ever was known; it follows the hunters and likewife the convoys that travel to their different ftations. They wait in flights, like ravens, for the decampment; and then they come and eat greedily all that has been left there, after which they go on, towards the new camp. They eat dead corpfes; their feathers are black, and the foft downy feathers under the wings, have the quality of ftopping the blood.

The *Flamingo* is of the fame fize, the end of its wings is black, the back white, and the belly flame-coloured *.

There are ftares of two kinds; the leaft are of the fize of the European ones: they are fo common that a hundred of them are often killed at one fhot; they are very good to eat but the inhabitants are obliged to guard their crops of maize and rice, which otherwife would be entirely eaten up by thefe birds; they are as black as jet, and have the tip of the wing of a fine bright red; their feathers are very fine, and the ladies

Vol. I.   B b   wear

---

* Flamingo, *Phœnicopterus ruber*. Linn.

wear muffs, and linings to their dresses of them*.

Here are parrots and parrokeets, and fine jays in great abundance: in the country of the *Missouris* there are magpies, only different from the European ones by their plumage, their black and white colours being shaded; the Indians make ornaments for their hair of them.

The eyes are taken with the beauty of nature unassisted by art; here she appears as she came from the hands of the Creator, before the fall of man. The ear of the traveller is enchanted by the songs of the birds, and especially those of the *mocking* birds, which are fond of being in his company, and seem formed on purpose to make him forget the fatigues and tediousness of the journey. Indeed as soon as the mocking bird perceives a man, he perches near him, and sings very agreeably, flying from place to place; and in a word, this bird is inimitable; it settles at the top of a tree, and mocks or mimics all
the

---

* These are the *red-winged stares* or *maize thieves* mentioned and drawn in *Kalm's Travels*, Vol. II. p. 74. *Oriolus phœniceus*. Linn.

the other birds; he likewise imitates the mewing of a cat. The mocking bird sometimes comes to the towns and houses, and appears enchanted and pleased when one plays on any instrument and even joins the concert; it is of the size of a stare, and of a bluish grey colour: it is easily tamed, if taken young *.

The *Pope* is of a bright blue round the head; on the throat it is of a fine red, and on the back of a gold green colour, it sings very finely and is of the size of a canary bird †.

The *Cardinal bird* is quite red, having the throat black, and a crest of feathers on its head, its bill is strong and red; it is a kind of sparrow, which is very fond of men, and comes to the size of a lark, but whistles during summer like a black-bird ‡.

---

* Mocking bird, *Turdus Orpheus* Linn. Kalm's Travels, Vol. II. p. 90. F.

† *Pope* is the male of the *Emberiza Ciris* Linn. known by the name of painted Finch. F.

‡ Cardinal bird is the *Loxia Cardinalis*, Linn. F.

The *Bishop* is blue mixed with purple and of the size of a linnet *.

The gold-finch is quite yellow, with the tips of the wings black †.

There is a bird they call the *Harlequin*, becaufe it is varied with many colours, and another called the *Swifs*, becaufe it is red and blue; the laft three fpecies only come to the *Illinois* in fummer.

The *humming bird* is no bigger than a large beetle, and painted with many bright and changing colours; it lives upon the fweet juice of flowers as bees do; its neft is made of a very fine cotton or woolly fubftance, and fufpended on the branch of a tree ‡. There are numberlefs unknown birds, which would make the account too long.

I have feen butterflies of great beauty; I found two on my voyages (that have been eaten

up,

---

* Bifhop, *Tanagra Epifcopus* Linn.

† Goldfinch, *Fringilla triftis*, Linn.

‡ Humming bird, *Trochilus Colubris*, Linn.

up by worms) the like of which I never saw; I never beheld any thing more magnificent! it seemed as if the author of nature had been pleased to throw upon their wings the finest and most vivid colours; the finest and purest gold appeared mixed among the other colours with admirable symmetry.

These butterflies were probably carried to the *Akanzas* by a sudden storm, for in the whole space of a thousand leagues which I have gone through, I have never found their equals. I desired some Indians, of the *Osages* nation, who live near the mines of *St. Barbe*, to bring me some of these butterflies: they answered, that in the country where they were to be found, the inhabitants were very ferocious, and had merely the forms of men.

Here are various sorts of ducks, but the most curious are those which perch on trees, having pretty strong claws at the end of their palmated toes; they build their nests upon those trees which lean over rivers or lakes, and when their young ones are hatched, they go into the water immediately. As to their feathers, they are shaded with the finest colours: the male has a crest upon its head. These ducks are the best to eat, they feed in the woods on acorns and beech feeds *.

On the banks of rivers there are birds called *Egrets*, they are exceeding white and the ladies employ their feathers as *aigrettes* †.

The *Pelican*, which the inhabitants of the country call great throat, on account of a pouch he has under his throat, is as white and as large as a swan, its bill is about twelve inches long; they make muffs of its skin, and precipitate the paste of indigo with its fat. This paste is made from a plant, the grain of which comes from the East Indies, for dying blue ‡.

The spoon-bill §, having a bill like a *Spatula*, an apothecary's instrument so called. There is likewise a bird called *Lancet-bill*, whose beak is

actually

---

*. This is the *Anas arborea*, Linn.

† Egrets, *Ardea alba?* Linn. the great white heron ? Forst. North. Am. Animals, p. 14.

‡ Pelican, *Pelecanus Onocrotalus*, β. Linn.

§ Spoon-bill, *Platalea Leucorodia*, Linn.

actually like a lancet. It is impossible to finish this matter, it would require whole volumes; I leave this detail to our learned countrymen, M. *de Buffon* and *Daubenton*, who have undertaken this vast work. I wish you may be content with this short account.

I am, S I R, &c.

*At New Orleans the 1st
of June, 1762.*

P. S. Before I conclude my letter I shall speak to you of two precious plants in Louisiana; which are the *Indigo* and the *Cotton*.

Indigo is a plant resembling the *Broom* or *Genista* very much. A kind of it is growing in Louisiana spontaneously, and commonly upon hills and near woods. That which is cultivated is brought from the West India isles. There are two crops of it every year. It grows to the height of two feet and a half. When it is ripe, it is cut, and brought into the place where it is to rot; this is a building twenty feet high, without walls; but only supported by posts. In it they make three troughs, one above another, the lowest is made so, that the water it contains, may run out of it, and out of the building. The second stands on the edge of this, so that the water it contains falls into the first, and the third is disposed in the same manner with regard to the second. The indigo leaves are put into the uppermost trough; with a certain quantity of water, and must putrify in it. The man who is at the head of the manufacture examines the indigo from time to time, and when he sees it is time to empty this trough, he turns the cock, and the water runs into the second trough; there is a proper time which must be well observed for doing this operation, for if the plant remains too long in this putrefying place, the Indigo becomes black.

As soon as the water is in the second trough, it is beaten till the overseer thinks it sufficient; it is use and habit by which one learns to seize upon the true moment. When the water has been well beaten, it is left to settle: the indigo forms a kind of sediment at the bottom of the trough; the water above it must have time to become clear, and is afterwards drawn off by means of several cocks placed above each other.

The

The indigo is then taken off likewife, and put into facks made of common fackcloth, where the remaining water may run off. After this it is fpread upon boards, and when dry it is cut into little fquare pieces, put into barrels, and fo fent to *Europe*.

In order to have feeds, it is neceffary only to let fo many plants grow up as are wanted; it grows more or lefs tall according to the nature of the foil, which ought to be light; in the Weft India iflands they have four crops a-year, on account of the great heat, but in *Louifiana* they cannot have above three; the indigo in the latter place is likewife not fo good*.

The cotton-fhrub is no bigger than a rofe-bufh, but fpreads more. It does not fucceed fo well in ftrong or rich grounds as in others; therefore that which grows in Lower *Louifiana* is inferior in goodnefs to that which is cultivated in the higher parts of that province.

The

---

* The indigo plant is, with Dr. *Linnæus*, the *Indigofera tinctoria*, and the indigo mentioned to grow fpontaneoufly in *Louifiana* is the *Sophora tinctoria*, Linn.; which, with a proper management, is faid to afford as good indigo as the celebrated *Anil* of the Indies and Egypt. F.

The cotton of this country is of the species called white cotton of Siam. It is neither so fine nor so long as the silky cotton, but it is however very white and very fine. Its leaves are of a lively green, and resemble spinage very much; the flower is of a pale yellow, the seed contained in the capsule is black, and oval like a kidney-bean: it is commonly planted in such grounds as are not yet fit for tobacco or for indigo; for the latter requires the greatest care.

The shrub is cut down to the ground every two or three years, because they say it bears more after it. The pistil of the flower changes into an acuminated capsule, of the size of a pigeon's egg, green at first, then brown, and at last almost black, dry and brittle.

When the cotton is ripe, the heat of the sun makes it expand; the capsule that contained it opens in three or four places with a little noise. Then it must be gathered quickly, lest it should be lost. Each capsule contains five, six, or seven seeds, of the size of pease; the cotton sticks to them, and it is therefore difficult to get the seeds out, except in time and with patience; for
this

this reason, however, many planters have been disgusted with the culture of cotton *.

I have not mentioned tobacco to you; it is likely that it is a native of the country, because the tradition of the Indians, or their *ancient word*, tells us, that they have always employed it to smoke in their calumets of peace. I shall conclude with an observation that has already been made, and which it is good to repeat, till somebody tries the experiment. The climate of *Louisiana*, and the hilly parts of that country, give reason to believe, that it would not be difficult to plant saffron there; the colonists would reap great advantages from it, and the neighbourhood of *Mexico* would procure them a quick and certainly an useful consumption.

---

* The people in the English colonies, and in China, employ an instrument which separates the pods from the cotton with great ease. F.

LETTER XXI.

To the same.

Reflections on the Population of America; *that Continent has not been unknown to the Ancients; it seems that it is connected with* Asia *on the Side of Tartary, from whence the People that first settled it must naturally be supposed to have come. A Digression upon the Way of preserving one's Health in* America.

SIR,

 Expect to set out for *France* very soon; and I take advantage of an opportunity that offers to write to you, before I leave this part of the world. After giving you an idea of the manners, customs, and of the history of the people with whom I have been during my voyages, I do not believe I could better conclude my narrative, than by some reflec-

tions

tions on the population of this immense continent; but this matter is so obscure, that we cannot now flatter ourselves to clear it up: many learned writers have already attempted to throw light upon it, but they have not succeeded; modern philosophy has endeavoured, with as little success, to draw advantages from it, and its reasonings and opinions have not even been able to seduce weak geniuses.

By reflecting attentively upon the old writers, every thing seems to convince us, that *America* was not entirely unknown to them. *Diodorus Siculus* seems to have spoken of it with precision enough: Father *Laffiteau* quotes a passage from that historian, and adds his reflections to clear it up. The *Phœnicians*, if we may believe the Greek author, after sending several colonies upon the coast of the Mediterranean, being enriched by their trade, did not go far beyond the columns of Hercules; that vast and unknown ocean, which they discovered on coming through the streights of *Gibraltar*, inspired them with a kind of horror, which they surmounted only by degrees: some bold navigators ventured out upon the ocean afterwards; but sailing along the coast of *Africa*, a violent tempest, of several days duration, carried them to an isle of very

great

great extent, at a great distance to the westward.
At their return they were very ready to speak of
their discovery, they embellished their accounts,
with all the fictions familiar to travellers of all
countries; and at all times. When the *Tyrrhe-
nians* became the masters of the sea, they were
willing to make a settlement there; but the
Carthagenians opposed it, fearing that their countrymen, attracted by what was said of this land,
should leave their country in order to settle
there; they likewise considered this new-disco-
vered country as a last resource for themselves,
in case some disaster should have overturned their
empire.

To this passage of *Diodorus Siculus*, Father
Laffiteau adds one of *Pausanias*. This writer was
inquiring, whether there were any satyrs; one
Euphemus, who was born in *Caria*, told him,
that, in a voyage of his, he had been carried by
a storm to the extremities of the ocean, where
he had seen several isles, which the sailors called
Satyrides. The people that inhabited them were
of a red colour, and had tails; the sailors trem-
bled, and endeavoured to avoid them; but the
contrary winds forced them to come near the
shore; the savages invested the vessel, and the
crew,

crew, in order to get rid of them, were obliged to deliver a woman to them.

Father *Laffiteau*'s reflection will appear very juft to you. " The defcription of thefe ifland-
" ers," fays he, " perfectly fits to the *Caraïbes*,
" who were mafters of the Antilles, commonly
" called the *Caribee* iflands, out of moft of
" which they have been expelled by the Euro-
" peans in thefe latter times. The complexion
" of thefe people is very red, and it is naturally
" fo; it being lefs the effect of the climate,
" than of the imagination of the mothers, who,
" finding the red colour beautiful, tranfmit it
" to their children *; their flefh is likewife arti-
" ficially red, for they paint themfelves every
" day with *rocou*, which ferves inftead of vermi-
" lion to them, and appear as red as blood by
" it. As to what concerns the imagination of
" the failors, who thought they beheld fatyrs,
" it only was the effect of fear, that made them
" take

---

* Every one will not agree with the Jefuit upon the effect of the mother's imagination on their children: the different colours of men from the feveral parts of the world, offer many more difficulties. All that has been written on the fubject has not explained this phenomenon; men who were originally white, muft have become black, red, and brown, (bronzed), by the union of feveral caufes.

"take false tails for real ones; almost all the
"barbarous nations of *America* wore this orna-
"ment, especially when they went to war."

The similarity which has been observed to exist between the manners of several *American* nations, and those of some of the oldest nations on our continent, seems to demonstrate that this country was not unknown in ancient times, and chiefly proves that the known or old parts furnished the new one with men; how could that similarity be explained, if this had not happened? How great a resemblance is there in the religion, manners, and customs of the *Indians*, with those of some ancient nations. These details will always destroy most of the bold systems which have been started on the population of *America*. If they were a colony of people escaped from the deluge, the universality of which is in vain contested, they would have brought anti-diluvian customs into *America*. Those nations that were born after this dreadful punishment, do they resemble their ancestors that were buried under the floods? We have not yet light enough upon this subject to make a just comparison; we can answer nothing to those who say, *That the Almighty hand, which sowed plants and fruits in all parts of the world, could likewise place*

then

LOUISIANA.

men there. An ingenious phrase is not always a reason: no one disputes this power of the Creator; but he has been pleased to teach us himself, that it was not his will to people the world so, and that he gave existence to two creatures, who were the origin of the whole human race.

All these opinions rest upon the course that men must have taken, in order to come from the old world to the new; and it is upon this difficulty that most authors found their writings. A more exact and extensive knowledge of our globe would annihilate all these difficulties. It is very probable, that there is a passage which unites *Asia* to *America*; I have already said something of it to you, in speaking of the elephants bones found in one of the countries I have gone through: this is not a new opinion; this conjecture has been made long ago. " *America*," says Father *Laffiteau*, " can be come at " in different places, and accordingly it may " have been peopled from all sides; this is be- " yond a doubt; it is but at a little distance " from the southern unknown countries; and " in the north, *Greenland*, which is *perhaps* con- " tiguous to this new continent, is not far from " *Lapland*. Those parts of *Asia* which bound it " towards the land of *Yeso*, probably make but " one

" one continent with, or are only at a little di-
" stance from *America*, if the streights that are
" supposed to be there go to the Tatarian sea:
" the ocean which surrounds *America* almost en-
" tirely, is strewed with isles, both in the nor-
" thern and southern seas. Men may have gone
" from isle to isle, either by shipwreck or by
" mere chance."

This author alledges many reasons to prove, that *North America* joins to *Tartary*, or to some country contiguous to it; the following is a very singular one: You know that *ginseng* is originally a native of the *Mantcheoux Tartary*, the *Chinese* or *Tartarian* name of it signifies, the *thighs of a man*. The *Americans*, who were long acquainted with it, and made use of it, called it *gareloguen*, which has the same signification. If *America* did not join to *Tartary*, or if the latter had not peopled the first, how could their respective inhabitants give names of the same signification to the same plant? I do not speak here of etymologies of words that have been corrupted, and which are only found by forcing them; their signification is here in question.

Captain *William Rogers* looks upon it as very probable, that some *Tartarians* passed over into
America :

America: he obferves, that the fhips which annually go from the *Philippines* to *Mexico*, are obliged to fteer to the northward; in order to meet with favourable winds, thofe which rife between the tropics being always contrary to them. He adds, that after paffing forty-two degrees of north latitude, failors often meet with fands and fhallows, which feem to indicate that they are near fome coafts. He imagines, that thefe coafts might well be fome continent unknown to *Europeans*, and uniting *California* with *Japan*; but fhould they not rather be the coafts of *Kamtchatka*, or of that new country to the eaft difcovered by Captain *Bering*?

To thefe obfervations I fhall add an abftract of a relation, publifhed in the *Mercure Galant* for November 1711. I fhall quote the fact, without making any reflections to confirm or contradict it; the author pretends to have got it out of a manufcript found in *Canada*.

Ten men refolved to go out upon difcoveries, with a view to get riches; they embarked in three canoes, and went up the river *Miffifippi*. After a long voyage, they found another river which flowed to the fouth-fouth-weft; they carried their canoes to it, and continued their navigation;

vigation; some time after, they arrived in a country which extended two hundred leagues, and was inhabited by a nation who called themselves *Escaaniba*.

The Frenchmen (for the ten travellers were of that nation) found much gold with these people. Their king pretended to deduce his origin from *Montezuma*; his name was *Agauzan*, and he kept a standing army of an hundred thousand men in time of peace. The *Escaaniba* women were white as the *European* women; they and the men of that nation had long ears, to which they fastened gold rings. One of their distinctions was, to let their nails grow: polygamy was permitted among them; they did not pay any attention to their daughters, who lived in the greatest liberty, without any one to watch over their conduct. Their country produced tobacco, various fruits, some common to *Europe* and *India*, and some that were peculiar to it; the rivers abounded with fish; their forests were full of game of every kind, and contained above all a great number of parrots. The capital was situated at six leagues from the river, which they called *Missi*, *Golden river*. They valued gold so little, that they permitted the *French* to take as much as they pleased with them: you may
con-

conceive, that they made a good ufe of this permiffion; each of them took for his fhare two hundred and forty pounds weight of gold. Their mines were in the mountains, from whence they brought the gold upon rivulets, which were dry during one feafon of the year.

Thefe people traded with a nation very diftant from them; and in order to make the *French* fenfible of it, they told them, that it required fix months to make the voyage. The adventurers happened to be with the *Efcaanibas* at the time when their caravan fet out to trade with thofe ftrangers; it confifted of three hundred oxen loaded with gold; an equal number of men, armed with lances, bows, arrows, and a kind of daggers, conducted and watched them: they brought back, in exchange for their gold, fome iron, fteel, lances, and other weapons.

I cannot afcertain in what degree we may truft this account; the adventurers conjectured, that the diftant country whither the *Efcaanibas* went, was *Japan*; in that cafe, there muft be a communication between *Afia* and *America*; fome Englifh writers, without attempting to difpute the authenticity of this account, believe, that the favages went to trade with the inhabitants of

Kamptchatka, or of some isle or continent near that peninsula. This communication will never be well ascertained whilst it remains undiscovered *. Conjectures explain nothing; they give probabilities, but go no further: however, be it as it will, it is very probable that such a communication exists: supposing there are streights that divide these two great parts of the world, they cannot have prevented men from penetrating out of one into the other, by crossing those streights. We must hope, that the ignorance in which we are at present will not last for ever; the discoveries which men shall endeavour to make in the great southern or Pacific ocean, will give us more light on this subject †. If, after making

---

* The modern geographical discoveries, and especially those made by the Russians, sufficiently evince, that the sea entirely divides *Asia* from *America*; there can be no doubt neither of *Japan*'s being an isle, and unconnected with the continent of *America*; it is true, however, that the sea which divides *Asia* from *America* near Cape *Tchukshi*, is very narrow, and not a sufficient obstacle to the migration of the nations that inhabit the north-east parts of *Siberia* into *America*; for a further hint concerning the population of that vast continent, see *Kalm's Travels to North America*, vol. iii. p. 125. &c. F.

† When these letters were gone to press, I heard that the English had discovered ten islands in that ocean. There is

making voyages that way, some streights be really found, it is no reason why they should always have been there: earthquakes may have divided the isthmus or neck of land which combined the two continents; many authors attribute the streights of *Gibraltar* to the same kind of event: the Mediterranean, they say, had formerly no communication with the Atlantic; many pretend, that *Great Britain* was joined to *France*; now the sea separates *Dover* and *Calais*: why cannot this be the case with *Asia* and *America* likewise?

The time in which the population of *America* was commenced, is as obscure and indeterminate as the manner in which it was peopled; every thing which is difficult to penetrate excites the curiosity of men; they wish to see something new, and to speak of it, and frequently they give

---

an account of it in the voyage of Commodore *Byron*, who has been so much talked of, and has proved the existence of giants, which was blindly believed by the ancients, rejected as chimerical by the moderns, and now confirmed by new discoveries. The next voyage which the English will make that way, will furnish us with more minute accounts; others will be encouraged to imitate them, and a perfect knowledge of the South Sea will clear up the difficulties concerning the junction of *Asia* and *America*.

give us their own chimerical imaginations as something real. Among the singular opinions which this subject has given rise to, I shall mention that of *Marc Lescarbot*, in his History of *New France*; Father *Laffiteau* shall still be my guide on this occasion, and from his work on the manners of the savage *Americans*, I shall take what I have to say on this matter. " *Les-*
" *carbot* has not scrupled to advance very posi-
" tively, and in a manner that goes beyond con-
" jecture, that *Noah* was not unacquainted with
" the western continent, (where *Lescarbot* was
" born); and that at least he knew it by fame.
" That, having lived three hundred and fifty
" years after the deluge, he himself had taken
" care to people, or rather to re-people that
" country: that, being a good workman, and
" an excellent pilot, and being charged to re-
" pair the desolation of the earth, he may be
" supposed to have conducted his children thi-
" ther; and it may have been as easy to him to
" have gone through the streights of *Gibraltar* to
" *New France*, *Cape Verd*, and *Brazil*, as it was
" to his children to go and settle in *Japan*, or
" as it was to himself to come from the moun-
" tains of *Armenia* into *Italy*, where he founded
" the *Janiculum* upon the banks of the *Tiber*, if
" we

" we may credit the accounts given by profane
" writers."

I doubt whether it is neceffary to go back to *Noah*, to find the period of the population of *America*; if, as is very probable, the *Tartars* went over into that continent, it muft have happened in the following times: a fet of people, who are not numerous, do not eafily leave the vaft country they inhabit; they do not fo foon endeavour to feparate from each other; they continue together, till, by having multiplied too much, they fpread more, or till fome other circumftances force them to leave their native country: fuch refearches are of little importance; they are mere matters of curiofity, and the difficulty of fatifying that ought to prevent men from employing their time in them. All that can be afferted with certainty is, that *America* feems to have been inhabited only of late.

Powell, an Englifh writer, mentions, in his Hiftory of *Wales*, that, in the year 1170, there was a war in that country for the fucceffion to the throne, after the death of Prince *Owen Gwinneth*. A baftard took the crown from the legitimate children; one of the latter, whofe name was *Madoc*, embarked in order to make new difcoveries;

coveries; directing his courfe to the weftward, he came to a country the fertility and beauty of which were amazing. As this country, was without inhabitants, *Madoc* fettled in it; *Hakluit* affures us, that he made two or three voyages to *England* to fetch inhabitants, who, upon the account he gave them of that fine country, went to fettle with him.

The Englifh believe, that this prince difcovered *Virginia*. *Peter Martyr* feems to give a proof of it, when he fays, that the nations of *Virginia*, and thofe of *Guatimala*, celebrate the memory of one of their ancient heroes, whom they call *Madoc*. Several modern travellers have found ancient Britifh words ufed by the *North American* nations. The celebrated Englifh Bifhop *Nicholfon* believes, that the Welch language has formed a confiderable part of the languages of the *American* nations; there are antiquaries who pretend, that the Spaniards got their double or guttural *l (ll)* from the *Americans*, who, according to the Englifh, muft have got it from the *Welch*. I fhould never have done, if I were to mention all their reafonings to prove the voyage of the *Welch* Prince *Madoc*. The Dutch brought a bird, with a white head, from the ftreights of *Magellan*, which the natives called

Penguin;

Penguin; this word is an old Welch one, and signifies *white head*; from hence they conclude, that the natives originall came from *Wales* *.

The *Englijh* are not the only people, who, according to our hiftorical romances, went to *America* and fettled there : *Bayer* pretends, that the *Normans* were the firft Europeans who ventured to fail to that country.

Doctor *Lochner* afferts that a *Bohemian* of a diftinguifhed family went to *Brafil*, and difcovered the ftraights of *Magellan*, before *Columbus* went to the New World; this Bohemian was called *Martin* †. Many German writers who

feem

---

* This, however, is a wrong fuppofition; for it appears, that the bird in queftion has a black and not a white head; but its name is Spanifh, and fignifies a fat bird, the *Penguin* or rather *Pinguin* being very fat. F.

† Our author miftakes the name of this man for that of his country: he was called *Martin Behaim*, a native of *Nurenberg* in Germany; his father was a noble fenator of that city: after ftudying mathematics, and efpecially aftronomy and geography, under the great mathematician *Joannes Regiomontanus*, he went to the *Netherlands*, then governed by the Princefs *Ifabella*, daughter to *John* I. of Portugal; he there obtained the command of a fhip, fitted out for the purpofe of making difcoveries: he fet fail in 1460, and,

failing

seem to wish that America should bear his name preferably to that of *Americo Vespucci*, have followed this opinion.

Whether these traditions are adopted or rejected, whether they are fabulous or true, it remains inconteftible that the *Americans* have the same origin with us; among all their errors, they have preserved some ideas that have a great similarity with those, which have been transmitted to us by writing: I shall mention to you a piece of an English differtation on the population of *America*,

---

sailing to the westward first met with the isle of *Fayal* one of the *Azores*, all which islands were afterwards called the *Flemish* isles from the first inhabitants, which *Martin Behaim* brought thither. He then returned, and obtained two ships, with which he cruized in the atlantic for some time, and at last discovered the fourth part of the world, and even went as far as the straights, now called *Straights of Magellan*; he laid down all his discoveries in a sea chart, which he presented to king *Alphonsus* the fifth, of *Portugal*. This sketch afterwards fell into the hands of *Christopher Columbus*, a *Genoese* who was at *Lisbon*, and first infpired him with a defire of visiting those unknown countries. When he undertook the voyage, he always followed the same course which *Martin Behaim* had laid down on his chart, and performed the voyage in as short a time as is done now. In the noble family of *Behaim* at Nuremberg, they still preserve among other curiosities a globe drawn with a pen, and coloured by that able navigator, in which all his discoveries are marked. F.

LOUISIANA.

America, in which many *American* opinions are collected, which owe their origin to the truths preserved by *Moses*. " The *Peruvians* believe,
" that there formerly was a deluge, by which
" all the inhabitants of their continent perished,
" a few excepted, who retired into caverns at
" the top of the highest mountains, and whose
" descendants filled the earth with inhabitants
" again. Some ideas, little different from
" these have been received by the natives of
" *Hispaniola*, according to what *Gemelli Carreri*
" relates. The old histories of *Mexico* likewise
" mention an universal deluge, by which all
" men, one man and woman excepted, perished.
" These two people, according to the *Mexicans*,
" had numerous descendants; but all their chil-
" dren were dumb, till a pigeon endowed them
" with the power of speech; they add, that the
" primitive language of the immediate de-
" scendants of the couple who survived the de-
" luge, was split into so many dialects, that it
" was impossible for them to understand each
" other; which after obliging them to separate,
" contributed to make them people the different
" countries of the earth. Some *American* na-
" tions have a tradition, that all men derive
" their origin from four women, which agrees
" pretty well with the *Mosaic* history, which
" makes

"makes all the nations defcend from *Noah* and
"his three fons. All thefe traditions manifeftly
"fhew, that the *Americans* are defcendants of
"*Noah*, and that various accounts of the *Mo-*
"*faic* hiftory are even come down to them.
"This is fufficient to overthrow the ftrange fyf-
"tem which attributes anceftors to the *Americans*
"anterior to *Adam*."

Does not this quotation anfwer all the arguments of thofe fyftematic writers, who will give us the fruits of their abfurd imagination as truths? Where could the *Americans* get thefe notions, if they were not all pofterior to the deluge, and defcended from nations that had preferved the tradition? It is eafy to explain, that by length of time, by the ignorance and the mutability of the *Indians*, they have immerfed true facts, which were committed to their memory, in fables. The want of monuments, characters or letters to write down thofe events, certainly impairs the purity of tradition; as foon as it is tranfmitted by word of mouth from father to fon, it muft be much changed after paffing through fo many generations.

The wars which the *Indians* ever carried on among themfelves, have contributed greatly to hinder

LOUISIANA. 399

hinder population; their small number has certainly been the cause of the nomadic life they lead; they ran through the woods in order to search for game, and settled in all the places where they found food in abundance, leaving them again in order to go further, whenever it began to fail them.

If they were more numerous their wants would increase; it would become more difficult to provide food for them all; this difficulty would open their minds, give them new ideas: they would feel that it was necessary to provide a subsistence more independent from mere chance; the fruits which the earth produces, would teach them to multiply them by cultivation; they would see all the uses of these productions, think of appropriating them to themselves, and succeed in it; in some places we see them already cultivate maize, they would soon cultivate other corn; one kind of knowledge would lead to another: they would settle in the country which they had cultivated, and be no longer such vagabonds as there are now.

The settlement of the *Europeans* in the northern parts has engaged many of these nations to come and settle in their neighbourhood in order

order to get that affiftance from them which they want; the defire which the *Europeans* fhew of poffeffing their furs and the eafe with which they can obtain brandy and fire-arms in exchange for them, often excite them to go through the woods and hunt in the extent of two hundred leagues around, in order to get thofe things, which become real wants to them; thus they are only apparently fixed; they preferve their love for a rambling life, and the period of their civilization feems as yet very diftant; perhaps they will deftroy each other before they come to it.

This is all that can be afferted with probability on the population of *America*; my letter would be too long, if I would only mention a hundredth part of what has been faid on this fubject. The fyftems and contrary opinions which have been long publifhed, would make confiderable volumes; I have endeavoured to confine myfelf to curious obfervations; thofe who think the *Tartars* have chiefly furnifhed *America* with inhabitants, feem to have hit the true opinion; you cannot believe how great the refemblance of the *Indian* manners is to thofe of the ancient Scythians; it is found in their religious ceremonies, their cuftoms and in their

food,

LOUISIANA.

food. *Hornius* is full of characteristics, that may satisfy your curiosity in this respect, and I desire you to read him.

I shall now quit all these discussions which ought to finish the account of my voyages, and shall speak of another subject, more useful to the human race, in regard to which observation and experience suffice to instruct us.

As it is the natural desire of man to live long, I hope it will not be foreign to my purpose, to shew in a few words, how one may preserve life and live long in *America*.

I shall therefore finish my letter by a small dissertation on the method of managing one's health. I remember to have read, in the *Holland Gazette* of the 3d of April 1687, that *Frederick Gualdus*, a noble Venetian, has preserved his life to the age of four hundred years; it is pretended, that he was possessed of the universal medicine. He left *Venice* the 7th of March 1686; having his picture with him painted by *Titian*, who was then already dead an hundred and thirty years. I am sure you will agree with me in saying, that exercise and sobriety procure a perfect health. The nations of *America* knew neither wine nor brandy two hundred and sixty years ago, when the *Europeans* came to them; they lived, as I have already said, on the flesh of wild beasts dried, roasted, or boiled with maize pounded in a mortar made of some hard wood. This food is wholesome, and makes a very good *chyle*. I have lived about two months upon these victuals, going up the river *Mobile* with the *Indians*, and can affirm, that I never enjoyed my health better in my life than at that time. Of all Latin proverbs, this is the best:

Plures gula occidit, quam gladius.

Voluptuousness and intemperance in eating and drinking, destroy more men than the sword. Therefore one ought to prescribe to himself a proper regimen of life, especially in the hot countries of *America.*

First of all, great care must be taken to be accustomed to the climate by degrees, and to abstain from eating all kinds of fruit, and drinking all sorts of liquors, till the body is used to it. People who are very replete with blood, may be bled from time to time, to prevent an apoplexy. A gentle purge will sometimes do well; the burning

burning heat of the fun muſt be avoided, and the air at night likewiſe.

When one has drunk too much wine, it is neceſſary to take four things; ſuch as lemon, which is very common there; by this means you will neither find yourſelves ill, nor be overcome by the vapours which commonly follow. If the quantity of liquor which has been drank heats the body, ſome refreſhing aliments muſt be ta-taken, but every thing that increaſes heat muſt be avoided: ſpirituous liquors ſhould be drank as little as poſſible, for they burn the blood, and eaſily cauſe a hot fever.

When you have eaten too much, ſtrong liquors are good to ſtrengthen the ſtomach, and help digeſtion; but if, on the contrary, it happens that you are heated by drinking too much*, they would prove very dangerous. Thoſe who are too much addicted to debauchery are almoſt always tormented with bad dreams, which fatigue them ſo much as almoſt to trouble their mind,

---

* It ought to be remarked, that, ſince the *Americans* have drank wine and brandy, they have like us ſhortened their days.

mind, becaufe the fumes of the wine, with which their body is filled, fucceffively excite their imagination. It is known by experience, that fober perfons, and thofe efpecially who drink water, fleep quietly, their fleep being neither too flight nor too heavy. It appears, from the fecond chapter of the Life of *Apollonius*, written by *Philoftratus*, that at Athens thofe who were afflicted with bad dreams applied to the priefts of the falfe deities, in order to be rid of them; they ordered them to abftain from wine for three or four days; this cleared their imagination, and produced a cure, which they attributed to their gods.

If, after taking too much food, you are heavy, and your members fatigued, fo that too great an abundance of nutritive juice occafions a plenitude in the whole body, and makes you tired; I believe that, in imitation of the *Indians*, fweating is an infallible remedy, when the natural heat is affifted with an exterior one; this remedy is infallible, provided it be applied at the firft appearance of the diftemper; the *Europeans*, in order to perfpire well, get between two blankets, and remain there covered up, the face excepted; they do not get up till they have

fweated

sweated well, and about an hour after the whole perspiration is performed. If this method of sweating is continued during some days, you find yourself so much eased, that your strength and appetite return, and you are surprised to see yourself so light and so nimble; for by the perspiration all the *viscera* are perfectly cleared of all their superfluities, without pain or any violence done to nature, which the ordinary medicines cannot do. In order to be healthy, this ought to be done thrice in the year, *viz.* in spring, autumn, and in winter.

My conclusion is, that diet, perspiration, and sweating compose an universal medicine.

Therefore I say, that nature should direct us in all things; from her we must learn the true means of preserving health, which she orders us to do upon pain of the greatest evils, and even of death. I have already told you, that the frequent exercises of the Indians of *North America*, such as dancing, playing at ball, hunting, fishing, and fighting, increase their natural heat so much, that it drives all the superfluities out of their bodies by perspiration. Why do the pea-
sants

fants live long, and are healthy, without the affiftance of phyficians! The perpetual labour they are employed in keeps them fo; exercife prevents their knowing the gout, gravel, and other infirmities, to which the richer people in *Europe* are fubject, on account of the refined tafte of their tables, and becaufe they make no more ufe of their legs than old infirm men. I have known fome, who, like Moliere's *Malade imaginaire*, filled their ftomach with as many drugs as an apothecary's fhop.

It has been obferved, in the hot countries of *America*, that the young *Europeans* die fooner there than the old ones; becaufe the former imprudently eat all forts of fruit, which caufe them a dyfentery; therefore it is neceffary to eat very little of them, till the body is accuftomed to the climate, after which, at the expiration of a year, this will caufe no further inconveniencies.

By obferving thefe precautions, I will warrant, that people will live longer in this part of the world than in the old one. There are now many people alive in *Louifiana*, who have been there ever fince its firft fettlement. I faw
a planter

a planter called *Graveline*, aged one hundred and eighteen years, who came hither with M. *d'Iberville*, in 1698; he ferved in *Canada* as a foldier for about thirty years, in the reign of *Lewis* the Fourteenth.

I am, S I R, &c.

End of the FIRST VOLUME.

www.ingramcontent.com/pod-product-compliance
Lightning Source LLC
Chambersburg PA
CBHW050848300426
44111CB00010B/1172